Aesthetic Conflict and the Evolution of a Riot:

Impact of Dewey's Global Movement and the Rise and Fall of a Tradition in Higher Education

B. Marie Brady-Whitcanack, Ph.D.

authorHOUSE®

AuthorHouse™
1663 Liberty Drive
Bloomington, IN 47403
www.authorhouse.com
Phone: 1-800-839-8640

First published by AuthorHouse   2/22/2011

ISBN: 978-1-4567-3556-2 (hc)
ISBN: 978-1-4567-3560-9 (e)
ISBN: 978-1-4567-3561-6 (sc)

Library of Congress Control Number: 2011902127

Printed in the United States of America

Contents

CHAPTER 1: INTRODUCTION

I am nocturnal, the philosopher
I've reached the level, that I deserve
I've reached the level, where I work best
I am the artist, I am depressed
I have switched off and all I want is
to kiss the roof of Heaven
just to confirm that this is Hell
(Hinterland, 1990)

The following text examines aesthetic conflict and the evolution of a riot at Iowa State University. The facts and discussion about the events are based upon a series of incidents personally experienced and reported to appropriate security personnel, administrators, government agency officials, and elected officials by the author over an approximate four-year time period while a doctoral student at the university. The book that follows is a discussion of the conflict and its possible causes. The consideration of causes includes identification of patterns as indicative of possible social psychosis from a Jungian perspective (Conforti, 1999). A hermeneutic analysis of the events also includes an explanation of field theory, the method of systems pattern analysis that could further explain the archetypal field and complex in play that resulted in progressive violations of boundaries.

Though this examination is primarily a hermeneutic analysis, hermeneutics and its close relationship to Jungian psychology and the development of archetypal complex theory based on the ancient Kabbalah (Wolfson, 1995) are examined. Though there are numerous texts that examine the use of the Kabbalah in the psychological theories of both Freud and Jung (Drob, 2000), this study explains the initial critical

1

thinking process of attempting to understand a conflict in process. Thus, the book follows in the tradition of Kolodny (1998) in her *Failing the Future: A Dean Looks at Higher Education in the Twenty-First Century* and Lovitts's (2001) landmark examination titled *Leaving the Ivory Tower: The Causes and Consequences of Departure from Doctoral Study.*

The present text is an analysis of the series of events and the evolution of a riot as a hermeneutic analysis that may be expanded into a "systems pattern analysis" from a Jungian psychological field theory perspective that could be replicated for use in analysis of other incidents at college campuses across the country (Conforti, 1999). For example, numerous riots occurred at Southern Illinois University in Carbondale, Illinois during the same time period as those at Iowa State University in Ames, Iowa. Both of these major universities were under investigation by the Federal Bureau of Investigation simultaneous to the escalating events. The readers must consider whether the evolving nature of riotous behavior at Iowa State University, Southern Illinois University in Carbondale (the home of the Center for Dewey Studies), and numerous campuses across the country are "celebratory riots" (Hacker, 2005) or are indicative of a greater challenge to the larger civilization.

The major focus on aesthetic conflict and the challenge of aesthetics as a core concept in higher education is our initial incident. Discussion of other challenges to civil behavior and tradition follows. We will begin with a discussion about what aesthetics is and why this concept has been central to education theory since the earliest formation of public education. For example, Wechsler tells us that "aesthetics plays the part of the delicate sieve of reality" (1978, p. 1). Others, from Heisenberg to Einstein, consider the aesthetic experience in fields such as science to be a process often used in the search for truth (Wechsler, 1978, When I speak of aesthetics in education in this study, I speak of its core of simplicity and beauty as well as balance, harmony, and unity. Aesthetics is an overarching concept that includes values theory and ethics. The conflict in aesthetics examined in this study is considered in its relationship to the demise of a doctoral program of study in home economics at one major state university. The significance of the loss of this foundational program will be better understood as the history of education and the challenge to traditions of Western civilization unfold.

The role of aesthetics as a core concept in foundations courses of home economics (later known as family and consumer sciences education) was challenged initially by direct and indirect hostile communications during curriculum planning meetings and doctoral course discussions during education foundations and theory courses in the doctoral degree program of study at Iowa State University. In addition, a series of physically aggressive acts and harassment directed toward the author as a student of traditional studies and this field of study progressed to what has been identified as "mobbing" (Davenport, Schwartz, & Elliott, 1999). The traditional curriculum of home economics, with roots tied directly to John Dewey and the Chicago laboratory schools during the rise of public higher education, subsequently experienced a decline; ultimately, this resulted in the doctoral degree program at Iowa State University and other major universities across the country being eliminated. Though the consequences of losing this area of study are only now (2010) beginning to be examined in relationship to increased social dilemmas, such as unplanned pregnancies among teens and young college-age students (Delaney, 2010), this analysis looks at some of the challenges to traditional course content and other conflicts specific to core concepts in education, such as aesthetics. The analysis also considers the rise and fall of home economics (family and consumer sciences) in higher education as well as the implications for general education and social changes theory.

I will argue aesthetics provides a criteria and reasoning structure in the search for truth, serving as not only a "delicate sieve of reality" (Wechsler, 1978), but also as a psychological and philosophical theory of balance and harmony in reasoning that establishes "aesthetics [as] the mother of ethics" (Muelder Eaton, 1997). For example, the relevance of aesthetics to modern education has been extensively examined by Buescher (1986) who describes various kinds of aesthetic knowing in the teaching of gifted children. In this educational setting, aesthetic knowing is a subtle process that dovetails across other cognitive processes. Buescher explains:

> The ability to experience, to imagine, to represent is a fundamental process of human intelligence. The process as well as the product that grows from it can have a deep, moving, and aesthetic character to it. Being able to experience what is subtle, to imagine what is interesting or useful, and to be able to adequately represent what has been experienced are each influenced by the conditions in which one lives ... Why do we have music or dance or

3

poetry or stories? Because it is only through these modes and others that particular kinds of human experience can be communicated. We have to do this as people. Human beings invented the forms that can meet that need to imagine and communicate. (Buescher, 1986, 7–15)

Defining aesthetics becomes an historic tour of philosophy within a historical context of psychology. Interpretation of concepts of aesthetics and aesthetic meaning within the current context of modern times is rooted in the hermeneutic process of interpretation. Collini (1992) explains that the "problem of textual meaning introduced by hermeneutics associated with Schleiermacher ... and the centrality of interpretation to understanding all the creations of the human spirit ..." (Collini, 1992) is central to the understanding of aesthetic meaning. The complexity of how meaning is to be interpreted within the context of communication will be a central concern in the discussion of aesthetics in education and its relevance to conflicts in understanding, such as conflicts between civilizations. The changing definitions of aesthetics, from a past centered in theology, to a core educational concept, to its current expanded meaning within the larger world context of global communication is also discussed (Huntington, 1997).

The philosophical life of the aesthetician is interwoven into the tradition of educational philosophy and psychology. For example, the traditional understanding of balance and beauty as a cognitive process of learning has its roots in ancient philosophical discourse as a goal of the learned person "to form more than to inform—to prepare people for the world by teaching the 'art of living'"(Romano, 2000, B11). Aesthetics philosophy as a way of life and mind was a key concept in the development of a theory of life and living.

In the modern world of intellectual activity the search for aesthetic balance is seen as central to scientific as well as artistic creation. "When scientists, however, reflect on their work, the development of concepts, and the theories that expound them, it is evident that intuition and aesthetics guide their sense of 'this is how it has to be,' their sense of right" (Wechsler, 1978, p. 1–2). Cycles of meaning may vary along with the dominant experiential themes of the times (Sorokin, 1928). Aesthetic balance may modify in meaning according to the cultural context of the times. However, the process of aesthetic knowing and reasoning follows traditional sequences of reasoning that are linked to cultural values. Cultural situations "inevitably secrete a further 'image of personal being'" that continues to question human values at every point (Collini, 1992). The cultural structure is influenced and influences the reality of the living condition (Wundt, 1921). Aesthetic learning and aesthetic knowing or reasoning become content as well as process for an educational imperative (Abbs, 1994). For example, Socratic questioning and aesthetic learning require a continued focus on creativity in relation to past and present philosophies of aesthetic knowing. Art embodies the logic of feeling, intelligence, and symbolic form (224). Yet, the teaching of creativity and critical thinking follow similar elements of structured reasoning. Paul (2009) links the critical thinking process and the creative processes in a fluid and seamless intellectual reasoning structure that is necessary for the modern educated person.

Artists and scientists share an aesthetic knowing when something is wrong. They seek truth and are continual questioners of the present meaning and relevance of things. They are ever in search of new knowledge (Van Manen, 1990). They are uncomfortable with an issue that remains stagnant and seldom accept things the way things are. They share an intuition in the identification of a phenomenological experience that just doesn't feel right. I experienced such an intuition and phenomenological experience that led to the research for this text. It began a search for why: Why were philosophies of beauty, balance, and aesthetics, so long a tradition of general education, now absent in many state universities (East, 1982)? There appeared a conscious effort to reduce the significance of, or eliminate altogether, those elements of beauty and aesthetics that still existed in the educational philosophies in education.

The process of the interpretation of meaning in communication and symbols, hermeneutics, like aesthetics, can be quite subtle. Meaning may be known to only a few participants and observers of communication, and in some cases, may be similar to cultic activities (Brady, 2000). On occasion, contextual discussions may manifest as war. The interpretation of interpersonal communication becomes an expression of meaning and interpretation of that specific, transmitted meaning. A work of art becomes "one of the most important battlefields of the interpretation of the validity of values *and* demonstrates in itself why it is precisely philosophical aesthetics that is developed by a bourgeois society" (Heller & Feher, 1986, p. 4). For this reason, an arts-based genre is one of the elements of a multifaceted methodology for consideration of the issues of communication and interpretation through aesthetics in education.

A false impression, depicting science and art as rivals, has been considered by various authors. Sir Geoffrey Vickers argued this point in a paper presented to the Massachusetts Institute of Technology in April of 1974. In Vickers' paper titled "Rationality and Intuition: The Causal and the Contextual," he argues aesthetics and science are not rivals, but placed in a role of adversarial combativeness that is neither correct nor appropriate for the creative process necessary in each. Wechsler (1978) clarifies Vickers' thesis in the following quotation:

> Why not aesthetics in science? Whence comes the implication that to find aesthetics in science is like finding poetry in a timetable? The answer lies in the sad history of Western culture which, over the last two centuries, has so narrowed the concepts of both Science and Art as to leave them diminished and incommensurable rivals—the one an island in the sea of knowledge not certified as science; the other an island in the sea of skill not certified as Art. (Wechsler, 1978, p. 143)

Because there has been some confusion as to the conflict between qualitative and quantitative research, I will state from the outset that this is not the issue under investigation in this research. The focus of this study is not the combative potential for science versus aesthetic philosophy, but the totality of meaning toward an interpretation of the underpinning conflict of social values manifested in incidents to be described (phenomena), and the interpretation of what appeared to be a challenge to the traditional educational philosophy of aesthetics in education as a manifestation of a possibly larger social conflict, the conflict between civilizations (Huntington, 1996/1997). To begin that interpretation required consideration of the ancient hermeneutic doctrine and a conversation with theologians and educational philosophers of the past. Proponents of the educational psychology of John Dewey, and theological collaboration with psychologists such as Carl Jung and William Wundt presented a logical analysis of this core concept of reasoning in an "ongoing and far-reaching dialogue" (Brown, 1990, p. 4).

This study also is a conversation with the past in search of aesthetic meaning for the present and future. Jessop and Van Manen argue aesthetics requires a canon of judgment, not a norm or canon of feelings, sentiments one could argue belong to the field of ethics (Jessop, 1969; Van Manen, 1990). Like beauty, aesthetics has value; it is not value (p. 276):

> Beauty, unlike goodness, has various orders—visual, auditory and so on—and in no one of these orders, still less in all of them taken together, is there one perfect degree or form, a *summum pluchrum* It is not a hierarchy of subordinate and super ordinate degrees, but a galaxy of brilliant individuals. (Jessop, 1969, p. 276)

In the words of my now-deceased husband, a psychologist and trained Jungian analyst, "Books are our friends. They will speak to you, if you know how to listen" (Brady, personal communication, discussions on Jungian theory with counseling partner and spouse, December 25, 1979). What does this hermeneutic notion mean? I would suspect this comment was intended to validate the Jungian perspective about layers of possible interpretations within a text and the transmission of communication. These layers of meaning and method of communication are taken from Kabbalistic hermeneutic traditions that were examined by Drob (2010) as central to the development of Jungian depth psychology and Freudian psychoanalysis. The identification of layers of meaning in communication has also been described by Eco (1996) in regard to interpretation and over-interpretation. Eco explains:

> But if books tell the truth, even when they contradict each other, then their each and every word must be an allusion, an allegory. They are saying something other than what they appear to be saying. ... Thus truth becomes identified with what is not said or what is said or what is said obscurely and must be understood beyond or beneath the surface of a text: The gods speak (today we would say: the

Being is speaking) through hieroglyphic and enigmatic messages. (p. 30)

The need for interpretation of intended communication and layering of meanings within language—spoken, written, and symbolic—have come to mind many times in the process of the quest to understand just what happened at Iowa State University. In attempting to listen and to learn those universal truths relevant throughout time, I will continue the hermeneutic tradition and have a conversation with the early philosophers of the profession of home economics through the presentation of the texts and hermeneutic traditions upon which they built a tradition. These brave and brilliant women set high standards of excellence in the study of all areas of intellectual activity while focusing on how such education impacts the family and the community, foundations of the society as a whole. The hermeneutic phenomenology will be incorporated into a concluding creative/critical thinking methodology (Brown, 1990, p. 4).

The early founders call and direct attention to the perennial paradigm, the issues and concerns of the times, which prompted the creation of the profession of home economic as early as 1902 (East, 1982). The profession was originally based on values and service to others (the family and community) and centered on issues of the soul, beauty, and the connection to the essence of God. Some might argue that the profession has moved far from its origins (Baldwin, 1989). Beauty has value, but is not value; by "scrutinizing anew those elements of thinking that have given rise to controversy" (Brown, 1981, p. 4), it is possible to improve the prospect for successful communication and interpretation of the meaning of aesthetics and beauty as theology in a current challenge to Western traditions (Huntington, 1996/1997; Jessop, 1992, p. 277; Weaver, 1948/1984).

Aesthetics in family and consumer sciences education curriculum, the result of Dewey's global movement and a return to a theology of beauty, is the collective theme and central point from which additional psychological and philosophical interpretations branches. The challenge for core concepts such as aesthetics, previously tied to a theology of beauty, to remain relevant will be ultimately considered within the context of the larger perspective of cultural conflicts. The starting point for the analysis is a position where aesthetics in educational philosophy is a central as well as a key concept for the theories of both Dewey and Hunt (a major founder of the profession of home economics education) during the last Enlightenment.

Determining the current philosophical status of aesthetics as a key concept of past educational traditions is also a central consideration in seeing the educational profession's possible loss of soul. The value and moral elements of aesthetic meaning, so long a tradition in education, are being challenged in university curriculum committees as "unnecessary concepts" in the now more "empirical science-oriented" curriculum (Reitmeyer, 1990). This search for meaning will be conducted through analysis of incidents experienced and related sociological research. What happened here and why? Were the experienced incidents isolated or part of a larger pattern of escalating conflict and violence?

The possible challenge to the values of the one-hundred-year tradition of higher education at land grand universities across the United States is considered from specific experiences of the author while in a doctoral program at Iowa State University. Comments made by students and some faculty seemed to challenge traditional values and ethical traditions of past educational foundations courses. For example, statements such as, "Whose values?" and "Whose morals?" were not stated within the context of a critical thinking analysis of ethical reasoning, but while examining traditional values theories in the educational philosophy of the profession. Such a challenge would seem to indicate confusion as to the meaning of morals and ethics in an educational philosophy grounded upon universal principles of right and wrong (Wall, 2003). Also, such challenges question the relevance of educational philosophy in an educational institution (in this study, Iowa State University) that is now predominantly sciences- and technology-oriented. Yet, returning to the initial quotations regarding the relevance of aesthetics in science and art, the reflection must include a synthesis and totality of meaning in the process of aesthetic value judgment as a philosophy of being. Critical/creative thinking becomes a necessary reasoning process in order to determine the appropriate response to what appears in this study to be a challenge of *all* traditional norms. Such a possibility requires interpretation of communication and clarification as to the intent of that communication as well as what lay beneath.

The analysis requires clarification of not only the meaning of aesthetics in educational philosophy, but also its foundation in the development of moral reasoning. For example, Baldwin (1997) has stated, "If social reason and human freedom are to prevail, the human life-world (culture, society, personality) must not be dominated by technical rationality and instrumental action" (p. 91). . Those universal principles of a theology of the soul manifested in a theology of beauty are in doubt at the institution examined, and quite possibly in other state universities nationwide, for it would seem unlikely that a theoretical conflict in one major university would be an isolated case (Hacker, 2005). As will be discussed, long-term investigations at the university by the Federal Bureau of Investigation resulted in findings of criminal activity that were linked to at least three other major state universities in the Midwest (White, 2000). This challenge seems consistent with concerns of a larger social challenge, a conflict between civilizations and the dominance of the traditional white male culture. Discussion of how this traditional worldview is being challenged as well as the consequences of that challenge will include the impact on aesthetic theory and moral reasoning.

Experiences at this university placed me outside the accepted circle of some in my profession in that it was my attempt to maintain a traditional aesthetic and ethical standard of reasoning and communication as central to the professions, with a continued focus on the family and the community, still considered the building blocks for the larger society. In fact, I was not even sure why there seemed a general atmosphere of confusion and a challenge to the traditional norms in higher education. I was not quite sure what was happening; was it a localized problem, a transition in the field of study, or a larger shift in the social norms of higher education? Perhaps it was some collective of practitioners measuring things, like blind men on an elephant, each believing he had found some unique piece, but missing the large beast in the room. Again, there seemed an attempt to create "class" warfare, when concepts of beauty were mentioned, that attempted to connect aesthetics and philosophical studies to an elitist perspective of the past. The new norm seemed to be a twisted theory of chaos as order and order as class elitism. Beauty, aesthetic sensibility, and morality were no longer themes politically acceptable in that traditional norms were being challenged in all areas of higher education and campus life. What was this about? My quest had begun.

I first began a search for new knowledge and meaning through the interpretation of a conflict first manifested in fine arts activities and works. As a symbolic method of communication of social norms, the fine arts provide an early glimpse into a change in process. It is a method of cultural and social communication. Chaos in communication indicated a deeper social problem. Particular works of art reflected what Baldwin (1989) has called social anomie and a breakdown of society, as a result of a loss of soul. I realized any inference as to the best explanation of this phenomenon required some background considerations. If, ultimately, there resulted an acceptance of a low probability of a final conclusion that a loss of soul of this profession was in process, an interpretive method of analyzing current issues in curriculum and aesthetics would provide a larger worldview. Implications might then be extended beyond the boundaries of this study (Graybosch, Scott, & Garrison, 1998; Sokal, 1996). The quantitative empirical method of analysis does not allow the experience of art and aesthetics as part of the context for analysis.

The dominance of empirical inquiry was not appropriate for this study and would force the research in the wrong direction. The counting of frequencies of occurrence of themes or terms would not provide the big picture. The very lack of an attempt to include issues of values, aesthetics, and morality may well have set the stage for the current moral dilemma in society (Baldwin, 1989). That this dilemma has been accepted as part of the current challenge to Western civilization is well established (Huntington, 1996/1997). What has been less visibly analyzed is how this conflict of civilizations and the world order are manifested in the college classroom and on college campuses across the country.

Various discussions about educational theory by Baldwin, Brown, and Richards (philosophers of education) were met with similar contentiousness. Questions of the need for clear speaking and communication in the 1995 philosophical dialogue sponsored by the Kappa Omicron Nu Honor Society echoed this observation of combativeness in academia (Brown & Baldwin, 1995). Yet, the profession's earliest leader, Caroline Hunt, made some of the most prophetic observations in 1902, which are similar to those of modern leaders such as Brown and Baldwin. We will begin our journey with a conversation with Hunt, because this remarkable woman began her career working with John Dewey at the University of Chicago. I will include Dewey's observations that were made during a joint conversation between the two that occurred early in the development of the laboratory schools in Chicago (East, 1982).

Dewey was developing a laboratory school for Domestic Science and

Industry. Hunt (in the tradition of Talbot before her) identified issues of her day. Hunt quotes Talbot's observations at the time: "Home economics is a subject for developing not mechanical or manual facility, not even hygienic habits, but the meaning of the physical, social, moral, esthetic, and spiritual conditions of the home to the individual and society" (Brown, 1985, p. 264). A moral philosophical base, which included concepts of aesthetics and beauty, was established (East, 1982, pp. 126–129). Thus, to challenge the consideration of aesthetics as a core concept in the curriculum was to challenge all that it implied, "the physical, social, moral, esthetic, and spiritual conditions of the home to the individual and the society" (Brown, 1985, p. 264). The aesthetic, social, and spiritual conditions of the home as the central core of the society would become the focus of an entire profession.

Dewey and Hunt were among the earliest advocates for public education as well as educational theorists. These early founders of public education in land grant universities would direct the development of educational theory for over 100 years. The early laboratory schools would become the foundation schools and structure for all educational theory for land grant universities across the nation and education theory in general up to and including the present day. The sister colleges in land grant universities were schools of home economics and the college of agriculture. From these foundations all other colleges would evolve, such as the college of arts and science, the college of fine arts, the college of business, among a few. Thus, the traditional educational theory established as a result of the research of John Dewey at the laboratory schools of Chicago was the foundations for all of higher education in public schools.

The conversations between Dewey and Hunt preceded the Lake Placid Conferences for home economics and the formation of home economics as a profession and the only access to higher education for women of that era. How ironic that we find Brown and Baldwin making similar calls for a theoretical reflection in their 1995 dialogue in the Kappa Omicron Nu Honor Society, *The Concept of Theory in Home Economics* (Kappa Omicron Nu, 1995, pp. 7–32). A more thorough discussion of the various qualitative inquiry methods relevant to this past tradition, Enlightenment, and current conflict, will be presented in the methods section. The primary methodological focus will be in the process of experience and phenomenological considerations of communication within the social context of meaning of daily life. Art and self-expression in aesthetics, being forms of communication as one concept of "being," will be discussed from their phenomenological and psychological (Jungian-hermeneutic) perspectives. Though the analysis will make some mention of the specifics of the home economics curriculum, the majority of the study focuses on general education, as, subsequent to this research document and the federal investigation, the college of home economics (family and consumer sciences education) doctoral programs have been terminated.

In addition to hermeneutics and psychological field theory, critical and creative thinking was considered from an arts-based genre, an analytical method that is also consistent with Jung's analytical perspective on how to interpret symbols and signs in communication (Whitmont, 1969). This analytical method becomes primary in our consideration of the role of aesthetics as a concept vital to education and "deep" psychology and the hidden meaning within all communication (Singer, 1994), especially aesthetics communication in the curriculum. The subtle symbolic meaning in all forms of communication is fluid, taking on cultural contexts. "In short, signs are not constituted by the interdependence between the expression itself and the reality for which it stands, whereas in the case of symbols there is a necessary relationship between the two" (Brown, 1981). Jung expounded upon personal mythologized symbols being expanded to reflect collective meaning through his three levels of analytical psychology. It will be argued that the various forms of communication, which will include art-based genre as communication, reflect a disintegrating society, in a Western culture that has lost its mystical sense of identity (Jung, 1961; Wundt 1980).

My own worldview has been influenced by a background in art (impressionist painting), music (voice), psychology (as a trained counselor married to a Jungian-trained therapist and treatment director), a doctor of philosophy in education theory and philosophy in general education, medicine, investigations, law enforcement, and political science. This multidisciplinary perspective has enriched and substantiated my interpretations and perceptions of the issues of aesthetics in curriculum from an eclectic and multidimensional approach, heavily oriented toward political science and psychological analysis. The choice of Dewey as the primary educational philosopher and particularly a focus on his aesthetics philosophy, along with the considerations of the Scottish Enlightenment, became more remarkable as the research progressed. Friends were calling from beyond the veil of obscurity. The significance of cycles of Enlightenment is more specific to the hermeneutics and phenomenological methods of inquiry and will be explained as well. Ashfield and De Bolla (1996) explain the significance of aesthetics during the Enlightenment: "Our senses of the self, society, science (in the sense of knowledge) are both derived from and dependent on models created during the eighteenth century: we are, to all intents and purposes, children of the enlightenment" (1996, p. 1). Thus, the relevance of aesthetics to not only the intellectual movement of the period, but the foundations of educational theory, with its original roots of women's studies in the field of home economics is without question. As a core concept in general education in most university curricula, regardless of whether it is housed in the colleges of sciences or humanities, aesthetics is held critical to the adequate education of an enlightened and truly educated person. Ashfield and De Bolla (1996) continue with the following clarification about aesthetics during the Enlightenment:

> More specifically in relation to the subject of aesthetics it fell to this period in particular to articulate the complexities of affective experience, and it did so in the context of an emerging new understanding of the construction of the subject. The new subject the site of various appetites and desires, was increasingly cut loose from the old certainties, which grounded and provided guarantees for the subject in a predominantly religious culture. It is this change from and epistemology based in theoretical belief and debate to one in which man must find from within himself the grounds of knowledge, which above all others distinguishes the enlightenment as the single most important moment in the history of the concept of the aesthetic (p. 1).

The type of data analysis used for this study moved from a consideration of content analysis to what became a very obvious need for historical and transcendental phenomenological hermeneutics. These methods are more appropriate to reflective examinations of the past Enlightenment. Again and again, those from the past who "stood on the backs of giants" and "the true ancients of the world and on the shoulders of those who have gone before" were calling (Baldwin, 1989; Gilbert & Kuhn, 1939, 1953, 1954, 1972, p. ix).

The process of incorporating a form of historical transcendental phenomenological hermeneutics in a search for a clearer interpretation and significance of meaning through communication would also require critical theory and thinking for a reflective critique and cause for action consistent with ethical reasoning (Baldwin & Brown, 1995). An explanation of a sort of experiential hermeneutics will be presented in the process of the journey of discovery. This particular aspect of the methodology lends itself quite appropriately to the incorporation of an earlier investigation of hermeneutic methodology in Brown's study, *Jung's Hermeneutic of Doctrine: Its Theological Significance* (Brown, 1981) and Eco's *Interpretation and Over Interpretation* (Collini, 1992). Brown's 1977 doctoral dissertation for the University of Chicago presents not only a rationale and justification for the hermeneutic phenomenology methodology, but provides a sequential link to the educational psychology and tradition of Dewey and Hunt via Jungian psychology and a hermeneutic doctrine in the interpretation of signs and symbols (Collini, 1992).

The journey through this history of philosophical masters allowed a path of historical reasoning and collective consciousness for the consideration of experience as a continuum, a simultaneity of time and space—truly a hermeneutic phenomenology. Consideration of the unique history of the now long-gone profession of (home economics) family and consumer sciences in the formative years of general education theory is central to the examination of conflict in education across the curricula. The "gentle child of academia" (home economics) would ultimately be left the victim of bullying; that is one reason for publishing the analysis presented in this study.

The gentle child, the gentle spirit of knowledge based upon universal truth and a theology of beauty is no more. Brown (1983), who moved from a graduate degree in political science to her doctoral degree in home economics, established benchmarks for that early educational profession that set the standard for future foundations courses in education theory still taught in modern education ethics, political science, and psychology courses. I also advanced from a graduate degree in political science to a doctoral degree in education. Thus, I find Brown's perspective regarding conflicts in cultural and social transition periods examined from the perspective of not only an education theorist, philosopher, and practitioner, but also a political scientist. Brown's doctoral dissertation states best the beginning and the end of why this study came to be, a critical reflection about a lost profession as well as the end of an era in education history and theoretical foundations. One of my own questions is do we really want to change the nature of the sublime?

Purpose

The purpose of this analysis was to review present and long-range educational theories in educational curriculum as related to concepts of aesthetics and conflict. Further, a goal of the analysis was to interpret indications of conflict in education theory as a paradigm shift away from traditional values education and the larger society in general. The ultimate consequence of various conflicts on the campus, the riots at both Iowa State University and Southern Illinois University, are the destructive events that will be briefly considered from the perspective of archetypal field theory in systems pattern analysis. Readers are directed to Conforti (1999) at the Assisi Institute for further details about the use of systems pattern analysis in conflicts. The current changes in educational curricula toward global standards required consideration of traditional educational theories, evolving in part from Dewey's heuristic educational philosophies that are centered on aesthetics (Zeltner, 1975). In these philosophies, aesthetics and beauty become analogous to a theology of beauty. The association between the development of home economics and family and consumer sciences later could be found in the general education focus of Dewey's educational theory.

The aesthetic link was examined within the context of a larger global paradigm shift in cognition and values theory in education. Dewey's philosophy continues to seem relevant in the globalization of education, so the fact that similar conflicts were occurring at Southern Illinois University, home of the Center for Dewey Studies, may be relevant, for example, if there is to be a central role for aesthetics concepts within global education (Zeltner, 1975). It is the link between aesthetics and cognition, visual stimulation (such as in art) and theories of social evolution in democracy which require a closer examination of Dewey's aesthetics, the Scottish Enlightenment, the arts, and a global enlightenment in progress (Curreri-Alibrandi, 1996).

Similar shifts in cognitive awareness seen in previous periods of enlightenment will be identified (Jauss, 1982; Man, 1982). The clarification of the role of aesthetics in these periods will focus special attention on the Scottish Enlightenment for possible indications of the new enlightenment in process. Dewey's aesthetic philosophy and progressive theory are the primary educational theories because of their relevance to a global movement that incorporates aesthetics concepts into the curricula as a given, progressive education as a pedagogical technique, and philosophical goals involving global democratization. The relevance of the underlying goal of global democratization as central in Dewey's aesthetics will help us further identify the significance of a challenge to aesthetics as also indicative of a challenge of Western civilization and global democratization (Dewey, 1946).

Goals of the research include the identification of the central role of aesthetic concepts and their origins in theology (Heidegger, 1992), in general education, and in family and consumer sciences and general education within this global movement (Zeltner, 1979). The cycles of aesthetics in educational theory, with Dewey's central aesthetics philosophy in relation to general education and family and consumer sciences curricula, have been examined to determine if and to what extent modifications in curricula are appropriate. Finally, the possibility of current challenges of aesthetics in education as a core concept being indicative of the larger challenge will be examined through critical thinking, with some final causes for action recommended.

Objectives

1. Recognize the human need for beauty and aesthetics by examining general theories of order versus chaos in an aesthetics philosophy. Dewey's theory of education and aesthetics philosophy are considered most specifically.

2. Identify the search for beauty and aesthetics in individuals and group behavior through personal expression and communication, demeanor, clothing, architecture, interactions, arts objects, music, and other forms of human communication consistent with interpretive methods of inquiry in the qualitative research tradition.

3. Examine the current trend in reconstruction of aesthetic value as a relevant component of general education and in family and consumer sciences education.

4. Identify connections of the enlightenment periods, specifically, the Scottish Enlightenment, and their relevance to a current revitalization of Dewey's aesthetics philosophy in the progressive educational movement as it applies to general education and inferences about larger social generalizations.

5. Consider the critique of current aesthetic consciousness, consistent with hermeneutics, phenomenology, and critical theory through critical/creative thinking, in the development of recommendations for action.

6. Examine the process of Jungian field theory and systems pattern analysis (Conforti, 1999), to examine the specific incidents of mobbing of an individual and a profession as an indication of an archetypal complex in play that resulted in a major riot at the university.

Research Questions

The study was designed to answer the following research questions:

1. What is the current role of John Dewey's aesthetics philosophy as it leads to a general progressive educational movement and its impact on education?

2. Are education college curricula consistent with the philosophical aesthetics (arts-based) trends that are occurring in general education?

3. Is there an identifiable enlightenment movement impacting the consideration of aesthetics as a necessary component to curricula in higher education?

4. Can systems pattern analysis assist not only in identification of a social complex in play, but also as a predictor events, leading to a revitalized profession of human sciences.

5. Is Jungian field theory and specifically, systems pattern analysis a viable exemplar to predict and modify destructive conflicts on university campuses?

Assumptions

It was assumed the historical records, communications, images, and antiquities of the periods examined and analyzed were accurate, valid, and correct representations, and not forged. Further, it was assumed the researcher, as research instrument, would present and portray interpretations as accurately as possible and provide triangulation for substantiation and objective analysis. The major assumptions for phenomenological hermeneutics were applied in the gathering and interpretations of data. Hultgren (1989) provides major assumptions to be considered in phenomenological hermeneutics methodology as follow:

1. Understanding is both epistemological (theoretical) and ontological (grounded on existence of God);

2. Understanding is intrinsically historical;

3. Understanding is linguistic;

4. Understanding always functions in three modes of temporality: past, present, and future;

5. Understanding is a dialectical process between self-understanding and what is encountered in the world;

6. Understanding is a happening, an event, and not a psychological process of comprehension.

7. Meaning or reality is socially constructed, not the property of some individual;

8. Knowledge is context dependent and human experience is context bound;

9. The knower and what is known are closely involved with one another; and

10. Inquiry is a moral endeavor (Hultgren, 1989).

Limitations

Time and finances limited the collecting of documents, communications, images, and the review of sound recordings, concerts, and art exhibitions for the period of arts-based data collection. Concepts of aesthetics were limited to general educational theory of aesthetics within the Western tradition. Concepts of aesthetics were limited to those applicable to aesthetics in general education and home economics, later family and consumer sciences, curricula in general. Although some consideration of aesthetics in textiles and clothing curricula was examined, it was with the intent of providing examples of personal and social manifestations of aesthetics in daily experience. Consideration of aesthetics within science was of a general nature in defining and examining global trends in an enlightenment process.

The discussions of aesthetics in music and fine art were limited to the examination of the experiential context of aesthetics in the larger, more general content of life experiences, not as a separate discipline, such as art criticism. All considerations of aesthetics within the philosophy of education were with the intent of finding hermeneutic value themes manifested through various forms of communications. The search for value themes within the context of aesthetics was targeted for the development of an educational theory from within a general educational framework.

Significance of the Study

Brown (1989) identified the qualities of good research and the significance of that research linked to information that makes an important contribution to insight and practice in the professions. This significance is further clarified as important if others learn something by reading the study. Brown recognized an absence of needed research and studies that interpret values orientation. This analysis provides a search for values orientation and interpretation of aesthetics within that context in the curriculum of family and consumer sciences and general education and leads toward recommendations for further action. The general move toward a multidisciplinary and trans-disciplinary process and content across all disciplines has been mandated by the U. S. Department of Education. For example, the mandate to teach critical and creative thinking as well as philosophical inquiry is a return to the earliest tradition of education theory introduced by John Dewey and the founders of home economics (family and consumer sciences) and now general education. The significance of identifying the early history of education and women's access to education as a component of the last Enlightenment movement is consistent with the consideration of the elements of critical and creative thinking, specifically, hermeneutics and phenomenology, as sub-categories of the critical and creative thinking process.

The stated limitations of the study are in concert with an awareness of a massive heuristic tradition of aesthetics, along with a continually evolving body of findings. The analysis limits considerations to aesthetics in development of a framework for values orientation and interpretation toward social action. The definitions and justifications for the research questions, during the process of an evolving interpretation, lead to the final critical appraisal of the findings. The research questions are incorporated and approached in a circular process and synthesis through symbols for awareness of aesthetics as a concept in our everyday lives. The revelation of what lies beneath these various forms of communication leads to a call for rational criticism and possible revision of our current position within the family and consumer sciences and general education curricula with a goal toward a more expanded worldview consistent with other disciplines and their incorporation of aesthetics curriculum in higher education (Costa & Liebermann, 1997; Paul, 1995).

Finally, the hermeneutics method of inquiry used in this study promotes a shared understanding of aesthetics and its relevance to the family and consumer sciences curricula and aesthetics cognition in general. The clarification of the significance of the Enlightenment movement in regard to hermeneutics promotes more meaningful understanding of aesthetics in its totality of experience, whether of art, music, clothing, or other existential communications, and of its perspective within a larger worldview phenomenon. The application of critical theory in the development of conclusions and recommendations for action are an appropriate follow-up to interpretations of meaning from a phenomenological and hermeneutic doctrine of cognition.

Clarification and understanding of aesthetics in daily living promotes a cause for action for its future inclusion in curricula content considerations in general education, policy formulation, and social action from a position of global social evolution. Consistent with the original intent of aesthetics as a core philosophy by Dewey in his progressive education movement, aesthetics as a core concept tied to a theology of beauty is also linked to the teaching of independent thought and democratic thinking. The challenge of the Western civilizations' traditional Judeo-Christian culture is thus not only a conflict of theological tradition, but also the democratic philosophy that is best understood through an overarching aesthetic knowing. The evaluation of that possibility is followed by alternative courses of action to respond to such eventuality.

Definition of Terms

Several terms are defined for use in the study. The following are general definitions applicable to the analysis:

Aesthetics: A philosophy of art and beauty where balance, form, ethics, and virtue are the harmonious balance of life as experienced (Heidegger, 1981/1993).

Art: According to Croce, art is one of the major forms of the human spirit, the work of the spirit in its aesthetical aspect. Spirit manifests itself as well in a logical and a practical synthesis, the latter exhibiting itself in the economic and moral activities of man. Croce refers to these various aspects of spirit as "the circle of spiritual activity." At the foundation of all knowledge is art, for intuition, the stuff of art, precedes concepts (As cited in Hofstadter & Kuns, 1979, p. 555).

Arts-based genre: The particular modes of inquiry that are composed of a constellation of ground rules, methodologies, and techniques within the inquiry tradition of the arts-based process, i.e., case study, ethnography, grounded theory, personal narrative, biography, discourse analysis, literary criticism, and art criticism, as related to the humanities and fine arts (Piantanida & Garman, 1999).

Archetype: Sharp (2009) states that the archetype appears in consciousness as a universal and recurring image, pattern, or motif representing a typical human experience. Archetypal images come from the collective unconscious and are the basic content of religions, mythologies, and legends in art. They also emerge from the collective unconscious in individuals through dreams and visions. The encounter with an archetypal image evokes a strong emotional reaction, conveying a sense of divine or transpersonal power which transcends the ego.

Complex: Sharp (2009) defines a complex as an emotionally charged unconscious entity composed of a number of associated ideas grouped around a central core which is an archetypal image. One recognizes that a complex has been activated when emotion upsets psychic balance and disturbs the customary function of the ego.

Critical science: The process, the course of action taken by individuals and groups to collaboratively examine and critique present social structures for the purpose of their own emancipation (Gentzler, 1999).

Critical theory: Is the outcome of the process, the end result of a process designed to expose inherent incongruities related to the social situations (Gentzler, 1999).

Critical thinking: An active, purposeful, organized cognitive process we use to carefully examine our thinking and the thinking of others, to clarify and improve our understanding (Paul, 1995; Topp, 1999).

Ego: Sharp (2009) defines ego as the center of consciousness and the seat of the individual's experience of subjective identity.

Hermeneutics theory: A worldview or philosophic orientation of essence. Historical inquiry is one of the hermeneutic processes of interpretation of human action where cognition is understood within the context of the social reality of the times. This concept is central in Dewey's discussion of reflection in critical thinking; Brown's discussion of Jung's hermeneutic doctrine (Brown, 1977); and Brown's philosophy of the profession (Brown, 1985), (Dewey, 1922).

Historical hermeneutics: A more specifically defined aspect of hermeneutics, as depth hermeneutics, in a systematic search for deep understanding or meaning and truth in the content of text, and of the ways in which persons subjectively experience (perceive, interpret, plan, act, feel, value, evaluate) the social world (Hultgren, 1989).

Intersubjectivity: The state involving or occurring between separate conscious minds, as the intersubjective communication made accessible to or capable of being established for two or more subjects. Intersubjectivity is the communication between individuals of mutuality and understanding (Baldwin, 1986; Morgaine, 1997; Whybrow, 1997).

Phenomenology: A twentieth-century philosophical movement dedicated to describing the structures of experience as they present themselves to consciousness, without recourse to theory, deduction, or assumptions. Phenomenology is understood as the experiencing of the world through the study of essence, according to Husserl, Heidegger, Ricoeur, and Gadamer (Hallery, C., Hurwitz, R., & Duffy, G., 1987).

Philosophy: The system of beliefs, traditions, norms, and values, which have led to the current mission of the professions of education and family and consumer sciences education.

Portrayal: A presentation of a critique of music, art, or objects, and/ or a dialogue concerning the interpretation of the aesthetics components relevant to the aesthetic experience (Piantanida & Garman, 1999).

Progressivism: The educational movement led by John Dewey though separate from him, emphasizing aesthetics as its core and democracy as its process in teaching and learning (Dewey, 1922).

Scottish Enlightenment: The intellectual movement of the eighteenth and nineteenth centuries, and the major participants in the intelligentsia of the European enlightenment movement. Enlightenment movements immediately following the Scottish Enlightenment and evolution of the Victorian society were still influenced primarily by the first Scottish Enlightenment in the fifteenth century and the later movement of the eighteenth and nineteenth centuries, and were thus considered part of the Enlightenment (Chitnis, 1986).

Systems pattern analysis: According to Conforti (1999), patterns are expressions of a field. Thus, hand in hand with field, form, and what will evolve or become, there is a pattern or repetition of action that is indicative of an archetypal field. The archetype is an intimation of the soul and substance in the material realization of the field. The symbol and metaphor of the field tells a very specific story. A story about, for example, a potential empty wine glass and a bottle of wine tells a specific story about the wine, the glass, and the metaphor of the wine.

Theory: The belief, policy, or procedure proposed or followed as the basis of action (her method is based on the theory that all children can learn). In this study, it means the educational worldview or dominant philosophy (Mish, 1994).

Triangulation: The practice of comparing results from data designed to measure the same construct but collected from different sources and/ or by different methods to increase certainty about the validity of the construct.

Organization of the Study

The study begins with an *introduction* that includes a statement of the problem or issue of conflict between the key concepts of aesthetics in education that also infers conflicts between civilizations, prompting this investigation, its importance of the issue in regard to current and future direction in higher education curriculum planning, and a list of definitions of terms. The *objectives* and *research questions* precede the *review of literature* in chapter two. The third chapter reviews issues of art and aesthetics in education; core knowledge programs, aesthetics in family and consumer sciences and general education curricula, Dewey's aesthetic philosophy, Dewey's concern for community, phenomenological aesthetics, and the Scottish Enlightenment. These areas of investigation form the framework for the historical transcendental phenomenological hermeneutic analysis and critical theory in critique of the problems presented.

I consider the development of a "universal history" as well as a potential renewed aesthetic movement toward a "point of perfection" as, for example, a new enlightenment, or, the final stage of social degeneration and decay (Jauss, 1982; Wundt, 1921). This "universal history" analysis is focused upon the consideration of Western civilization, and an assumption of general knowledge of the "shrinking" Western influence (Huntington, 1996/1997) from the position of the traditional white male culture. This past tradition and that of manifest destiny in relation to Christ-consciousness and the "concept of history and the various stages of mental culture" are considered from the perspective of a "transcendence of a history of a single people," Western civilization (Wundt, 1921, p. 512). Thus, the process of revelation of meaning in hermeneutics becomes also the hermeneutic methodology of "becoming" (Brown, 1977).

The chapter also provides a more in-depth description and rationale for the use of historical transcendental phenomenological hermeneutics and the *methods and procedures* of conducting the research. The section explains the evolving nature of qualitative interpretive inquiry leading to the research findings.

The *interpretation* presents the major findings of the research in the fourth section. The *conclusion, implications, and cause for action* evolve from the findings and are presented in Chapter 5, along with a summary, recommendations, and future research where appropriate. Included in Chapter 5 are recommendations for further study and analysis using Conforti's (1999) Jungian analytical field theory and systems pattern analysis for implications as to the archetypal complexes in play at Iowa State University and other major universities, such as Southern Illinois University, where civil disturbances continue to present security issues.

CHAPTER 2. METHODOLOGY

Or ever the silver cord be loosed, or the golden
bowl be broken, or the pitcher be broken at the
fountain, or the wheel broken at the cistern, then
shall the dust return to the earth as it was; and the
spirit shall return unto God that gave it.

(Ecclesiastes, 12:6–7)

Background Considerations about the Hermeneutic Sciences, Critical Thinking and Systems Pattern Analysis

Baldwin (1989) tells us that knowledge is developed through human beings who communicate through speaking and interpretation of actions in dialogue with others. Included in this dialogue are considerations of the past and different cultures about common concerns of human life. Thus, knowledge is concerned with universal concepts and information. The historical context of individual lives and universal history has led to the development of social behavior and language of social conduct, and development of a sense of what is morally right. Hermeneutics attempts to answer questions through moral critique (Paul, 2000) and comprehensibility of truth and rightness of norms through philosophical inquiry (Baldwin, 1989).

An imbalance in the interpretation of the human dimensions of communication and symbols in the empirical sciences by, for example, ignoring issues of morality and values has led to anomie and a breakdown of cultural traditions. The development of adolescent psychopathology in social violence is only one manifestation of cultural fragmentation in the challenge of traditional norms (Brady, 2001). The dominance of empirical science, in the choice of quantitative methodology over qualitative methodology in research analysis and the ignoring of human social implications, has led to a loss of practical moral reasoning, communicative competence, and moral sensitivity within the American society (Baldwin, 1989). This was not the original intent of empirical analytic inquiry at the time of its inception (Wright, 1873). However, the loss of the incorporation of values as a concept linking the process of ends and means has resulted in this imbalance in empirical analytic reasoning and inquiry (Dewey, 1922).

Baconian pragmatism (in reference to Sir Francis Bacon, the prophet of pragmatic conception of knowledge) is expounded on as a scientific method within the context of society and change where moral reasoning is considered of primary importance (Eisley, 1967). From this perspective, the ultimate goal of knowledge is progress, but progress with a goal toward an improved human condition. For example, in the nineteenth century Bacon warned:

> that while we have been reasonably successful in obtaining command of nature by means of science, our science is not yet such that this command is systematically and preeminently applied to the relief of human suffering. (Wright, 1873, p. 89)

Bacon explained that the dignity of knowledge in the archetype or first platform, knowledge in God, is wisdom (Weinberger, 1985). Thus, morals must also be considered within the context of time and space and the process of change (Dewey, 1920, 1948). The new form of inductive reasoning designed by Bacon emphasized the search for new knowledge. Bacon noted his concern for the process of ends and means in alerting investigators that, at the perfecting of his design and a speeding up of its application, the primary intent should remain the production of "a prompt harvest for mankind," a harvest of knowledge that improved the state of existence for mankind (Farrington, 1964). The concern for a systematic inductive reasoning with focus on interpretation of human communication toward social action is to be found in hermeneutic inquiry

(Heidegger, 1993). Ethical dilemmas, such as the ends and the means, are more consistently applied through the application of this qualitative method of inquiry, versus quantitative inquiry alone, especially where social issues are at stake. The use and applicability of empirical inquiry does not preclude the relevance of qualitative research. Eco clarifies the specific adequacy of hermeneutics as appropriate for linguistic phenomena:

> Hermetic thought states that our language, the more ambiguous and multivalent it is, and the more it uses symbols and metaphors, the more it is particularly appropriate for naming a Oneness in which the coincidence of opposites occurs ... Hermetic thought transforms the whole world theater into a linguistic phenomenon and at the same time denies language any power of communication. (Eco, 1992, p, 32)

The power of communication is contingent upon mutual understanding between parties—intersubjectivity. The use of universal symbols in the translation process for clarification of ambiguous language aims at accurate interpretation of the intended meaning of communication.

General Considerations About Hermeneutics

Hermeneutics has been defined generally as the science of interpretation (Brown, 1989). Hermeneutics research serves to promote shared understanding and mutual agreement and the renewal or repair of communications about meanings in human existence (p. 268). Radnitzky (1968, 1970, 1973) explains that hermeneutic science is concerned with the objectification of human cultural experiences with the intent of interpreting human interaction and identifying normative patterns. Thus, hermeneutics is very similar to systems pattern analysis in Jungian psychology (Conforti, 1999). We will consider normative patterns in this study as they relate to cycles of enlightenment and conflict which precedes enlightenment. I would argue that systems pattern analysis is quite similar to hermeneutic patterns, as may be seen in the following description of patterns in psyche and nature as explained by Conforti (1999):

While patterns are ever present in the outer, natural world, we also see the clustering of archetypal material into recognizable patterns within the cultural and social domain. Each culture, in response to some intrinsic sense of meaning, creates rituals and customs expressive of it. (p. 14)

In addition, I will consider two levels of hermeneutics involving interpretive or human sciences and inquiry at the level of hermeneutic theory and philosophical hermeneutics as explained by Brown (1989). The use of hermeneutic philosophy results in more full disclosure of the subject matter and the explication of universal meaning in everyday life (Brown, 1989, pp. 274–275). However, I will add to the philosophical discussion a consideration of the psychological interpretive process, where relevant to our examination. Thus, the analysis of cycles of social change and the meaning of communication in challenging existing Western civilization will require the hermeneutic disclosure of subject and explication of universal meaning. The search for an archetypal field theory, where a cluster of behavior may indicate development of an archetypal field, a complex, of social psychosis, will also be examined.

This analysis considers hermeneutics as a science in the attempt to understand the meaning-content of symbolic systems of various forms of human communication. Yet, like aesthetics in general, the need for consideration of intersubjectivity and the structure of reality is most often applied to the philosophy of hermeneutics. Historical hermeneutic inquiry has a fundamental interest in communication and consensus for social integration with a focus upon the historical relevance of reality as influenced by past generations and social mores. It provides "another way of knowing; another way of viewing the world" within a context of religious ideology, as this is the central concept of universal history (Baldwin, 1989; Wundt, 1921). This other way of knowing is more intuitive, yet may be conducted in a systematic process of reasoning, which includes concepts of religious ideology (Brown, 1977; Finlay, 1981, pp. 308–309; Wundt, 1921).

I will include further descriptions of the characteristics of hermeneutic study from the philosophical perspective of, for example, Schleiermacher, and the more recent modern emphasis on text as emphasized by Gadamer, Seidel, and Eco who clarify intent. Like Eco, Seidel attempts to explain the significance of the intent of communication and the actual responsibility of the reader or listener in the communication process:

Thus, the task of interpretation is understood as seeking to grasp the spirit, the Muse, that inspires the author and is present [again, hopefully] in the inspired text produced, whatever that "text" may be. ... The hermeneutic of motivation, intention, intent, and inspiration is then applied to a variety of "texts," in ascending order, from the level of sense, through understanding, to science, to the psyche of psychology, the social, etc. Such a phenomenology of Spirit does not proceed dialectically, however, but hermeneutically, while at the same time recognizing that such a process can occur only if Spirit "were present and wished to be present at the start and all along the way." (Seidel, 2000, p. 9)

Though concepts of human science, hermeneutics, and phenomenology are often used interchangeably, the method of order in the interpretation and descriptive process should be explicated. The process of hermeneutic phenomenology is based upon traditions of German and Dutch "osmosis" of sorts in that either one can transcend this description and interpretation in the process of what Van Manen calls "the spirit of human science scholarship," or regress (Van Manen, 1990, p. 3). "Phenomenology describes how one orients to lived experience, hermeneutics describes how one interprets the "texts" of life, and semiotics is used here to develop a practical writing or linguistic approach to the method of phenomenology and hermeneutics" (Van Manen, 1990, p. 4).

The rationale of hermeneutics is concerned with knowledge produced through human interaction. Thus, thoughts, language, or any other form of symbolic interaction, such as music, poetry, and painting, in communication within the world of nature and societies are intertwined in hermeneutics (Brown, 1977, 1985). As a method of inquiry, hermeneutics provides a sense of mutuality in an enlightened social order (Brown, 1985). Dewey has identified this process in education as follows: "Education should provide a variety of kinds of experience, for example, with nature, in social life, and in art and aesthetics so that active reflective participation in these experiences would enable the individual to develop autonomy and creativity" (Brown, p. 307).

We find in hermeneutics "the affinities of phenomenology and pragmatism" by the focus of theories of Dewey and Bacon (empiricists) in the hermeneutical method of inquiry (Boydston, 2000). Further, Dewey's "instrumentalism" is a guide to ethical analysis and criticism bridging scientific knowledge and morals (Brown, 1985). Thus, one of the fundamental purposes of criticism in philosophical studies and the development of rational insight and justification is best met by the hermeneutic method of inquiry (Brown, 1985, p. 125).

A historical analysis of archival records and communications for aesthetics theory, with special emphasis on Dewey's educational philosophy and the Scottish Enlightenment, has been conducted (Gilber & Kuhn, 1939). Although other periods of intellectual enlightenment are mentioned within the context of hermeneutics (Hultgren 1989), time constraints limited the study to the consideration of the Scottish Enlightenment. There is one extension of the Enlightenment concept presented by Gaetano Curreri-Albrani (1996), though it is not identified as an Enlightenment movement. His presentation of what he terms "visual plural-dimensionalism" is very much consistent with an enlightenment process on a global scale that is applicable to consideration of a modern enlightenment movement (Chitnis, 1986).

Within the method of hermeneutics, especially in reference to the spoken language, concepts are interpreted within the context of the current times for their meanings. For example, the meaning of the word "prejudice" is often not the modern meaning of "prejudice," such as social bias. For example, Hultgren (1989) speaks of such a term in discussing Gadamer's interpretation of dialectic hermeneutics: "It is here where he says hermeneutic problems come in and he suggests that a fundamental rehabilitation of the concepts of 'prejudice' is required from the Enlightenment's interpretation." In this context, "prejudice" is to be interpreted to mean anticipation of meaning, a preconceived notion of meaning. Thus, separating the true prejudices by which we understand from the false ones by which we misunderstand is a crucial task of hermeneutic conversation (dialectic) in the art of conducting a conversation (Hultgren, 1989, p. 48). Therefore, there is an attempt to discern and interpret meaning within the context of the times and make application of the information and communication to the current times.

The examination includes analysis of modern themes and recurring patterns somewhat similar to the meaning of aesthetics during the Scottish Enlightenment. There are some references to aesthetics within the context of hermeneutics when speaking of the Enlightenment. This will be clarified later, as there are cycles of enlightenment in addition to the Scottish Enlightenment. This included general consideration of such ideas as the "heartbeat" of the earth, and a series of vibration changes in the cycles of the earth's base frequency changes, i.e., Schumann Resonance (8 cycles to 13 cycles) and Fibonacci Series (the fundamental code of patterns of life on earth, i.e., 1,1,3,5,8, and now, 13). Conforti (1999) also considered Fibonacci patterns (p. 14) in the development of a field theory in Jungian systems pattern analysis. My examination of the enlightenment cycles also follows closely and is similar to processes identified by Hutcheson during the Scottish Enlightenment period in the use of such concepts as beauty and virtue in patterns of balance and form (Kivy, 1973).

Hutcheson, one of the earliest researchers of aesthetics, was also identified as a man who "stood on the backs of giants" of the past traditions. What constituted an Enlightenment, and the Scottish Enlightenment, led to the evolution of Victorian society immediately afterward (Chitnis, 1986). The Enlightenment for this dissertation is the period of the Scottish Enlightenment and the hermeneutics process of Gadamer and Habermas (Palmer, 1969). For, as Gadamer has asserted, "Modern historical research is not only research but the transmission of tradition and that the foundation for study of history is hermeneutics" (Hultgren, 1989, p. 49). Thus, our conversation with the past is also a clarification and conversation with the present and future through hermeneutics.

Patterns of Thought as Phenomenological Research

Cycles of changes of cognition have been identified by the sociologist Sorokin (1928) in his studies of the fluctuations, rhythms, and cycles of social processes and habits of thought (Heidegger, 1992). The notion of time and social thought being linear was consistent with the interpretation of reality at the time (Sorokin, 1956, p. 728). Now, we find science and society in the process of readjusting their interpretation of reality to fit the needs of science once more (Baldwin, 1989), and simultaneity of processes requires multiple dimensions of concurrent thought and actions. Again, the current research in science concerning changes in earth rhythm (similar to changed in brain wave patterns from sleep to awakened states of consciousness) and a rhythmic "heartbeat" of the earth suggests that the earth is about to awaken. The changes in the scientific analytical process have come as a result of reflective acts and folding back upon time in the critical analysis of existing patterns of thinking within a particular discipline (Brown, 1985). This provides the purpose of reflective history as part of hermeneutic phenomenology and a search for truth, whether scientific truth or social truth (Heidegger, 1988).

The significance of this early consideration of multidimensionality is relevant for our use of hermeneutics and phenomenology and concepts of knowing, such as osmosis. Arguments for "the phenomenal character of space and time are repeated with little change in the Transcendental Aesthetic," similar to the thought that it is "clearer and better than the Aesthetics treatment, and gives time the priority which space has in the Aesthetic" (Findlay, 1981, p. 80). The relevance of aesthetics from the perspective of theology is in its relation to notions of evolving consciousness and the universal history of religion in relation to progressive concepts of independence, freedom, and individual as well as social actualization.

Key Elements of Phenomenological Research

The general guidelines for developing concepts of descriptive phenomenological research as a component of interpretive hermeneutics must include essential elements. These elements are presented by Hultgren (1989) as follows:

1. The turning to the nature of lived experience by: a. an orienting of oneself to the phenomena; b. the formulating the phenomenological questions; c. the explicating of assumptions.

2. The application of existential investigation by: a. using personal experience, b. tracing derivations of words, idiomatic phrases, and obtaining experiential descriptions from others and in citations.

3. The application of phenomenological reflection, uncovering thematic aspects from descriptions, and composing linguistic transformations through deep questioning. The use of phenomenological writing by: a. attending to the speaking of language, identification of varying examples, and writing and rewriting.(Hultgren, 1989, p. 52)

Rules of Validity and Reliability

Hultgren (1989) also developed guidelines for using rules of validity in the interpretation of qualitative research and has provided the following rules:

1. The rule of intention asks (Hultgren):

    a. What are the person's intentions in relation to the primary ideas being communicated through projects to which actions are directed, and motives, and reasons?

    b. What are the persons' frames of reference (background, goals, assumptions, and values, experience, and interest) from which they speak?

    c. What is the ongoing "grammar" of the situation (words in relation to the whole of the communication)?

2. The rule of context:

    What is the immediate, biographical, group, or institution relating to the communication? (Hultren, 1989, p. 56)

These rules of validity and guidelines were utilized in participant and non-participant observations, listening, and reading in the literature review. Visual symbols, as an essential part of human communications systems in industry, technology, and daily life, were considered within a framework of the phenomenological method of aesthetics critique. This allowed a process to interpret symbolic messages through thematic analysis (Hicks, 1993; Holsti, 1969; Krippendorff, 1985; Weber, 1990).

Validation

The validation of interpretations and inferences was achieved through specific examples, both positive and negative aesthetic exemplars (unanticipated results from the environment or the teaching method) (Posner & Rudnitsky, 1997). Inferences were made from the data collected and the methods of reporting, i.e., the observed and interpreted meanings, and triangulation through cross-references of interpretations with previous aesthetics researchers. Background research considered such authors as Mann, Hegel, Foucault, Habermas, Lyas, Michelis, Dondis, Matias, Knieter, Morris, and Paul. Additional aesthetics educators in our own profession were considered, including Dendel, East, Baldwin, Brown, Hunt, Hultgren, and LeBaron Hilton.

Method of Data Collection

The collection of data was by a combination of review of archival records, heuristic literature review, field observations, and arts-based genre in the portrayal of the Scottish aesthetic, specifically. The dominant data analysis method was to use an interpretive method of inquiry through historical transcendental phenomenological hermeneutics (Baldwin & Brown, 1995). The optimum technique for the study of human behavior is claimed to be indirect, through an analysis of communication, whether paintings, writings, music, essays, texts, songs, or any type of communication (Dondis, 1973). This methodology section has been further developed into specific procedures for the process of the qualitative research and historical hermeneutics/phenomenological method with critical theory and thinking applied in a final critique of interpretations and findings (Hultgren & Coomer, 1989).

Concepts of Continuous Literature Review

The outcome of phenomenological inquiry or hermeneutic

phenomenology was an increased awareness of different ways of thinking and acting. The search for new alternatives of interpretation of existing and new knowledge through aesthetics intelligence, leading to actions to better serve the good of mankind, is an ongoing process. A constant reassessment of the state of being and interacting in this process of evolving has occurred within the body of research and interpretation. Just as the state of being is not constant but ever changing, so too is the need for updating, reflecting, and re-evaluating key concepts of experiencing, such as aesthetics cognition, as part of cognitive evolution and the acquisition and search for new knowledge (Costa & Leibermann, 1997).

The construction of a full interpretive description of some aspect of the life-world, remaining aware that a lived life is always more complex than the explication of the meaning revealed, is the goal of this discussion:

> The aim is to construct an animating, evocative description (text) of human actions, behaviors, intentions, and experiences as we meet them in the life world. To this purpose the human scientist likes to make use of the works of poets, authors, artists, cinematographers—because it is in this work that the variety and possibility of human experience may be found in condensed and transcended form. (Van Manen, 1990, p. 19)

In this study the researcher also discusses experiential data: "[T]he author, the poet, the artist, transforms (fictionalizes, poetizes, re-shapes) ordinary human experience in infinite variety" (van Manen, 1990, p. 19). The difference is that this artist-as-researcher expands the phenomenal process by using historical transcendental hermeneutic phenomenology. The hermeneutic process "aims at making explicit and seeking universal meaning where poetry and literature remain implicit and particular," and the use of phenomenology is subsequent to hermeneutics in a spiral fashion. The hermeneutic circle or spiral explicates, "human science starts where poetry [and art] has reached its end point" (p. 19). Phenomenology begins where art ends.

Major Assumptions of Phenomenological Hermeneutics

1. Phenomenological hermeneutics make clear what is unclear and enable the researcher to understand cultural phenomenon by bringing meaning into full human awareness;

2. The guiding interest of the research is centered on what shapes our lives and how we should live;

3. The research is done from a point of view that values as central to communication;

4. The focus of the investigation is in the meaning in communication;

5. The research incorporates the major assumptions of hermeneutics listed earlier;

6. Questions focus on experiences and perceptions;

7. Methods of validation involve intersubjectivity; and

8. The central traditions of phenomenology; hermeneutics, history, and ethnography lead to interpretation (Van Manen, 1990).

Critical Theory

Critical theory has as its goal emancipation from ideological or repressive conditions arising from everyday life (Baldwin, 1989). Its validation is through rational discourse. Critical theory has been defined by Gentlzer (1999) as "the end result of a process designed to expose inherent incongruities related to social situations" (p. 23). While critical theory is the outcome, critical science is the process, "the course of action taken by individuals and groups to collaboratively examine and critique present social structures for the purpose of their own emancipation" (p. 23). Like hermeneutics methodology, critical inquiry and theory assume four types of validity claims (Habermas, 1979).

Critical Thinking as a Critical Science Process

All reasoning has or leads to implications and consequences. Further, all reasoning is based on data, information, and evidence. All reasoning is expressed through ideas or concepts, such as our present consideration, the concept of aesthetics in educational curriculum. The processes of inferences and/or interpretations lead to conclusions. To systematically analyze and test the accuracy of our perceptions, the process of critical thinking through universal intellectual standards is applied. Paul(2000) offers questions that assist in reaching the ultimate goal of critical thinking by addressing the universal standards.

The process of thinking critically regarding the presentation of verbal and visual symbolic communication in regard to aesthetics is a key concept in the process of challenge and is necessary when reflecting upon the meaning of the communications discussed. Further specifics as to methodological process are presented in Chapter 5.

Summary Considerations of the Design Methodology

The need for philosophical reflection in the dominant empirical analytic inquiry has had a negative impact on the global society (Baldwin, 1989). The majority of recent scientific research has ignored human need and moral practical reasoning. As a result no moral growth in human understanding or moral sensitivity has occurred to a satisfactory degree, communicative competence has declined, and social fragmentation continues (1989).

The call for rational modes of inquiry must consider technical, hermeneutic (interpretive), and emancipatory (critical theory) issues in relation to key concepts in general and family and consumer sciences education in the specific (Brown, 1993).This fundamental justification forms the significance of the historical transcendental phenomenological hermeneutics inquiry of this dissertation. The more specific procedures of phenomenological method in critique of examples of communication through music, art, design, and other aspects of aesthetics in daily living are presented in the *interpretations* and arts-based genre portrayals to follow (Johnson, 1998, Spring).

The larger concepts of aesthetics cognition, the Enlightenment, and general moral philosophy relating to the current crisis in aesthetic awareness are considered simultaneously through the method of hermeneutics. *Conclusions and implications* for actions are reached through critical theory, critical inquiry, and critical thinking (Paul, 1995).

General Concepts in Qualitative Research

The study followed a purposive, naturalistic, non-random sampling of smaller sample sizes, utilizing qualitative approaches, rather than positivistic, random, or non-random larger samples in quantitative approaches. In that quantitative refers to the what, how, when, and where of a thing, its essence and ambiance, and qualitative refers to meanings, a qualitative method was most appropriate (Berg, 1998, pp. 10, 100, 112). The larger concepts of aesthetics and beauty in philosophy were funneled down for systematic selection and samples more focused to the context of education in data collection by the various methodological strategies. The methods for quantitative research—random, non-random, stratified, cluster random, two-stage random, systematic, convenience, and purposive samples—did not fully provide this funneling process.

The approaches for qualitative study include: ethnology, ethnography, ethnography of communication, ethno-methodology, field study, participant observation, oral history, phenomenology, case study, connoisseurship/criticism (such as art criticism), investigative journalism, non-participant observation, human ethnology, and natural history, which allowed a larger field of methodology from which to begin the evolving process of a qualitative research method. The qualitative methodological inquiry was, thus, found to be more appropriate.

The general format, then, is a funneling from the larger general philosophical concepts of aesthetics to the more specific aesthetics, and ultimately to a focus on a theology of beauty as it concerns higher education curriculum within a global curriculum. The use of hermeneutic phenomenology and art-based genre with examples of expressionist and impressionist art works that I painted prior to and after the Scottish workshop, are offered as personal life world experiences and expressionist symbols of the historical hermeneutics context consistent with Jung's three levels of hermeneutic interpretation of symbols (Brown, 1995).

Data collection instruments: The classification of who and how for the qualitative research method—interviewing, focus groups, ethnography, sociometry, unobtrusive measures, historiography, and case studies—have been combined in phenomenological hermeneutics (Berg, 1998, p. 4). The researcher was used as the instrument, as observer, in addition to collecting the paper and pencil notations, scheduled interviews, and anecdotal records for gathering the information. Examples of data produced include researcher-completed and unobtrusive observation for qualitative research, and forms the core of the data for interpretation.

Plan for research design, procedure, or approach: Methods for achieving "validity" and "reliability" of the findings (using appropriate qualitative terminology) in this qualitative research included validity: appropriateness, meaningfulness, usefulness. These were evidenced by: content, criterion, construct, and by reliable data in a reliable instrument (or researcher as an unbiased instrument (aesthetic disinterestedness), in development of warranted conclusions. The use of valid instruments with questions well formed, unbiased samples, and cross checks in literature review for qualitative relevance, was conducted as a cognitive process. The storing of data in a safe place for recall and keeping field notes was performed to control for threats to internal validity. Qualitative validity was further ensured by: saving notes, organizing files for historical /current versions of research drafts, saving backup discs and hard copies of information and drafts in alternate locations, and copyright during the draft dissertation process of both written and arts-based works.

Focus groups: Hypotheses for future research information, for instrument development, new ideas, needs assessment, and checks on validity were indirectly conducted by informal individual and group observations, i.e., current use of focus groups for marketing toward adolescents in the mass culture. Identification of a range of many different ways of thinking about the topic was attended to by considerations of various forms of hermeneutics (see the specific evolving definition as examined by MIT research in artificial intelligence in the definition section). Open-ended questions were held internally by the researcher on an ongoing basis, i.e., the researcher was observer and participant, and updated as the analysis evolved.

Non-standardized depth interviews: General unstructured conversations to gather information allowed informants freedom to identify issues and responses in relation to their own perceptions of aesthetics. This was an ongoing process by participant observations at the art workshops and conversations with other artists and musicians during the investigative phase of information gathering, for example in the Scottish workshop and the Iowa State University art workshop. The researcher does not assume to know all the questions relevant to the topic nor whether or not an equal depth of meaning is understood by subject terms. To augment observations, to gain rapport with informants, and to gain additional information when unfamiliar with respondents' lifestyles, religion, ethnic and cultural customs, and attributes, was the justification for the use of hermeneutics as the most appropriate method for an intuitive perspective. This is consistent with established protocol for such research and was implemented (Van Manen, 1990).

Participant observations and case study: Participant observation may include non-interventive and empathetic strategies, but the purpose for this discussion was to gather information on more than one case. In the analysis, the participant observations at the International Workshop in Scotland, and observations of antiquities during a site visit to Rosslyn Chapel, in Roslin, Scotland, were conducted to further clarify issues identified in the art studio at Iowa State University and the significance of symbolic meaning in search of the larger meaning of social issues. The idea of a single case study may be in the experiences of the researcher as interpreter of her own world. While participating in these activities, information was gathered by observations of community, homes, housing, amusement, and religious institutions as a part of the overall milieu or *Volkerpsychologie* (Wundt, 1921). The case study of the International Art Workshop in Glasgow, Scotland had as a primary purpose the gathering of a great deal of information about one particular case or phenomenon, which could be generalized to similar cases in interpretation of the larger meaning (Brown, 1995). For this dissertation, the applicability was to prior art studio experiences at Iowa State University during the summer of 1997 and those of Glasgow in 1999. Subsequent details regarding the riots at Iowa State University and Southern Illinois University are taken from news media accounts and not personal experiences. Sources are identified where discussed.

Member check and audit trail: To ensure reliability, member check, such as in content analysis, was conducted by returning to informants or key informants and seeing if the emerging items or topic sounded correct (double-check interview notes and meaning or interpretations by the researcher with similar research, in this case analytical psychological interpretation in establishing the meaning of symbols). An audit trail, referring to the researcher's field notes and note taking (the how, when, who, and why, and when new themes emerged as part of critical/creative thinking and philosophical inquiry), was implemented by dividing the research into phases of process and content to verify the accuracy of the researcher's analysis. That such research is consistent with the hermeneutic spiral resulted in the continual refinement of general to specific themes and examples of meaning of aesthetics and "aesthetic knowing."

The records of how the researcher came to these conclusions may be interpreted by the stages of observation and topics for analysis. No formal coding was required, as is normally presented with content analysis. As has been mentioned, content analysis did not address the interpretive issues to a satisfactory level for this particular discussion. However, a general search for themes evolved during the hermeneutic process and was part of the plan for the audit trail and memos to show follow-through in thinking. This may be seen by a review of the very early stages of dissertation statements of topic issues and the general direction in the evolving investigation, with initial intent to use hermeneutics from the first presentation and acceptance by the committee of the topic of research of aesthetics.

Participant observation and non-participant observation: Participant observations where the observer becomes a participant in the situation to be observed to gather data (overt) may impact data gathered. In this case, the participation in the art workshops included both the workshop at Iowa State University and the International Workshop in Glasgow, Scotland. Non-participant observations, where the researcher was observer but did not directly participate in situations, such as during music presentations, were incorporated into direct participation in painting workshops. This naturalistic, case study, simulation, and observations (covert), have averted questions of ethical issues of data gathering, sometimes identified in this sort of data collecting (in attempts to secretly gather information). However, for purposes of this dissertation, the need to attempt to incorporate concepts of aesthetic literacy and comprehension had no impact upon the participants and other observers of the art workshops and concerts, especially, as painting was done in the researcher's room for most of the workshops (as a result of negative exemplars to be discussed as unanticipated outcomes).

Review of literature in historiographic method of data collection: An archival review of literature in the tradition of aesthetic philosophy focused on the history of aesthetics, aesthetics in education (such as Dewey's aesthetics philosophy), the history of aesthetics in family and consumer sciences curricula, and aesthetics concepts within enlightenment movements, especially the Scottish Enlightenment, were targeted for interpretation. The introduction to the problem, as stated in the first portion of the methodology and procedures, is expanded to incorporate the phenomenological method for an aesthetics analysis. This becomes especially significant within the context of process of synergistic phenomenology as defined by Jung in his analytical psychological method and his hermeneutics of doctrine (Brown, 1995)

Participant and non-participant observations in data collection: Again, participant and non-participant observations of aesthetics activities, e.g., fine arts, classical music, museum tours, utilized the phenomenological methodology format for a sort of thematic content analysis in aesthetics. Preliminary interviews with instructors of art, arts council participants, the Iowa Office of Cultural Affairs, were conducted to develop the themes in aesthetics relevance in education and current trends, such as in strategic plans for economic development, were considered and evolved during the gathering of data (Palmer, 1999). The phenomenological methodology was utilized in the analysis of these conversations as well for themes that recur, further indicating aesthetic content considerations as part of a larger curriculum movement in aesthetic knowing and *Volkerpsychologie* (Brady, 2001).

The need for some true application and experience of art in the production and viewing of actual pieces has been identified by the curriculum expert Timmerman, in Posner and Rudnitsky's (1997) textbook, *Course Design*. Timmerman has presented course outlines in art appreciation in her chapter, "Survey of Western Art" (Posner & Rudnitsky, 1997, pp. 229–248). She cites what she terms "negative exemplars," which result from a non-aesthetic environment, such as a messy studio, or lack of actual pieces of art for experiential analysis. This became more relevant in the interpretive phase of the research and a search for meaning with respect to the Scotland art studio and arts-based example of this genre.

A search for aesthetic themes: The research was conducted within the context of hermeneutics methodology, as discussed earlier, with special focus on past themes of aesthetics within the context of the literature review. Content analysis as a method of data collection and translation of these themes was considered but rejected as not an extensive comprehensive methodology for this study:

Recurring themes and patterns of intellectual activity related to aesthetics are identified in relation to general education and family and consumer sciences education. Kaelin's (1971) phenomenological method of aesthetics critique and evaluation was considered and modified in its application. It was applied in a modified form to aesthetics content as it relates to curriculum and development and the final rationale for inclusion of aesthetics in curriculum content for general education in higher education.

To recognize those activities and examples of aesthetics in an enlightenment movement, it was also necessary to provide examples of negative exemplars, or unanticipated outcomes not consistent with concepts of aesthetics in education found in a review of the literature. These negative examples or exemplars were seen as indications of an anti-intellectual counter movement to an enlightenment movement.

A thematic analysis was conducted to identify recurring themes in aesthetics movements in relation to economic development, social change, and legislative acts in the United States and abroad, e.g., the enlightenment movements, especially the Scottish enlightenment, as these events relate to cycles of aesthetics activity in general. This analysis was then applied to family and consumer sciences curricula. Heuristic examination of literature and artifacts was conducted consistent with time and financial constraints.

Observations and interviews: The search for aesthetic content in higher education curricula and other areas of daily life from a phenomenological perspective was general in nature, from those areas which might be expected—textiles and clothing, and interior design. However, attention was given to the presence or absence of a theme of aesthetics in the early history of the profession as compared to the present content encountered in this examination, specifically, in family and consumer sciences education in higher education. Aesthetics as a term was not a noted theme of any kind for the total doctoral program of study, examined while the researcher was in the doctoral degree program in family and consumer sciences education. It was generally implied within course content under such terms as multiculturalism. This lack of specific identification of a key concept in the founding philosophy prompted in part the historical review of the significance of aesthetics within the language of the that profession as well as the discipline of general education during its formative stages.

Use of human subjects in research for observations and interviews was not required, as all conversations and observations were of a public nature, without any need to consider confidentiality of records or comments. The need for actual on-site observations of art works, at museums, and aesthetics projects, have been identified by authors of various teaching methodologies, as addressed earlier by Posner and Rudnitsky (1997). The unexpected outcomes in a non-aesthetic art studio environment, and aesthetic decay as indicative of the larger social fragmentation, are consistent with established concepts of aesthetics in art in observations made in actual studio situations. A phenomenological discussion of the positive and negative exemplars and the meaning within the context of arts-based genre is discussed in the findings (Posner & Rrudnitsky, 1997). This activity became relevant to interpretations of larger social issues, often first manifested in the symbolic representation of arts.

The researcher contacted potential interviewees and participants in aesthetics activities and arranged these activities, along with field observations, museum site visits, and other opportunities for unobtrusive observations of communication through symbols. Field journals, where appropriate, were developed by the researcher, kept, and transcribed, along with interview notes and reflections. Criteria for selection of on-site visits, activities, and completion of actual artwork were developed consistent with time and financial constraints. Some actual art works, such as paintings and drawings during the Scotland workshop, were completed, consistent with experiential considerations of the aesthetics process for analysis; with the theoretical findings of the aesthetics content and process analyzed by analytical psychological considerations (Brown, 1995) and critical/creative thinking (Costa & Liebemann, 1997). An interpretive discourse of actual works of art rendered by researcher and other archival examples are compiled and included in the discussion of findings.

A report of findings in the form of a written research document, examination of fine art presentations, and exhibitions, journal articles, and public discourse, incorporating the historical transcendental phenomenological hermeneutics construct has been completed. Text and examples of the Scottish aesthetic, for example, Rosslyn Chapel, descriptions of photographs, drawings, and paintings are discussed from the perspective of an arts-based genre in the portrayal section. The methodology was limited by time and availability of artifacts, concert attendance, conversations, literature review, and further oral and nonverbal discourse during the evolving qualitative dissertation process.

CHAPTER 3. REVIEW OF LITERATURE

There's an aesthetic dimension to everything.
Every school environment, every teaching act,
every setting you create to spend time in, enhances
or diminishes the quality of life. Whether you're
teaching science or art, the challenge is to make it
beautiful

(Eisner, 1990).

Aesthetics as a Philosophy of Being

The disciplines of aesthetics, art history, and art criticism have been components of general education and aesthetic knowing across centuries and cultures (Dewey, 1934; Navone, 1996; Olson, 1997). Dewey (1939) quotes Plato on the topic: "[T]he rhythmic and harmonious elements of art, like a breeze blowing in a goodly place, may from earliest childhood lead us peacefully into harmony with the beauty of reasonableness. One so nurtured will, beyond others, welcome reason when its' time comes and know it as his own" (p. 291).

What is meant by aesthetics, and why is it necessary in curricula? What are the major theories of aesthetic value in education? What are the social, political, and cultural forces impacting aesthetic taste and expression? What responsibility does the student have to understand notions of aesthetics? Finally, why should we teach students concepts of aesthetics in family and consumer sciences education curricula?

The earliest notions of aesthetics may be found in quotations from Xenophanes and Heraclitus, in an attack against poetry, "The poet errs in saying: 'would that strife might perish from among gods and men.' There would be no harmony without high and low, no animals without the opposition of female and male" (Gilbert & Khun, 1972, p.1). At the height of the Greek tradition in the fourth century BCE, Plato speaks of "the ancient quarrel of poetry and philosophy" (Gilbert & Kuhn, 1972, p. 1) for control of the fount of wisdom. Both poets and philosophers claimed possession of the fountain of wisdom. The ancients, the bards, the poets, the word workers, from notions of universal language and meaning, have attempted to claim wisdom in symbolic communication. The ancient language of wisdom is transmitted through time by the word. The notion of a linking by more than mere attitude or perception to some transcendental process of communication through symbol and word requires a more specific example. Hartman (1989) describes of teaching of "traumatic history without increasing inappropriate psychological defenses."

Hartman tells us of a seventeenth-century poem that has its roots in the "forgotten catastrophe: a red rash marking the disease, posies of flowers to ward off the smell of death and perhaps death itself, and the burning of contaminated materials and corpses" (p. 436). The poets communicate knowledge "transformed from a traumatic into a bearable truth" (p. 436). The search for communication of truth, the font of wisdom, is further explained by Gilbert & Kuhn (1972):

> The idea of a fount of wisdom became the fount of the universe and the cosmology, psychology, and "techne" (purposive human action), forced the emergence of aesthetics as metaphysics of beauty and the soul's response to the process of creation of the beautiful. It was Pythagoras who first prepared a true philosophy of art and beauty, in numbers and music. Thus, the Pythagoreans saw the universe as "a kind of divine music box." Parallel elements were created between the soul, stars, and planets in an aesthetic harmony. (Gilbert & Kuhn, 1972, pp. 8–9)

The notions of value or quality in aesthetics were becoming linked by more than mere attitude or perception (Hospers, 1969). As part of a continuing study of the connection between science and aesthetics in Germany in the mid-seventeenth century, King Maximilian II, of Bavaria, commissioned seven volumes by the Royal Academy of Sciences. From these commissioned studies, Lotze developed a series of lectures on aesthetics. In turn, from these lectures, a clearer meaning of aesthetics and beauty as a state of process or theology of the soul may be seen in the following quote from this text of some antiquity:

> But we are told that the beautiful is not given to man in the form of a concrete intuition, or of a finished concept whose marks may be distinguished and read off in order by the aid of logical processes. The beautiful is rather given to man in the form of the Idea. No individual, therefore, can fully compass it, can have more than a share in the understanding of it—according to the degree of his attainment in the culture of its appreciation. (Lotze, 1885, p. viii)

> The term aesthetics has been applied to useful arts, operative, or mechanical arts, technic (technical), or applied arts, ornamental arts, arts of design, and aesthetic arts. When there is attention to an effect upon the senses, with mental results, the concept of aesthetic utility is more correct. Thus, all of the listed forms of art may produce aesthetic utility through production of not only material but mental result (Raymond, 1906).

> The aesthetic utility and mental response to beauty is as a result of complement, counteraction, and balance. These three concepts form the development of the same principle of beauty and complement, produces unity from things different; counteraction applies to the underlying principle of complement to things not complementary by nature; and balance applies to the same principle to things that may not be counteractive or complementary. All produce a sense of harmony. Thus, just as confusion may exist in nature, and may be introduced into art for contrast or

variety, its intent is to produce harmony, not to produce chaos. (Raymond, 1906, p. 284)

A similar notion of balance, harmony, and rhythm remains "immortal" and constant throughout the times into the modern age. Raymond's principles of counteraction, complementariness or complementarity, and balance are seen in contemporary abstract art by painters such as Kandinsky in the beginning of the abstract art movement around 1947. "That is beautiful which is reduced by internal necessity, which springs from the soul." (Kandinsky, 1949, p. 75). Kandinsky has been identified as one of the first modern artists of the soul. This may be seen in the following quote addressing his (Kandinsky's) approach to beauty of expression through art:

> There is nothing so curious of beauty or so absorbent of it as a soul. For that reason few mortal souls are able to withstand the leadership of the soul that gives itself to beauty ... The artist continues to clarify his concept of beauty as neither meaning contemporary external beauty nor inner morality, but that quality which enriches and refines the soul. Any color is then intrinsically beautiful, causing spiritual vibration. This vibration can enrich the soul, so outward ugliness has potential for beauty. (Kandinsky, 1949, p. 75)

It would appear here that Kandinsky expresses a similar interpretation of the principles of harmony and balance as those presented by Raymond some four decades earlier. Consistent with this "modern" connection of beauty and aesthetics as linked to the soul, Hunt defines beauty in the early history of home economics (East, 1982, p. 126):

> Beauty is a term, which is difficult of exact definition. Primarily it denotes a quality of a material object by means of which the object gives pleasure through the senses. We are not, however, satisfied with this restricted use of the word, and stretch it to mean a quality of an immaterial thing like life or character, which inspires admiration by appealing to the intellect rather than to the sight or to the hearing.

Esthetics is the philosophy of beauty. A narrow conception

of its province makes it concern itself exclusively with beauties like those of form and color and design. A broader and better conception brings into its province all beauties, including those of lives in harmony with their physical surroundings and their social environment. (East, 1982, p. 126)

Questions About Aesthetics Education

There is an ever-present renewal of concern for aesthetics as a necessary way of learning and knowing which, as we have seen, spans time and cultures (Costa & Liebemann, 1997). Redfern identifies the aesthetic response in a survey of the department of education and science for primary education in England. Like concerns expressed in America, the basic issues of aesthetics in education are consistent across member nations of Western civilization. Redfern defines aesthetics education as follows, "Aesthetic education may arise in connection with work in any area of the curriculum," and responses included music, arts, and crafts, under the heading of "aesthetic and physical education" (Redfern, 1986, pp. 1–4). Formal ballroom dancing is then both aesthetics and a sports category. The attempts to incorporate concepts of truth or fact in a philosophical dimension of aesthetics and beauty are clarified in another example from the English primary school:

If, further (again sometimes mentioned in the official literature), aesthetic considerations enter into matters to do with, say, dress (including, of course, school uniform); the way pupils and teachers take meals (for example, the layout of tables, the manner of eating and drinking); how individuals sit, walk and generally move about; the appearance and treatment of books, equipment, notice-boards and the school building as a whole-if, that is, there is what Roger Scruton (1979) calls "an aesthetics of everyday life"—is it to be expected that experience of the arts (for example) automatically carries over to wider contexts? And can there be any justification for teachers caring about and taking responsibility for aesthetic education within the arts but not in the everyday sphere (assuming for the moment that arts education does involve the aesthetic). (Redfern, 1986, p. 3)

The significance of separating the mere transmission of emotion in communication in art, and the aesthetics of art, is well developed in the Redfern example. Art is not necessarily aesthetic if it lacks the concepts of harmony and unity in connection to a value base, such as Kandinsky's concepts of vibrations of the soul. Participation in a practical art activity, for mere creativity without more formal considerations of the past history of aesthetics in relation to value movements and spirituality, simply promotes hedonistic pleasure-seeking of a lower order of experiencing (Redfern, 1986, p. 22). It has been this tendency to suppress the historical connection of aesthetic imagination from historical, scientific, or philosophical imagination that has led to much confusion (p. 23). To detach considerations of morality (ethics) from the definition of aesthetics as a process or action only does not foster the education of sensibility to social restrictions of deportment and cultural norms. The "greedy organism of the self" seeks only its own pleasure (Murdock, 1979; Redfern, 1986, p. 22).

Redfern considers aesthetics a necessary part of education that requires some appreciation of works of art. If this results in an appreciation of aesthetics in art, but not outside of art, aesthetic education is said to be lacking and inadequate (Redfern, 1986, p. 97):

> They [curriculum planners] further claim that "arts teaching in schools inevitably incurs a considerable responsibility in this sphere, as do other areas of the curriculum such as Craft, Design and Technology and Home Economics. Courses in these last-mentioned subjects would certainly seem to involve aesthetic appreciation of the particular sorts of objects with which they deal, and might even be seen as rather less than successful if they did not result in pupils becoming more perceptive also about the wider aspects of the environment in which those objects are set. ... Yet it seems somewhat optimistic to suppose ... that experience in craft, design and technology will necessarily extend to

an aesthetic concern with the man-made environment in general; nor can development of aesthetic discrimination in home economics be expected to carry over to aesthetic appreciation of, say, feats of engineering skill. (Redfern, 1986, p. 97–98)

The discourse presented by the survey questions in the English schools becomes central to discussions about curriculum planning in the United States. The trivialization of aesthetics as a historical component of Western civilizations' theological foundation in education has resulted in negative effects on its interpretation by the larger public. Its once central role in education philosophy and educational curriculum in Western civilization has been obscured. "The word beauty is a little embarrassing; there is something old-fashioned about it, like a country girl wearing her mother's dress ... rather than the much cooler and more stylish term the aesthetic" (Turner, 1991, p. 1).

The experience of beauty in the aesthetic brings a quality of inexhaustibility of depth (Turner, 1991, p. 12). Turner identities not only a theory of beauty, but an explanation of why it has been rejected as a central cultural goal in the last two centuries (p. 16). What Turner later clarifies is three themes of his text on beauty, "Shame, the triumph of modern consciousness, the idea of the political left—the gauche—and its corollary, the political right—le droit," have led to the decay of beauty as an ideal, and as a technical enterprise in the last two centuries (Turner, 1991, p.17–32).

> Let us attempt to sum up the ugly, then, as any decay or reduction of a deeper beauty into a shallower one. A deep beauty has many hierarchical levels and needs them to articulate and maintain the differences of its elements. A pretentious ugliness is one that possesses more hierarchical levels than are necessary, and thus it displays structure of a deeper beauty but not its substance of differences; a reductive ugliness is one that possesses fewer levels than necessary, so that the genuine differences belonging to a deeper beauty are lost and destroyed (or deconstructed). The falsity that is essential to ugliness is precisely the disjunction between the form and substance of hierarchical depth. (Turner, 1991, p. 12)

Things may be moving back to center, at least in higher education, if a 1998 article in *The Chronicle of Higher Education* is any indication of the slow process of change. Many new books with topics of aesthetics may now be found, Humanists are attempting to set and define artistic standards for the new century (Heller, 1998). A goal for a "new and improved" version of aesthetics criteria is stated.

With the movement now in place, some conflict will likely also follow for "control" of the definition of concepts like beauty and aesthetics. Until some discourse occurs through hermeneutic inquiry into the valuation and critique of the current situations, confusion as to purpose and standards will continue. Yet, the philosophical connection of aesthetics to beauty and a value orientation, as to the soul, is the consistent hermeneutic doctrine of such pivotal psychologists as Carl Jung.

Jung's Hermeneutic of Doctrine

Unlike Freud, Jung was not only an empiricist, but a metaphysician or theologian in regard to the unconscious and the symbolic dimension of meaning in all psychic life. His concern for the revelatory potential of symbolic communication prompted some to accuse him of attempting to create a new religion. Brown (1981) identifies Jung's hermeneutic of doctrine with it central core, a quest for the essence of soul. His hermeneutic of doctrine with a centrality of search for meaning through depth psychology builds upon the *Volkerpsychologie* of his predecessor, Wilhelm Wundt (1921):

> It is Jung's passing utterances on revelation and faith, and his more extensive discussions of the God-question that sees in "the depths of the human soul" what is disclosed to it with the power of a revelation, then the content of such a revelation is presumed to emanate from the soul, then, Burber tells us, it is really a question of the soul experiencing itself. And so, to his mind, Jung's psychology of religion is at its heart a religious psychology, a "religion of pure psychic immanence," in which no distinction

is possible between the subject and object of religious experience. (Brown, 1981, p. 16)

The hermeneutic doctrine of Jung's psychology of religion was grounded in the symbolic as central for understanding his style of thinking and method of interpretation. Yet it is Jung's hermeneutic of doctrine, his thought processes, that moves in many directions and on many levels simultaneously, which is central to this hermeneutic consideration of aesthetics.

> He jumps from clinical to cultural materials and then back again, bridging between personal and collective worlds of imagery and meaning, between modern and ancient times, between West and East, etc. In so doing he digresses, amplifies, and "free associates" to the point where it is exhausting to follow him. To compound these difficulties, the terminology he employs is oftentimes fluid and at many points ambiguous. For these reasons, Jung's thought has invited misunderstanding, confusion and even consternation. (Brown, 1981, p. 1)

In a similar process to Jung's fluid free association, the interpretation of the meaning in communications presented regarding aesthetics must be equally vague yet relevant to the level of the reader. Interpretation and/ or over-interpretation (Eco, 1992) within the context of the times and the experiential foundation of the participants in communication becomes significant. That Jung attempted to assign universal symbolism creates a starting point for the creation of a hermeneutic doctrine. His body of principles, tenets, dogma, and teachings focus on the relevance of an "explicitly positive evaluation of the religious dimension of human life" (p. 2). Like those theologians researching his hermeneutic of doctrine, who entered into conversation with him throughout time, we too will continue an "ongoing and far reaching dialogue with Jung" (p. 6), and others. We will participate in a modified delineation and exposition of aesthetics and a return to a theology of beauty, focusing on those "issues of symbol and hermeneutics and their role in theological reflection" (p. 7).

The hermeneutic symbolism creates language that crosses disciplines and unites science, art, and language in its synthesis of meanings. The underlying meaning of concepts, such as those Turner (1991) labeled a "theory of the bio-cultural evolution of the sense of beauty," and "revised neural structures in the hominid brain," are now what some scientists consider components of "the cognitive revolution." A developing new science, the cognitive sciences, returns to free association and depth psychology for transmission of meaning centered on beauty, revealed through hermeneutic doctrine. Hermeneutic doctrine has been central in artificial intelligence research at MIT since 1986 (Mallery, Hurwits, & Duffy, 1987). The "cognitive revolution" hopes to include the arts, in that "aesthetics makes its home" in philosophy, rather than psychology (Freeland, 1999). The "cognitive revolution" of 1999 is fighting the same battle over the possession of aesthetics as Xenophanes and Heraclitus in ancient times (Gilbert & Kuhn, 1872).

The "cognitive revolution" also includes examples of how aesthetics and visualization in science are "part of a trajectory of thinking in art and architecture that rises about the highest planes of analytic reasoning" (Siler, 1990). The "planes of analytic reasoning" discussed in the new science are compared to the transformation of "various degrees of enlightenment." Like Buddha, the neurocosmological practice involves phases of initiation "from the passive viewing of familiar objects and images (the known and the pictured) to the gradual, active letting-go of all recognizable forms (the act of embracing the unknown and the unpictured)" (Siler, 1990). This process does not seem very different from Bacon's earlier process of induction, with the now exclusion of the divine.

Jones's (1988) interpretation of the significance of phrenology during the Scottish Enlightenment and the "ordering of the mind" are presented for review as to the visual correlation of Siler's "planes of analytic reasoning" in our present discussion. More detailed textual explication will be presented later in the review as it relates to layers of consciousness in architectural design during the Scottish Enlightenment.

A discussion of the potential for misdirection may be seen in Bacon's "The Apology to the Divines: The Charitable sources of Pride." Here Bacon discusses Solomon's "supreme or summary law of nature":

> Man's spirit is God's lamp, with which he searches the inwardness of all secrets. Therefore, no parcel of the world is denied to man's invention and inquiry. If such is the mind's capacity, then there is no danger in any proportion

or quantity of knowledge. Only the quality of knowledge, not the quantity, is venomous or malignant and could cause swelling. The divines further say that experience shows how learned men have been arch heretics, how learned times incline toward atheism, and how contemplation of second causes "derogates" from our dependence on God, the first cause. (Weinberger, 1985, pp. 50–51)

The movement toward what Siler (1990) calls a GUT ("Grand Unified Theory") and TOE ("Theory of Everything") in development of a more complete worldview is like art in the making. Layers of rhythms of interplay between the "brain" and the "cosmos" is what the action from head ("GUT") to toe ("TOE") exchange in this interplay of "process morphology" and "an ocean of interrelated themes" (p. 17). Process and processors are presented in "metaphorms" where there is a comparative study of unlike systems "in relating the concept of a society to the consolidated human brain" (Siler, 1990, p. 217):

We think as neurocosmologists when we relate a fundamental insight from quantum physics which maintains that the universe is one extraordinarily intricate energy pattern of sorts. The wholes and parts of this pattern are linked together like brain cell-assemblies, all of which work in concert in the process of creation. ... A more poetic—and precise—way of describing this linking process was supplied by Hofstadter in his eloquent description of the part-wholeness of a fugue. "Fugues," writes Hofstader, "have that interesting property, that each of their voices is a piece of music in itself; and use of a fugue might be thought of as a collection of several distinct pieces of music, all based on one single theme, and all played simultaneously." ... By exercising your mind's propensity for metaphorming—for "fugue listening"— you connect unsuspected relationships between these acts and the materials of the mind and universe (Siler, 1990, p. 225).

If we follow the logic of a unified theory of a concert in balance and aesthetic cognition, we must also consider the connection in social theory, such as the relationship between the development of aesthetic cognition and the development of leaders (Kenyon, 1998). There is a need to do more than frame language in the metaphors of the arts in the development of leaders. The cognitive processes required in the creation of the arts and the methods for developing them in relation to aesthetic cognition could be applied to leadership development. Similar to Siler's symbolic activity in aesthetic thinking, formal aesthetics education is "a journey to the soul" (Kenyon, 1998).

Kenyon (1998) identifies the processes for the education of leaders as the same as that found in aesthetic education, "an art of problem framing, an art of implementation, and an art of improvisation" (p. 76). Like leadership, aesthetic artistry requires imagination, craftsmanship, sensibility, and authenticity (p. 76). The elements of music "pitch, rhythm, dynamics, and timbre" (p. 77) and the dynamic interplay in the "concert" of interaction in the greater whole follow the return to similar concepts of a ("GUT") General Unity Theory (Siler, 1990).

With all these metaphorical references to aesthetics and art, there must be experiential considerations as to the manipulation of art within the Big Science movement. Art and aesthetics should in some way reflect the reality of the society within which they exist as a form of communication. Thus, concern for notions of "mass culture" and the identification of its "leveling" process must be considered. Like earlier criticism of aesthetics, "art" becomes a victim of the oppressive nature of "mass culture" (Horkheimer, 1941). Horkheimer points to the interaction between critical theory and empirical research for the interpretation of the impact of the modern mass culture on art. Horkheimer notes his satisfaction that for the first time (in 1941) these ideas have been presented and applied to the American subject matter.

The impact of society and the prevailing impact of "the plastic surgery of the prevailing economic system which carves all men to one pattern" was the focus of concern by Horkheimer (1941). This conclusion is shared by Weinberger (1985) and Siler (1990) in their descriptions of cognitive production and a unification theory, in that acts of creativity are not separate forms in the society in which the creative act occurs:

> Yet works of art—objective products of the mind detached
> from the context of the practical world—harbor principles
> through which the world that bore them appears alien and

false ... Not only Shakespeare's wrath and melancholy, but the detached humanism of Goethe's poetry as well, and even Proust's devoted absorption in ephemeral features of *mondanite*, awakens memories of a freedom that makes prevailing standards appear narrow-minded and barbarous. Art, since it became autonomous, has preserved the utopia that evaporated from religion. (Horkheimer, 1941, pp. 291–292)

Horkheimer (1941) argues that pure art has become more entertainment than the reflection of the individual's state of being, e.g., as deserted and in despair. The lack of norms of a society, or the anomie of the individual, is not allowed to manifest itself in true art, as it is no longer marketable. Thus, the mass culture within an oppressive society may dictate by market forces the communication of reality or promote lies (Baldwin, 1985). The concern for the cognitive sciences and the arts is increasing because of the power of film in the new art and its impact upon the mind of the mass culture.

The artist is no longer working from his own mind, but the mind of that culture: "His intellectual acts are no longer intrinsically connected with his human essence" (Horkheimer, 1941, p. 295). Abbs (1994) presents a similar thesis when he explains a creative and aesthetic learning and thinking process in art as follows:

Art embodies the invisible logic of the life of feeling and sentience and, in so doing, brings it to conception and consciousness. Once this is clearly recognized the common education distinctions between cognition and affect, between meaning and expression, between objective and subjective, between public and private break down and give way to what would seem a more valid differentiation between kinds of knowledge, between kinds of intelligence, between kinds of symbolic forms, between kinds of public language. (Abbs, 1994)

Horkheimer (1941) speaks of Adler and his book on "aesthetic problems." In his attempt to view art independent of time, and "to raise art above history and keep it pure, he betrays it to the contemptible trash of the day" (p. 296). The notion of art as advertising, with Walt Disney "the great master" in reaching children and simple folk, angers Horkheimer, because Disney uses Raphael's blue horizons as part of his landscapes. He sees this as similar to using the Sistine Madonna to advertise soap or toothpaste (p. 297). "A dogmatic definition of the beautiful protects philosophy no better from capitulating to the powers-that-be than a concept of art derived from the uncritical applause of the masses, to which it bows only too readily" (p. 297). Though Adler's intention in his book is to present the concept of morality and principles in art education, Horkheimer finds his concept as "unhistorical as his concept of art" (p. 297).

If we accept the idea that "art matters philosophically because it matters humanly," the subject of aesthetics within the context of philosophy must be considered. Philosophy has claimed as its fundamental aspiration the understanding of human experience. Art undertakes the expression of human experience. Yet, though most philosophers identify the need for a value theory, and aesthetics is a value theory, there remains trivialization and marginalization of aesthetics within philosophy (Devereaux, 1999).

If a central concern of aesthetics in today's society is the relation of aesthetic and moral values, how can philosophers aspire to understand the nature of value without attention to aesthetic value (Devereaux, 1999)? The issues of government subsidies for the arts in relation to moral values and seeking justification through aesthetics does not address some of the issues of using the communicative potential of such art to spread hate under the cloak of symbolic communication. An example is the painting of the Madonna with feces and the act of defecating on stage as performing art (Staff Writer, Chronicle of Higher Education, 2000). The symbolic communication is the obvious hate of an entire body of Catholic people by the ridicule of their universal symbol, the Madonna. This example is one of knowing but not aesthetic knowing. Buescher (1986) clarifies this aesthetic concept of knowing and communication in relation to gifted children:

> The ability to experience, to imagine, to represent ... is a fundamental process of human intelligence. The process as well as the product that grows from it can have a deep, moving, and aesthetic character to it. Being able to experience what is subtle, to imagine what is interesting or useful, and to be able to adequately represent what has been experienced are each influenced by the conditions in which one lives ... Why do we have music or dance or

poetry or stories? Because it is only through these modes and others that particular kinds of human experience can be communicated. We have to do this as a people. Human beings invented the forms that can meet that need to imagine and communicate. (Costa & Liebmann, 1997, p. 108)

If there is a growing call for the inclusion of arts and aesthetics education in curricula, will concerns similar to those presented by Horkheimer in 1941 be allowed to enter the conversation? Mann (1998) addresses some of the potential conflicts in his book, *Aesthetics*, when discussing "form," in that "Plato valued measure and proportion in art, and []Aristotle valued unity and wholeness" (Lorraine, 1999). Similar to the earlier concepts of Raymond in 1906 and Kandinsky in 1947, Mann finds that "all elements are eliminated that do not contribute to the completion of an action, or that are not essential to a unified whole." "Yet, it is often due to incongruities, deviations or inessential elements that works are so effective: true organic wholes may be 'too perfect' to engage us" (Lorraine).

The consideration of multiple aspects of an aesthetics movement must be taken within the context of history, as Horkheimer pointed out in 1941 and Baldwin in 1989, in her call for hermeneutic and critical theory for interpretive inquiry (Baldwin, 1989). The interpretation of opposites in the symbolic representation between the aesthetic and its counterpart, the grotesque, presents the current interplay for dominance of a developing cultural evolution or fragmentation. Yet, general educational curriculum development presents a move toward a standard of creative/critical thinking and philosophical inquiry rooted in tradition.

Art and Aesthetic Education as a National Agenda

Modern day concern has been unanimously voiced by six major education reform networks in the development of core knowledge programs and the arts (Olson, 1997):

Accelerated Schools Project, Stanford University

Coalition of Essential Schools, Brown University

Core Knowledge, Charlottesville, Virginia

Project 30 Alliance, University of Delaware

National Paideia Center, Chapel Hill, North Carolina, and

The Fourth "R": The Case for Music in School Curriculum.

As in the American reformers' research findings, Hungarian researchers found the academic records of children attending music primary schools to be significantly higher than for those of children in schools without music training (The fourth "R," 1998).

Discussion of Core Knowledge Programs and the Arts

Presidents Bush and Clinton both identified the arts as part of a national agenda in Goals 2000 (AFT, 1996) in the establishment of the National Education Standards and Improvement Council, Goals 2000, and the National Arts Consortium's K–12 Standards. Olson (1991) explains that these initiatives point to an opportunity for expansion and strengthening of arts programs in America's schools (p. 110). The Olson study made recommendations for doctoral and postdoctoral research into the application of the "fine arts" in the classroom. Some of the recommended research in general areas includes:

1. Qualitative research on the connection between aesthetic cognition and leadership in gifted and talented students (similar to the study on leadership and aesthetic cognition by Kenyon, 1998);

2. Relating developmental psychology to the arts (aesthetic knowing and education of gifted children;

3. Physiological correlates to musical experience (Gordon, 1974);

4. Imagery, psychology, and the arts (Jung and Wundt); and

5. Perception and the arts (Berlyne, 1974).

Art has been included in the "core knowledge sequences" by the National Education Commission of Time and Learning. These core courses in curriculum form what is termed the "core knowledge" program. They are an attempt to reinvigorate cultural literacy in our schools as part of the core knowledge framework (Olson, 1997, p. 114). Iowa primary and secondary educators identified a similar "core knowledge" concept for the inclusion of the arts (Hunter, 1999). Though the arts generated over 2000 jobs and 31 million dollars in revenue in Iowa in 1998, Iowa is listed 46th in the nation in tax money spend on the arts. The identification of creativity, aesthetics, and the arts is crucial for economic development and education (Estes, 1999). This would follow the argument of a unification theory or (GUT) for the manifesting of more than aesthetics metaphors in the social consciousness and evolution. To determine if there is a larger movement, identification of an underlying aesthetics philosophy directing these activities must be considered.

Thus, there is a need to review the current aesthetics status within not only the context of general education, but also in other areas, such as: economic development (Water Resources Planning and Management Conference, 1997); transportation (Heder, 1980); the environment (Berleant, 1992); landscape design (Bourassa, 1991); building construction (Holgate, 1992; Nervi, 1965); city parking (Smith, 1988); regional planning (Bagley, 1973); and general quality of daily life issues in relation to aesthetics components (Dendel, 1971). There appears to be a re-evolving global sociology of the concept of the "good life," as identified by early home economics researchers (Eaton, 1989). This requires a reassessment of these early concepts of aesthetics and current global paradigm shifts in consciousness.

Before we consider such a shift in general education curricula, we must examine the sister movements of Dewey and his aesthetics philosophy and Hunt and her role in the development of home economics. Before we consider Dewey and his aesthetics philosophy, we must first consider a larger enlightenment movement which impacted the educational philosophy to follow and may well have set the framework for not only that progressive movement, but the current enlightenment movement. In addition, it would seem Dewey's evolving aesthetics philosophy was tied directly to those intellectual events and contemporaries of the European

Scottish Enlightenment, such as T. H. Green (Dewey's role model), and others, as we will discover (Lamont, 1934; Ryan, 1995).

Phenomenological Aesthetics and the Scottish Enlightenment

Ecker, Executive Director of the International Society for The Advancement of Living Traditions in Art, presented an argument for a "phenomenological aesthetics" for well-being in the twenty-first century (Ecker, 1998). He argued a connection between aesthetics, balance, and a sense of well-being. As a process of investigation and cognitive development, Ecker experimented with the methodological use of phenomenological hermeneutics in teaching students the use of "levels of discourse—criticism, met criticism, theory, met theory—to delimit their investigations and to insure that their 'knowledge claims' were grounded in their 'aesthetic experience' of an 'object/event'" (Ecker, 1998, p. 6). He writes the article as a review of Kaelin's contributions to the topic of "phenomenological aesthetics," yet he sees himself in Kaelin's work (p. 5), much like Bacon in Dewey's.

The dominance of an "aesthetic experience" (p. 6) within the concepts of Bacon and Dewey may also be found in Scottish universities during the mid- and late-eighteen hundreds. The duality of personalities crossing through time, when it comes to "aesthetics and the notion of aesthetic inquiry as educational research," is evident in early promoters, like Campbell, the poet. During the Scottish Enlightenment, he was instrumental in attempting to draw an intellectual core to London:

> [T]o bring to the capital men like his former professor who would "chase vulgarity from the character, habits and pursuits, and from the very idioms and utterance of the vulgar wealthy" would form what later became known as "Scotch knowledge." (Chitnis, 1986, p. 169)

Quite similar to Dewey's concepts of the interconnectedness of the environment and the conditions of life within the total existence, Miller and Smith demonstrate the Scottish concern for society and conditions of life during the Scottish Enlightenment. Miller speaks of the development of the origins of class rank in response to the desperate conditions of the time:

> The poor are naturally dependent upon the rich, from whom they derive their subsistence; and, according to the accidental differences of wealth possessed by individuals, a subordination of ranks is gradually introduced, and different degrees of power and authority are assumed without opposition, by particular persons or bestowed upon them by the general voice of society ... [Man's] first efforts are naturally calculated to increase the means of subsistence, by catching or ensnaring wild animals. ... Accordingly as men have been successful in these great improvements, and find less difficulty in the attainment of bare necessaries, their prospects are gradually enlarged, their appetites and desires are more and more awakened and called forth in pursuit of the several conveniences of life; and the various branches of manufacture, together with commerce, its inseparable attendant, and with science and literature, the natural offspring of ease and affluence, are introduced, and brought to maturity. (Chitnis, 1986, pp. 2–3)

The social philosophy of the Scottish Enlightenment resulted in Miller's concept of economic progress:

> The general theories of survival in a mix of economic progress are consistent with Smith and Hume (Ogose, 1989). Followed to its conclusion, this concept will result in ... opulent families (that) are quickly reduced to indigence; and their place are supplied by professional people from lower orders; who by the purchase of land, endeavor to procure that distinction which was the end of their labours ... The general evolution of the society would result from the historical approach, in that the "political arrangements of society would be at their least sophisticated in the primitive phase and become increasingly elaborate as society advanced in wealth and possessions." (Chitnis, 1986, p. 3)

For Miller, the mechanics and laborers, who were the most numerous persons in a commercial nation, would be cut off from information, and as their superiors advanced in knowledge, they would become "involved in a thicker cloud of ignorance and prejudice." They then were in danger of being duped by their superiors and of being degraded. Thus, "to keep the common people in ignorance was absurd, abhorrent and provided only temporary security" (Chitnis, 1986, p. 6).

These were the political and social debates in the early nineteenth century and during the Scottish Enlightenment. It is difficult to fairly assess the proposals within the evolved conditions of our own society. The general state of societal poverty, illiteracy, and despair required a response within the framework of the reality of the times. Education for the masses was unheard of. Arguments as to the logic and need for such education was presented in light of the power structures of that time. The lectures which followed were an attempt:

> "to enlighten those who are destined for the functions of government, and to enlighten the public in respect of their conduct[.". This] no doubt followed a concern for "the difficult first decade of the nineteenth century when the French economists (and Adam Smith consequently [Ogose, 1989]) were believed to have been responsible for the excesses of the French Revolution. (Chitnis, 1986, p. 26)

The concepts of morals, values, and "aesthetic experience" within the same context as social revolution and process of evolution creates the same dichotomous interplay as we will later find in Dewey's reconstruction theory (Dewey, 1920, 1948). And, like Dewey's Laboratory School in America, a Mechanics Institute in England (1823), which later became the Birkbeck Literary and Scientific Institution, and finally Birkbeck College, was justified by the philosophical "Scottish" approach. In a "new plan for education in England," these Enlightenment founders:

> argued in the face of those who saw the education of working men as a danger that a more likely threat to public order was ignorance: knowledge begets prudence. The savage is proverbially thoughtless and improvident; and in the exact proportion as he becomes civilized, he

acquires the habit of looking forward and regarding the more remote as well as the immediate consequences of his actions ... Working men encouraged to pursue knowledge would generally be the friends, and the effectual friends of improvement in all our institutions ... The possession of knowledge ... must produce the same effect upon the working classes that the possession of wealth does upon the rich; it gives them a direct *interest* in the peace and good order of the community, and renders them solicitous to avoid whatever may disturb it. (Chitnis, 1986, p. 166)

Concern for social order soon after the French Revolution was primary in Europe. Though promoted through "Scotch knowledge" by a limited number of a "particular aristocratic set and their entourage" within the Whig Party, it illuminates the process of intellectual backgrounds and personal networks and "revitalized the demoralized party." A cast, called nobility, was formed, from which along all the great functionaries of government could be appointed in most countries of Europe; and in process of time, the more important charges could only be given among a small number of families In an article titled "The Dangers of the Country" in the *Edinburgh Review*, 10, pp. 11–12, Jeffrey Francis (quoted in Chitnis, 1986, p. 101) examines this concern:

The opening of the eighteenth century was a time of very bitter hardship for Scotland (Daiches, 1964, p. 5). Famine from cold, failed harvests, and frozen harvests devastated the country's agriculture. Thousands were starving. In 1698, an estimated two hundred thousand persons were in desperate state of poverty and beggars. The significance of ownership of land meant "the power to try, judge, and punish a tenant" (p. 6).

The improvements being made in the condition of agriculture and therefore of living conditions in Scotland were largely influenced by the examples of Holland, where many lawyers and landowners went from Scotland to law school to study Roman Law, and English farmers, now part of the newly established Union between Scotland and England. Here they also picked up new agricultural methods. To improve methods of farming on one's estate, to import seeds, to plant trees—these became favorite preoccupation of the more enlightened Scottish gentry in the eighteenth century and sometimes went along with an interest in literature and the arts (Daiches, 1964, p. 7).

The concentration of *literati* in Edinburgh was an attempt to realize the "Heavenly City" in stone, of the eighteenth-century philosophers of the Enlightenment (Daiches, 1964, p. 70). That the evolution of world history was tied to the Western tradition of Judeo-Christian manifest destiny is too often unconsidered in our present day reflection of issues. Yet, this Western theological foundation was central in the evolving "Heavenly City" of Edinburgh. Edinburgh became known in Britain as the "Athens of the North," with ideas for city planning and other social improvements begun by Sir Patrick Geddes. These plans for city and social improvements were to spread to the entire Western civilization. Daiches presents Geddes general concepts for the developing city of Edinburgh:

> He [Geddes] expressed concern "about the organic nature of a city's growth," with his concepts of relationship between environment, function, and growth and the relationship between place, work, and folk besides the ideas implicit in the plan," [ideas which] were continued on both sides of the Atlantic, by Geddes' student, Lewis Mumford (Daiches, 1964, p. 73).

It should be evident that this concept of environment and conditions of living became a central concern of Dewey's aesthetic in his educational philosophy and his belief in social evolution through democratic processes. The Enlightenment on both sides of the Atlantic would produce the golden age of Scotland and remarkable men, including: philosopher Hume; Song-poets Burns and Sir Walter Scott; biographers Boswell and Lockhart; portrait painter Sir Henry Raeburn; the greatest British architect of his century, Adam; and the medical dynasty of Doctors Monro, of Edinburgh's Medical College, which later became the most respected medical school in the world. Thus, every aspect of the human intellect was impacted by the Scottish Enlightenment. No greater achievements could be found in such a tiny nation in so short a time without return to "the Age of Mackenzie or to the Age of Pericles" (Daiches, 1964, p. 74).

The same strange duality of a "simultaneous seductiveness and anachronistic meaninglessness ... with sentimentality and shrewdness" is evident in the formation of such associations as the "Royal Society of

Edinburgh" and "the Highland Society of Scotland. This duality might be compared to the current conflict between those concerned with the superficial "aesthetic sensual surface" as compared to "aesthetic knowing" and moral critique (Paul, 1991). With interest in both economics and in the fine arts of the Highlands, the practical application of an evolving phenomenon of evolution was combined with economic necessity (Daiches, 1964, p. 76). The so-called "Scottish man of feeling," Henry Mackenzie, typified this duality in review of poets such as Burns:

> [I]mitating the strain of moral and sentimental reflection to be found in the later eighteenth-century English poets, (Burns) suppressed his original genius to produce sententious and rhetorical effusions of comparatively little merit and possessing no relation at all to what might be called the Scottish centre of the poet's imagination. (Daiches, 1964, p. 76)

Whether this suppression of the more primitive Scottish *literati*, less polished than the English, ended in a sort of balance in the development of the origins of poetry is still debated.

> A theory of language based on a theoretical anthropology and a theory of poetry based in turn on this and on both a theoretical and an empirical psychology (with John Locke and Neo-Platonism also involved) lay behind much of the rhetorical theory of the eighteenth century Scottish critics. ... But the apparatus of the Enlightenment employed to purvey a rhetorical analysis of works of literature soon produced yet another paradox of the Scottish culture, the co-existence of a coolly rational tone and method with a belief in the moral value of feeling. (Daiches, 1964, p. 82)

> The Jacobite movement had its effect on Gaelic poetry to an even greater extent than it had on Scots song, and we need not pause once again to note the paradox which made the Stuart line in the eighteenth century the champion of Scottish nationalism and the cause of the Highlander. (Daiches, 1964, p. 95)

71

The truly Scottish tradition of Gaelic poetry of the Enlightenment presents a hermeneutic tradition of palimpsest communication (Brooke-Rose, 1992). Yet, the Gaelic poetry did have a renaissance of sorts in the eighteenth century. Here, too, there is an ironic paradox of such Gaelic poets, for Mackay and Macintyre were influenced by Pope, their rival (Daiches, 1964, p. 95). Donn's parish minister had translated some of Pope's poetry into Gaelic and used these translations in his monthly prayer meeting (p. 95).

Though best known now for his translations of the Iliad, Pope was a member of a satirical group of young writers in London, including Swift. Pope, a Catholic, and Swift were caught in the conflict of the day. Pope used his writing as an opportunity to speak against Whig politics and the money culture that he felt attended it (Brooks-Davies, 1996). In fact, he became the main satirical poet of his century. Thus, the strange rivalry of society and creativity in the Scottish paradox remains similar to what we will find in our investigation of Dewey and his aesthetics philosophy and progressivism in education as a means of modeling citizenship. Similar to what we will find with Dewey's progressive movement in America, the later part of the Scottish Enlightenment called for a "Sketch of Education Legislation Needed for England," which was sent to Lord Russell in 1839 (Chitnis, 1986):

> The ignorance of the lower classes in any state encourages superstition, impairs industry, and corrupts the manners of the people; the most fruitful sources of prosperity in peace and security in war. He had stated the same objection more publicly in his *Report on the training of pauper children* (1839): "The great object to be kept in view in regulating any school for the instruction of the children of the laboring class is the rearing of hardy and intelligent working men, whose character and habits shall afford the largest amount of security to the property and order of the community" and he stressed that children should know the connection between property and the value of labour: ... Now the sole effectual means of preventing the tremendous evils with which the anarchical spirit of the manufacturing population threatens the country, is by giving the working people a good secular education, to

enable them to understand the true causes which determine their physical condition, and regulate the distribution of wealth among the several classes of society. (Chitnis, 1986, pp. 159–160)

The *literati* were to attempt all manner of philosophical and economic experimentation in dealing with the misery of the larger population. Edinburgh during the Enlightenment was to become the center of, again, the most respected medical schools of the times. Scottish physicians, like their counterparts in the humanities, were stimulated by the classroom teaching (Chitnis, 1986, p. 56). The associations of the Scottish universities and medical schools formed what we may now consider "learning communities" to promote association and friendship among students and scholars.

> The societies also found their origins invariably in the age of Enlightenment during which various societies for the mature community of university towns arose (for instance, the Select Society and the Royal Society of Edinburgh, the Political Economy Club in Glasgow and the Wise Club in Aberdeen) and became the generation and development of new ideas. (Chitnis, 1986, p. 56)

Most significant to our discussion of the societies and the new knowledge and ideas generated during this Enlightenment is their relationship to aesthetics and the arts, and the origin of "aesthetic disinterestedness" (Kivy, 1973). During this Enlightenment, Hutcheson, a predecessor of Hume, published his philosophy of aesthetics in 1725: *Inquiry Concerning Beauty, Order, Harmony, Design, and Inquiry into the Origins of our Ideas of Beauty and Virtue.* This work became a dominant force in the Enlightenment in the development of the "modern system of the arts" as a separate and autonomous discipline through "aesthetic disinterestedness" (p. 5).

> Absolute beauty for Hutcheson occupied a realm of pure form: a realm that included visible and aural forms, man-made or natural, animate or inanimate; and intelligible forms as embodied in the constructs of scientific theories. A form—be it a geometrical figure, a celestial phenomenon, a plant or animal, a theorem in physics—occasions the idea of beauty to the extent that it possesses *unity amidst*

variety. By far the largest and most widely appreciated class of such forms is that of natural beauties: "In every part of the world which we call beautiful there is a surprising uniformity amidst an almost infinite variety." But for those capable of theoretical understanding, mathematics, the natural sciences, and metaphysics offer too the *unity amidst variety* that is beauty's prerequisite … But art owes its major effect to relative beauty and to morality. (Kivy, 1973, pp. 6–7)

Whether in nature or by works of man, the sensation of mental response to beauty remains the same, based on response to uniformity of pattern and rhythm. The same notion of regularity is found in animals, lending a systematic procedure for identifying and classifying various animals by species (Kivy, 1973, p. 44). The uniformity in nature, for example, the harmony of sound, results from unity or uniformity of pattern (p. 46).

Hutcheson's notion of pattern, uniformity, and harmony in the creation of aesthetic space, would be expanded into a theory of interior space by Charles R. Mackintosh in his development of design for the Glasgow School of Art. Though built in 1844, The Glasgow School of Art would be transformed in the late nineteenth century. The "art of space, the house as a work of art," led Mackintosh to see "interiors whose perfection of form made them self-contained forms of art" (Buchanan et al., 1989).

The criticism of Mackintosh's concern for uniformity and aesthetic interior space seems ironic, considering the previous architectural movement of the Enlightenment (Jones, 1988). As early as 1783, the Glasgow University was bequeathed a large sum of money from William Hunter, the first Professor of Anatomy to the Royal Academy, for the building of a special museum. A detailed description of the building reveals the appropriateness of the title of Jones's chapter, "Buildings and the Ordering of Minds and Bodies," The designs show a number of interesting phenomena in spatial structure as discussed in the following:

First, that art and knowledge (paintings and books) are far deeper into the building than nature and medicine (natural history and anatomy). Second, that the central dome acts on both the main floors as a transitional space, where there is a movement from the visible, or surface phenomenon, (shown on the diagram by a dotted circle) become the junction of a three-pronged fork—the two sided prongs in each case having the same deeper penetration, both actually, in space, and metaphorically, in concept. Thus on the ground floor we move from the natural philosophy of visible object to the anatomy of invisible structures; on the first floor from visible art (painting) to invisible knowledge (books). It is not coincidence that a central dome—the dominant *motif* of cosmic unity in European architecture from Hadrian's Pantheon onwards—should have been the formal means to accompany the functional and spatial devices used to express this complex idea. (Jones, 1988, pp. 217–219)

Mackintosh attempted to find the sublime and beautiful in a "cosmic unity" for the interiors of his art school. The theme of beauty was central to his personal philosophy. The search for beauty as "cosmic unity" was evident in his 1902 lecture:

Art is the flower—life is the green leaf. Let every artist strive to make his flower a beautiful living thing— something that will convince the world that there may be—there are—things more precious—more beautiful— more lasting than life. (Robertson, 1996, p. 6)

The long tradition of beauty in relation to a "cosmic unity" continued, being revitalized on occasion, as each new generation found its significance. Notions of aesthetics and beauty have appeared within the same context as sciences for all time; one questions why such notions fall in ill favor throughout time. In perhaps a similar process of those change cycles, from hieroglyphics and "hieroglyphs of the soul" (Jauss, 1982, p. 177), with its "multiple concepts all superimposed upon one another," like a palimpsest icon, we have moved toward the linear sequence of the Greek alphabet, and continue to attempt to reduce reality to a more simplistic concept (Shlain, 1991). The move to "rationalism" in an attempt to separate reality from a higher context of God has consistently returned societies to a more primitive state, in the linearity of space and time, and cycles of civilizations (Shlain, 1991, p. 31). The lack of pattern, and attempt by Euclid to connect space "by an imaginary web of straight lines *that in fact do not exist in nature*" is further verification of the relevance of the Enlightenment's concern for "aesthetic cognition," hermeneutic spirals, and universal history (p. 30).

The Scottish Enlightenment was "the single most important moment in the history of the concept of the aesthetic," and "it has become commonplace to suggest that aesthetics began during the enlightenment" (Ashfield & De Bolla, 2000, p. 1). Aesthetics in "ideal presence" and "ideal being" becomes phenomenal and the hermeneutics of a theology of the soul. For, "in the British tradition there is a consistent refusal to relinquish the interconnections between aesthetic judgments and ethical conduct" (p. 3). Thus, a search for beauty is also a search for soul within the aesthetic milieu.

The possible trend toward another global enlightenment through the now revitalized progressive movement as a continuation of the previous enlightenment movements will lead us to the initial aesthetics philosophy of John Dewey. The present movement will be considered within its global social context.

Dewey's Aesthetics Philosophy

Zeltner begins his discussion of Dewey's aesthetics philosophy with an explanation of the rationale for Dewey's writing *Art as Experience*. Dewey expressed a desire "to restore the continuity of aesthetic experience with normal processes of living and the notion of beauty in everyday life" (Zeltner, 1975, p. 15). His unique interpretation of how the environment impacts and is impacted by humanity is consistent with the hermeneutic philosophy then and now. Let us consider a quote from Dewey's proposition carefully:

> Life consists of phases in which the organism falls out of step with the march of surrounding things and then recovers unison with it either through effort or by some happy chance. And, in a growing life, the recovery is never

mere return to a prior state, for it is enriched by the state of disparity and resistance through which it has successfully passed. If the gap between organism and environment is too wide the creature dies. Life grows when a temporary falling out is a transition to a more extensive balance of energies of the organism with those of the conditions under which it lives. (Dewey, 1922, p.181)

Dewey saw all experience as potential for growth or death. If we consider the concept of beauty as being that state where the soul searches for home (Navone, 1996), the significance of a state of distress in the process of life or death becomes more meaningful. For example, if the soul seeks beauty in such states, there can be no rational justification for that life which takes force from falsity or evil (Navone). If we accept that beauty and truth are one with the Creator, its opposite is death and the great deceiver who seeks to bring about that death.

If we accept further that the Creator is the source of all life force, the manifestation of the essence of life being love, anything contrary to that reality is not truth or beauty. It is not a far reach to include concepts of a "just and civil society" as components of truth and the aesthetics of mind, and Dewey's concern for patriotism and citizenship in the "creation of a more humane and just world" (Andrsejewski & Alessio, 1999, pp. 1–25). The concept of totality in a unification theory or a unification concert in the inner connectedness of all things and events becomes more meaningful in the global movement. Here, the argument as to whether aesthetics is a theory, a philosophy, a practice, or a method, seems irrelevant, if taken within the context of totality and a Theory of Everything (TOE) (Siler, 1990).

The idea at the time of "two orders of existence," dominant in Greek philosophy, and what Dewey interpreted to be a duality of "truth," was contrary to his own definition of truth. His long effort was to argue that truth and knowledge could not exist in the noumenal region (being) and a phenomenal, or transitory (non-being) reality. Truth or knowledge was to exist in both the order of the universe and the order of the individual mind trying to know the universe (Tuggle, 1997).

This struggle for unity evolved into Dewey's development of American pragmatism or instrumentalism (p. 37). The struggle for a correct definition of truth becomes intertwined with the essence of communication and symbolism in the arts (Heidegger, 1981/1993). The significance of such books by Dewey as *Art as our Heritage* (1940), reflects similar concerns about the potential for propaganda as Horkheimer expressed in 1941:

> Intelligence in politics when it is identified with discussion means reliance upon symbols. The invention of language is probably the greatest single invention achieved by humanity ... The nineteenth-century establishment of parliamentary institutions, written constitutions and suffrage as a means of political rule, is a tribute to the power of symbols ... "Propaganda" is the inevitable consequence of the combination of these influences and it extends to every area of life. (Tuggle, 1997, p. 21)

The process of inquiry and search for knowledge as a form of truth was Dewey's underlying concept "of logic and theory of knowledge" (Tuggle, 1997, p. 219). Yet, there seems to be confusion in his writing as to the unconscious metaphysics of his writing and his openly strong belief in God. In discussions of Dewey's, *Whitehead's Philosophy* (1937), concerning principles presented by Plato and Aristotle, he identifies this truth which "seemed to descend directly via pure intellect, out of the ether of reason, situated next to God or perhaps in his own intrinsic abode" (Tuggle, 1997, p. 219). This statement appears in conflict with his earlier objection to the Greek philosophy of "two orders of existence" (p. 37). The error of Dewey's logic in this is near that of Locke, as expressed in *An Essay Concerning the Human Understanding* (1690):

> First, a Child having framed the *Idea* of a *Man*, it is probable that his *Idea* is just like that Picture, which the Painter makes of the visible Appearances joined together; and such a Complication of *Ideas* together in his Understanding, makes up the single complex *Idea* he calls *Man*, whereof White or Flesh-colour in *England* being one, the Child can demonstrate to you, that a *Negro is not a Man*, because White-colour was one of the constant simple *Ideas* of the complex *Idea* he call *Man*: And therefore he can demonstrate by the Principle, *It is impossible for the same Thing to be, and not to be, that a Negro is not a Man.* (Tuggle, 1997, p. 19)

Thus, a sequential linear logic based upon false initial assumptions of the accuracy of life experience and observations alone, does not guarantee truth. Tuggle's example above best epitomized the argument for the limitations of quantitative empirical reasoning.

Considering the metaphysical bent in all of Dewey's writing, especially in his discussion of aesthetics and God, it is difficult to understand why this led to his pragmatism as a means of resolving the Greek philosophy of "two world orders." The issues of "progressive organization" and a holistic view of self-knowing (Greenberg & Tobach, 1990, pp. 48, 75) forming a "cognitive system" independent of "thought processes" (p. 31) also seems in conflict with Dewey's postulates in *Art as Experience* (1934):

> Art is a quality that permeates an experience; it is not, save by a figure of speech, the experience itself. Esthetic experience is always more than esthetic. In it a body of matters and meanings, not in themselves esthetic, *become* esthetic as they enter into an ordered rhythmic movement toward consummation ... Shelley said, "The great secret of morals is love, or *a going out of our nature* and the identification of ourselves with the beautiful which exists in thought, action, or person, not our own. A man to be greatly good must imagine intensely and comprehensively." What is true of the individual is true of the whole system of morals in thought and action. While perception of the union of the possible with actual in a work of art is itself a great good, the good does not terminate with the immediate and particular occasion in which it is had. The union that is presented in perception persists in the remaking of impulsion and thought. The first intimations of wide and large redirections of desire and purpose are of necessity imaginative. Art is a mode of prediction not found in charts and statistics, and it insinuates possibilities of human relations not to be found in rule and precept, admonition and administration. (Dewey, 1934/1980, pp. 326, 349)

Art is to Dewey the mechanism with which to unite the material and the ideal, the "two world orders," when he states in *Art and Experience* (Dewey, 1939, 1980) that:

> While art itself is the best proof of the existence of a
> realized and therefore realizable, union of material and
> ideal, there are general arguments that support the
> thesis in hand ... After all, even though "spiritual" and
> "material" are separated and set in opposition to one
> another, there must be conditions through which the
> ideal is capable of embodiment and realization—and this
> is all, fundamentally, that "matter" signifies. (Dewey,
> 1934/1980, p. 27)

Art as one process for the experience of the aesthetic became separated
from its original place in the daily lives of persons in societies (p. 10).
Dewey's goal was to return to daily experiences in order to discover the
"esthetics quality such experience possesses" (p. 11). Yet, the experience
(consumption of art) and the expression of the aesthetic (the actions of
man) may be seen as one and the same. The good a man does is interred
with his bones; the evil lives after him. One must question at this point
whether Dewey felt the aesthetic experience could be maintained as a
constant, or some passing experience, still separate from the "ideal" more
"spiritual" realm of reality, more as a mystical experience:

> It explains also the religious feeling that accompanies
> intense—esthetic perception ...a world within a world ...
> [W]e are citizens of this vast world beyond ourselves,
> and any intense realization of its presence with and in us
> brings a peculiarly satisfying sense of unity in itself and
> within ourselves. (Dewey, 1934/1980, p. 195)

He hoped, through art, to teach the experience of the cosmos, as "[a]
work of art elicits and accentuates this quality of being a whole and of
belonging to the larger, all-inclusive, whole which is the universe in which
we live" (Dewey, 1939, 1980, p. 195). The expressionist portrayal of the
opening lines of the poem by Hinterland in Chapter 1, or the psychological
impact of human suffering as a result of love of person or love of ideal,
result in the same experience of devastation as at the time of the original
loss.

> As we have already seen, the value of an art work in its
> specific capacity as a work of art is a value for its own sake
> that is *posited*, and it presupposes positing art's universal

value for its own sake. (For the universal concept of art posits value: it contrasts a non-value, in the form of mass culture, to itself). The whole process of the emancipation of art is nothing but this value debate ... There is a difference between some current post-modern movements and the "universal freedom of reception" in that "many do not wish to receive a given thing at all." ... The end result of such recognition may be that artistic activity and life activity become nearly identical ... [C]ould a creative and productive aesthetic universe of freedom arise in the place of universal art, where everybody could be an artist and the aesthetic sphere would not be isolated or in transcendental opposition to life but an imminent ethos." (Heller & Feher, 1986, p. 93)

In the course of its conceptual emancipation, art assumed quasi-religious features and reproduced categories of grace, mystery, divine promise, salvation, prophetic expectations, revelation, and the absolute. This observation is the fundamental argument by Brown (1995) in his discussion of Jung's hermeneutic of doctrine. The underlying unity of the psyche is expressed in the free-flowing exposition of the subconscious in the creative act. There is a personal, collective, and potential meaning in such expressions, which allow for appreciation of individual art for a larger society, beyond individual expression and meaning. Arnold Schoenberg writes in one of his letters to Kokoschka in 1946 about one of his admirers:

[U]nfortunately, like my own followers who admire Hindemith, Stravinski and Bartok as much or even more, he too has too many gods, Klee, Kandinsky, etc. Yet "thou shalt have one God." ... to maintain the claim of universality, the artist has to take the work to a spiritual market and reckon with the varying contextualization of recipient strangers. (Heller & Feher, 1986, p. 95)

If there is a universal aesthetics movement, its aim at relieving the misery of the mass culture would likely provide Dewey with hope beyond his own life. The cult movement demonstrated in the March 2000 pornographic performing arts exhibition at the San Francisco Art Institute may be considered such mass culture and its current decline (Chronicle,

2000). The notion of defecating on stage as performing art was to be challenged not only on grounds of public decency but aesthetic or artistic relevance. Some might argue this exposition of degradation simply reflects the reality of the culture in decline, and this is the mission of art, again, not aesthetics.

It is the concept of mass culture that Dewey laments in his time, as well as the terrible living conditions that were the daily reality for the majority of persons. That culture was one of despair and marginal survival. The reality of the environment of the last century is lamented by Dewey in the following:

> I can think of nothing more childishly futile, for example, than the attempt to bring "art" and esthetic enjoyment externally to the multitudes who work in the ugliest surrounding and who leave their ugly factories only to go through depressing streets to eat, sleep and carry on their domestic occupations in grimy, sordid homes. The interest of the younger generation in art and esthetic matters is a hopeful sign of the growth of culture in its narrower sense. But it will readily turn into an escape mechanism unless it develops into an alert interest in the conditions which determine the esthetic environment of the vast multitudes who now live, work and play in surroundings that perforce degrade their tastes and that unconsciously educate them into desire for any kind of enjoyment as long as it is cheap and "exciting." (Roth, 1962, p. 12)

Dewey's concern for the aesthetic experience as compared to the creative process in the production and experience of fine art are better explained by his aesthetic philosophy of life. If life was to have meaning for man, it must have aesthetic meaning in and through nature (Roth, 1962). The enrichment of the human experience outside the most basic of existence is in the self-realization of man's potential, through aesthetic experience (p. 34).

Here aesthetics is the successful integration of the human with his environment, outside of misery. It is in the sublime, the aesthetic experience, that man can find the opposite of his oppressive state. Interacting with and improving his environment, man participates in his own and the environment's evolution (Roth, 1986, p. 140). This principle is developed by "evolution of the material universe" and "human creativity in self-realization" as Dewey's two key concepts (p. 141). Yet, by habits of the mind (Dewey, 1922), moral reasoning may be directed or misdirected through life experiences. The environment becomes a part of the experience of the mind, and the relief from environmental misery may lead to further destruction of the moral character of those in states of environmental despair. Dewey addresses this reality with his own recommendations for action:

> There must be change in objective arrangements and institutions. We must work on the environment not merely on the hearts of men. To think otherwise is to suppose that flowers can be raised in a desert or motor cars in a jungle. Both things can happen and without a miracle, but only by first changing the jungle and desert. (Dewey, 1922, p. 22)

To change the jungle and the desert was more a challenge than to modify the individual reaction to it, as Kabat-Zinn (1994) explains this difficult dilemma in his book *Wherever You Go, There You Are*. The practice of meditation as a means of self-repose was as likely a practice for Dewey, who spent a great deal of his time in isolation from others. As is evident in Jackson's book on Dewey, His was the life of the mind" (Jackson, 1998, p. #). Thus, if Dewey believed the integration of the environment with the inner world of the individual was necessary for self-realization, there seems some conflict. A solitary man who chose to spend little time outside his own rooms would indicate a lack of desire to interact with his environment (p. 164). Yet, this ambiguous and dichotomous process of writing is the rhythm of "[t]he integral nature of an aesthetic experience [which] forced him to twist and turn as he goes along" (p. 44). Major concerns for Dewey in developing his "reconstruction" theory were environment and experience and how these affect the present. The control of his own environment for "reconstruction" may be a small part of the reason for his isolation and realization of his limited ability to impact that larger environment (p. 46).

Dewey's Reconstruction Theory

"To conceive of the past affecting the present, as the operation of habit" (Jackson, 1998, p. 46) allows alterations of the past and the present. These alterations of habit of mind became what Dewey termed *reconstruction* (p. 46). Reconstruction was to Dewey a method of applying "intelligence" in systematic inquiry into human and moral subjects (Dewey, 1948). Thus, the kind of method of observation of which Dewey speaks is quite similar to hermeneutics in its focus on context in relation to society. "[T] he principle of continuity of experience means that every experience takes up something from those which have gone before and modifies in some way the quality of those which come after" (Jackson, 1998, p. 46). Thus, Dewey reveals a palimpsest reconstruction of Bacon's earlier philosophy:

> Like Bacon, the need for a systematic process of inductive reasoning was not the goal, but the tool toward a greater purpose, the improvement of the human condition. Bacon … admonishes those who search out knowledge to take care that they consider what are the true ends of knowledge, and that they seek it not either for pleasure of the mind, or for contention, or for superiority to others, or for profit, or fame, or power or any of these inferior things; but for the benefit and use of life, and that they perfect and govern it in charity. (Raskin, 1987, p. 52)

Dewey's idea of a reconstruction of philosophy, with aesthetics as its basic premise of experience, was prompted by a belief that the subject matter and problems of philosophy grow from the stresses and strains in the community from which the disciple springs. According to the specific problems that constitute a crisis and turning point in history, the nature of philosophy will change (Dewey, 1948, p. v). For Dewey, the theory of reconstruction and continuity of experience also presupposed the use of good and bad experiences as a means toward growth, in this case, physical, moral, and intellectual growth (Jackson, 1998, p. 47). Therefore, for Dewey, as for Wundt (1921) and Bacon (Jackson, 1998) before him, there is a continuity in the progressive evolving of universal history and collective consciousness through ethical and moral critique (Paul, 2000).

Dewey was again in agreement with Bacon concerning the concepts of growth in relation to knowledge (Raskin, 1987, p. 52). "In any case, learning meant *growth* of knowledge, and growth belongs in the region of becoming, change, and hence is inferior to *possession* of knowledge in the syllogistic self-revolving manipulation of what was already known— demonstration" (Dewey, 1920, 1948, p. 31). Process as content, like critical thinking and creative thinking, so vital to aesthetic knowing, was the foundation of Dewey's progressive and aesthetic educational philosophy. Further, demonstration of what was known became action learning. Dewey (1920) states: "Making a living economically speaking will be at one with making a life that is worth living" (p. 211).

> If a few words are added upon the topic of education, it is only for the sake of suggesting that the educative process is all one with the moral process, since the latter is a continuous passage of experience from worse to better. (Dewey, 1920, 1948, p. 183)

Education then becomes life-long learning, a continuous process until death. The conflict with Dewey's theory at the time was not with morality, but the idea of core knowledge and memorization. There seems to be some confusion about practical outcome-based activities in general education and his Laboratory School, and action art (Jackson, 1998, p. 172). Dewey's concern for community was primary; his concern for life as experience and interaction with the environment and with other persons was the central focus in his aesthetic philosophy. Interaction, reflection, and experience are seen as central to Dewey's educational philosophy (Smith, 1998). The sharing in a "common life," the thinking process, and reflection are necessary for critical thinking, development of the individual in self-realization, and shared evolution (Roth, 1962; Dewey, 1934).

> There is no reason why, Dewey argued, humans could not undertake the same reconstruction of their social and political institutions (including those devoted to scientific research) so that our intellectual efforts generally are harnessed to the enrichment of human life. (Tiles, 1988, p. 179)

Dewey's aesthetic theory in relation to life and education is said to be his philosophy, and thus, "Dewey's philosophy *is* aesthetics, and all that he meticulously worked on in the area of logic, metaphysics, epistemology, and psychology is brought to culmination in his understanding of the aesthetic and art" (Zeltner, 1975, p. 3).

> Poetry, art, religion are precious things. They cannot be maintained by lingering in the past and futilely wishing to restore what the movement of events in science, industry, and politics has destroyed. They are an out-flowering of thought and desires that unconsciously converge into a disposition of imagination as a result of thousands and thousands of daily episodes and contacts ... When philosophy shall have co-operated with the course of events and made clear and coherent the meaning of the daily detail, science and emotion will interpenetrate, practice and imagination will embrace. (Dewey, 1920, 1948, pp. 212–213)

A similar notion of the interplay between aesthetics and cognition in relation to social evolution and democratization is seen in Curreri-Alibrandi's theory of "visual perspective" (Curreri-Alibrandi, 1996):

> [Where t]he relationship between symbolic VP (visual perspective) stimuli and individual social awakening becomes readily apparent observing the development of events in our own twentieth century, as the diffusion of VP images gains unprecedented proportions ... This new tool of mass-communication, added to its later evolutionary developments into cinematography and television, will unequivocally demonstrate that the perceived need for freedom and objective control, relative instigation for the pursuance of personal and communal goals and ideals, are directly connected to the spread of popular use of these visual technologies. In other words, the quest for freedom and object control will always be greater in the presence of a larger consumption of perspective-visual information. (p. 151)

The notion of visual perspective and cognitive stimulation in connection with evolving movements of democracy and freedom may seem a far stretch. The fact that past cycles of enlightenment were concurrent with periods of revolution, such as the Russian and French revolutions and the last Scottish Enlightenment, does cause one to pause. The idea of mass culture and mass communication with not only mental stimulation and social change potential, and a connection to cognitive evolution is a consideration. The current attempt to associate science and art as creative parallel worlds may be such a subtle link. Curreri-Albrandi (1996) theorizes that an examination of art history reveals that artists turned inward and developed greater intuition and foreknowledge to an expanded degree after the invention of the camera (pp. 151–171). Further, visual stimulation, whether early on in painting for the elite, or later and more so through photography for the masses, led to a cognitive evolution which resulted in a search for freedom.

Dewey's Progressive Education and Home Economics

Dewey's name has consistently been associated with "progressive" education (Dworkin, 1959). Yet, what is now meant by "progressive"? The integration of general educational issues, such as the progressive education movement, was as much a part of the social history of the profession as its origins in aesthetics philosophy. Hunt continued her own efforts and focus on domestic issues, while Richards more closely aligned herself with the women's movement of the time (Stage & Vincenti, 1997). While Richards published *The Art of Right Living*, Hunt would later publish *The Life of Ellen H. Richards: 1842–1911* (Stage & Vincenti, 1997).

Whether they were mentor and student or recycled prophetesses, the significance of Richard's early efforts in the development of the profession in bacteriology was more than an effort that "cleanliness might be sought for moral and aesthetic reasons" (Stage & Vincenti, 1997, p. 48). That Richards entered MIT under the "camouflage of domesticity" and was allowed a "special corner of the chemistry laboratory, 'very much as a dangerous animal might have been' attests to the reality of education for women in 1870s" and the significance of the reality for women within the context of the times (Stage & Vincenti, 1997, p. 21).

As more men moved into the profession in the 1950s and 1960s, "a growing sense of embarrassment at the field's strong vocationalism and explicit links to teacher education" and "such female domination constituted proof that the field was out of date" (Stage & Vincenti, 1997, p. 96). The University of California at Berkeley dumped the department of household science in 1955 "as an embarrassment to the prestige of the great university they hoped to build up at Berkeley" (Stage & Vincenti, 1997, p. 102). The separation of educational philosophers from the "mix" of technical and scientific education was well on its way. Hunt and her home economics, like Dewey as the "philosopher as sage" and his progressive education, was part of "'an outmoded philosophical tradition' that was to make way for the imbalance of empirical analytic inquiry ... for a time" (Ryan, 1995, p. 22).

The Current "Progressive Project" may not be what Dewey had originally had in mind for progressive education. In fact, he had refused to involve himself with the Progressive Education Association in 1919, though he did accept an honorary presidency in 1928 (Dworkin, 1959, p. 113). Yet, there are some varying definitions as to what "Progressive Education" means today. For most of the nineteenth and twentieth centuries, "progressive education" has been "used to describe ideas and practices that aim to make schools more effective agencies of a democratic society" (University of Vermont, 2000). This definition may be somewhat different from Dewey's description in 1928, in a chapter from a book by the same title, *Progressive Education and the Science of Education* (Dewey, 1928):

> All the schools, I take it for granted, exhibit as compared with traditional schools, a common emphasis upon respect for individuality and for increased freedom; ... They all display a certain atmosphere of informality, because experience has proved that formalization is hostile to genuine mental activity and to sincere emotional expression and growth. Emphasis upon activity as distinct from passivity is one of the common factors ... respect for self-initiated and self-conducted learning; respect for activity as the stimulus and centre of learning; and perhaps above all belief in social contact, communication, and cooperation upon a normal human plane as an all-enveloping medium. (Dworkin, 1959, p. 115)

Yet, concepts of integrating such a theory still prevail. An example of Dewey's understanding of the evolving "progressive education" movement may still be seen. Spira (2000), Associate Director for Scripps Clinic Wellness Programs, in La Jolla, California, cites some of the more basic of Dewey's principles of progressive education from Europe and America on a current Internet website (Spira, 2000). He relates the significance of Dewey's educational progressivism within the context of the new technology. The appropriate use of progressive principles as compared to "essentialist education" is presented for integration of technology-based distance learning. Concepts of individualization and action-based learning are the dominant themes in the discourse (Spira, 2000).

Taken to the most extreme, "those exploitive motives are universal in politics" (Ryan, 1995, p. 27). A new "progressive utilization theory" has evolved (Proutist Universal, 1998). PROUT, like TOE, is an acronym; it stands for "PROgresssive Universalization Theory, and TOE stands for the "The Theory of Everything," a socio-economic philosophy that synthesizes the physical, mental, and spiritual dimensions of human nature. A stated goal of PROUT is "to provide guidance for the evolution of a truly progressive human society" (Proutist Universal, 1998, p.1). The organization's goals include economic democracy, world government, and universal rights. They claim 20 million people who demonstrated at the 1998 Davos Conference against "The Globalizers of Misery." Headquartered in Copenhagen, Denmark, they claim global networks, and promote their theory as "superior to Adam Smith's or Karl Marx's," according to Galtung, Founder of the UN Institute of Peace Studies (Proutist Universal, 1998).

The more traditional progressive education movement, called the John Dewey Project, is located at the University of Vermont, Burlington, Vermont. It, too, claims a global following, with a Center for World Education in Burlington. Their focus seems to be on multiculturalism in arts and culture (Vermont Intercultural Dialogue, 2000). Yet, some faint echo of the earlier beginning movement of Dewey and his associates at the University of Chicago may still be gleaned from the new movement. Like Dewey's new school, "the focus on an aesthetic logic of sorts may be seen ... The point is again to remind the reader that however 'high' high art may be, it is rooted in everyday experience, and the rhetorical force of the claim that even abstract thought is similarly rooted and the two are connected in their origins is obvious enough" (Ryan, 1995, p. 257).

Aesthetics in the Family and Consumer Sciences Curriculum

The need for aesthetics education in daily living is well established by educational theorists, such as Dewey, in the development of his educational philosophy (Gilbert & Kuhn, 1939). The early history of the profession of home economics mirrored the philosophies of general education and included aesthetics as a core concept (Brown, 1993; East, 1982; Navone, 1996). Like general education in the mid- to late-nineteenth century, the early history of home economics included these concepts as necessary for improving the quality of life for individuals and the families (Hilton, 1972). The current revitalization of Dewey's educational progressive theory, with underpinnings of aesthetics philosophy in daily living, may now be expanded to include the global multicultural college classroom (Farrar, 1998).

Hunt (1982) presented a paper, "Revaluations," to the 1901 Lake Placid Conference. In her paper, she quotes from Carpenter's *Art of Life*: "To create around oneself an external world which answers to the world within is indeed a great happiness and the fullness of life" (p. 52). It is evident in the titles and contents of these early professional papers present the significance of values and moral foundations in the early years. The significance of the home as an extension of the self and the identity of the expressive freedom of the family unit remained a constant theme for Hunt. The value of the inner life of the self and society lay in free expression. The free expression "secured by careful examinations of values, simplification of material surroundings, discarding of useless conventions and traditions, and research on better health and social conditions" may have begun as Hunt's personal philosophy, but became the "creed" attributed to Richards (East, 1982, 47). Regardless of which wonderful lady followed the steps of Dewey or a chain of Enlightenment philosophers before him, is of little significance now. That both were in Chicago during the development of laboratory schools and the early experimentation with progressive education, as a component of aesthetics concepts as key in home economics becomes meaningful (Ryan, 1995, p. 6).

Perhaps, like Dewey's educational movement, home economics "belonged to an outmoded philosophical tradition" (Ryan, 1995, p. 22). Yet, as we have discussed, there seems a revitalization of the progressive movement, aesthetics cognition in leadership, and science. With this new movement, a change has occurred. "Moral philosophers did not talk about science, and philosophers of science did not talk about aesthetics; everyone went in fear of mathematical logicians, and everyone thought that 'analysis' was the essential philosophical technique." "Philosophical analysis" was, in the jargon of the day, "value-neutral" (p. 22). The dominance of empirical analytical tradition had silenced, temporarily, the value-based interpretive method of inquiry and reason.

The early identification of aesthetics and beauty as key concepts in home economics is due in part to Hunt. The foundation of Dewey's aesthetic educational philosophy, the need for the actual education of homemakers and housekeepers as to this necessity, was reintroduced at the Sixth Lake Placid Conference on Home Economics at the University of Wisconsin. Among the responsibilities which "the home will never delegate," Hunt presented the following rationale:

> Second, the home is responsible for the education of the beauty sense. We, as a nation, need a better architecture, a better art. We need a form of building that enhances and does not contradict and destroy the beauties of natural scenery—an art which shall penetrate to the commonest things of life and give us more beautiful houses, more beautiful furniture, and more beautiful clothes. If we are to secure this better art and better architecture, this greater beauty in everyday life, the child in the home must become accustomed to good color, good form and suitable ornamentation. He must learn to recognize the beauty which lies in the life in harmony with its material surroundings and with its social environment. The home can never delegate its responsibility for the cultivation of taste. (East, 1982, p. 71)

The significance of aesthetics and beauty as key concepts for the "domestic economy" course, as home economics was called at the time, began at Iowa State University prior to 1885–1886 (Sherman-Eppright & Storm-Ferguson, 1971). Welch, wife of the first President of Iowa State University, began the Department of Domestic Economy in 1875. In her lectures "she frequently expressed her concern for the beauty of the home, taste in dress, and appreciation of the arts" (Sherman-Eppright &

Storm-Fergusson, 1971, p. 105). The country girl had gone to town in her mother's dress. Even now, comments about Hutcheson and Dewey, and a belief in a philosophy of beauty as a theory of values, bring a knowing smile (Santayana, 1955). To some beauty is no longer seen as a linguistic manipulation into a higher form of aesthetic science, but is a moral philosophy of person and spirit in its own right.

Iowa State University and other land grant universities had preceded their own theoretical battle over the place of beauty, aesthetics, and art. The funding for the formation of land grant universities in 1862 was followed by the first course in domestic economy at the college level in 1871. The introduction of art courses began in 1885, with the wife of the first president as instructor. By 1926, what ultimately became known as the Department of Applied Art had grown to ten art laboratories teaching design courses, handcrafts, and art appreciation. By the fall of 1970, the department had grown to four majors: interior design, art education, advertising design, and general and applied arta and crafts, with prerequisites in art history, drawing, and painting. By that same year, 564 men and women were enrolled (Sherman-Eppright & Storm-Fergusson, 1971, p. 275).

We have now studied the sense of beauty in what seem to be its fundamental manifestations, and in some of the more striking complications which it undergoes. In surveying so broad a field we stand in need of some classification and subdivision; and we have chosen the familiar one of matter, form and expression, as least likely to lead us into needless artificiality. (Santayana, 1896, 1955, p. 162)

> Psychology attempts what is perhaps impossible, namely, the anatomy of life. Mind is a fluid; the lights and shadows that flicker through it have no real boundaries, and no possibility of permanence. Our whole classification of mental facts is borrowed from the physical condition of expressions of them ... in our sense of beauty, an appreciation of sensible material, one of abstract form, and another of associated values, (in) which we have been merely following the established method of psychology. (Santayana, 1896, 1955, pp. 162–163)
>
> Christian theology, based on the historical revelation that God is the Creator of all things, assumes that we can

know the truth, and love the goodness, and delight in the beautiful of all things because the Creator first knows and loves and delights in all creation. (Navone, 1996, p. v)

It is from this historical perspective that we will begin to examine the actual experiences to which historical transcendental phenomenological hermeneutics will be applied. The movement during the course of the presentation of the interpretations and findings is somewhat similar to Heidegger's circular moving of *Being and Time* around to *Time and Being.* I mention these titles as examples of the circles of the process of what may be a "hermeneutic circle" in process. The "uncivil discourse" and conflicting interaction and challenge of the traditional norms, meaning of aesthetic concepts may be understood by reflecting upon Heidegger's exposition of the terms of the hermeneutic circle of spiral and phenomenology:

Heidegger moves from a phenomenological hermeneutics of human being toward a fundamental ontology of Being. In this work he uncovers layers of experience, analyzing things of nature *(Vorhandensein)*, artifacts *(Zuhandesein)*, and the core of human being in its basic structure of care. All three constitute the original, indissoluble unity of being-in-the-world. (Heidegger, 1972, p. vii)

This literature review is augmented by further detailed clarification where applicable. The evolving nature of hermeneutics inquiry often necessitates additional review of historical texts in elucidating the conflict that precipitates a *trigger event* in the next phase of analysis, critical/creative thinking. The significance of such events (trigger events) in manifesting social crisis and conflict will be clarified after the interpretation chapter (Jauss, 1982). At this point, it should be pointed out, the importance of attention to the detail of daily living becomes central in the hermeneutic phenomenological method of interpretation as described by Van Manen:

This is the world of the natural attitude of everyday life which Husserl described as the original, pre-reflective, pre-theoretical attitude. In bringing to reflective awareness the nature of the events experienced in our natural attitude, we are able to transform or remake ourselves in the true sense of *Bildung* (education). Hermeneutic phenomenological research edifies the personal insight

(Rorty, 1979), contributing to one's thoughtfulness and one's ability to act toward others, children or adults, with tact or tactfulness ... it is the science of being and becoming. (Van Manen, 1990, p. 7)

It is the progress of humanizing human life and humanizing human institutions to help human beings to become increasingly thoughtful and thus better prepared to act tactfully in situations ... to produce *action sensitive knowledge.* (p. 21)

It is this challenge to a demeanor of *thoughtfulness* and *sensitive* interaction in its production of *action-sensitive knowledge* (Van Manen, 1990) that prompted investigation currently in progress. The growing "uncivil discourse" and interaction in challenging the core concepts of aesthetics as grounded in a theology of beauty that also presented growing evidence of a larger challenge of traditional norms at every level of experience in the Western traditional white male culture. Interpretations of the trigger events progress via the hermeneutic spiral to the next level of exposition in chapter 4: Interpretations. The background presentations of general terms and history are further augmented and detailed in the progressive hermeneutic process through more detailed explanation of events as experienced through phenomenological reflection.

CHAPTER 4. INTERPRETATIONS

> The artist is always engaged in writing
> a detailed history of the future because
> he is the only person aware of the nature
> of the present.
>
> (Wyndham Lewis,
> cited in Shlain, 1991, p. 97)

Introduction

We have examined general terms and historical events concerned with aesthetics in education and home economics. The methodology and use of hermeneutics and phenomenology, as components of critical/creative thinking were presented. The historical background investigation revealed the long tradition in general education and home economics with underpinnings in aesthetics philosophy and historical hermeneutics, consistent with the psychology of the times. The Western cultural tradition was the "ground" from which these two aspects of education evolved (home economic and progressive education).

The significance of the Scottish Enlightenment and its impact on the larger world intellect was considered, along with its role in the establishment of aesthetics as a discipline. I will next examine the more specific trigger events that occurred at the university and continue to refine the hermeneutic spiral of this phenomenological exposition. Not until the final chapter will the more formal process of Socratic questioning and reflection move toward resolution and recommendations. The historical background discussion with the ancients brings the reader to the present, where there is a reexamination of the role of a theology of beauty. Thus, the methodology requires a move from general to specific and back toward a general big picture once more, following the tradition of the hermeneutic spiral of reasoning. The final chapter is one of critical thinking toward a reasoned judgment consistent with ethical reasoning (Wall, 2005).

I will next ask a general question. What is the current role of Dewey's aesthetics philosophy and the progressive educational movement? More specifically, how does Dewey's philosophy about teaching global democratization impact family and consumer sciences education; what is the impact of the loss of this profession on global democratization? Are family and consumer sciences education college curricula consistent with the philosophical aesthetics (art-based) trends that are occurring in general education? These driving questions require clarification. For example, the challenge to Dewey's aesthetic movement in curricula and the confusion and puzzlement that resulted from the department's curriculum committee meeting in challenging this movement also indicated a challenge to the traditional role of aesthetics and education in family and consumer sciences. The present chapter considers some of the most basic issues of aesthetics, its place in daily living, education, and fine art, or a modified form of applied art.

Whatever the aesthetic cognition, creative endeavor, or sublime experience of life, the constant interplay and attempt for balance, harmony, and unity become the aesthetic themes of reality. To perceive and produce objective knowledge as to the significance of aesthetics requires "a philosophy of method" and an avoidance of the historical schema and reductionist methods of natural science (Maller, Hurwitz, & Duffy, 1987). The significance of a "conversation" as a discourse is a vital process in the hermeneutic currents and phenomenological hermeneutics. A process of self-reflection in the synthesis of a "genre of language" creates the circles of spirals of hermeneutic understanding, "literary evolution," and the development of a "theory of the aesthetics of reception" and "aesthetic knowing" (Costa & Liemann, 1997; Jauss, 1982, pp. 32–33; Maller et al., 1987). A search for causality of conditions and symbolic meaning are not the context of phenomenology alone. The life as experienced, especially in relation to aesthetic meaning and beauty, is the focus of hermeneutic phenomenology. For example, the great philosopher Descartes (Heidegger, 1972) states: "All consciousness is consciousness *of* something. Thus, there is no such thing as a world less subject (exemplified by Descartes's *re cogitans*), nor is there a world in any meaningful, phenomenological sense of that world without human beings" (Heidegger, 1972, p. viii).

The use of language processing and common-sense reasoning requires understanding of historical concepts of earlier hermeneutics in pulling the deepest history of meaning (essence) from within the text, verbal, or symbolic communication, for a central or core meaning in the communication. Thus, the "conversation" becomes one not only with the past, and the meaning within the context of that past, but also one of relevance to the current evolving significance of aesthetics in a present enlightenment. Separating the earliest applications of concepts of beauty and aesthetics from their spiritual roots would be changing the very dialectic and design of reconstruction of previous knowledge bases (Heidegger, 1982; Navone, 1996).

The significance of manifest destiny in an evolving universal Christianity was understood during the last Enlightenment (Wundt, 1921). To understand the meaning of aesthetics within the context of theology at the founding of the profession of home economics and in Dewey's progressive education is vital in order to understand the current challenge to its relevance now and in the future. This is to consider the hermeneutic spiral of history and a spiritual history linked to aesthetics and ethics.

One fundamental rationale for the study of art and aesthetics within the context of cultural reality is a concern for structural realities as expressed in the artworks that are left for future generations to decipher. An example would be the Egyptian hieroglyphics of the ancient world and the American Indian cave paintings. The works demonstrate not only the worlds of the individual artists, but the worlds and belief systems in which they lived. We may find emotional similarities common to all humans that may be presented in different styles of the day, or the fashion of the times. But, if the phenomenological hermeneutics process is successful, some core knowledge base should be transmitted and cognitive development should occur (Jauss, 1982). Continual return to the initial questions should remain primary. For example, what is the current status of and need for aesthetics education? What are the arguments or reflective contemplation of meaning, and general observations? The issues form the hermeneutic circle of reasoning. Brown (1981) has termed this process as Jung's hermeneutic of doctrine. The hermeneutic of doctrine is also the thinking process that reveals meaning through what Gadamer termed the "triadic unity of hermeneutics process" and his "horizons of reading" (Jauss, 1982, p. 139).

A goal of aesthetic awareness is the perceiving of the significance of aesthetics and beauty in everyday life. However, I am not sure this is a modern reality, nor am I sure that there is an ongoing awareness or a general understanding of aesthetics in family and consumer sciences education curricula during the late twentieth century and the beginning of the new millennium. In addition, there does not seem to be a general awareness of the role of aesthetic philosophy and why it played such a very important role as an underlying foundation of Dewey's progressive education movement.

Although it may not be necessary to explicitly state such goals and objectives in curriculum development, my own belief is that there should be some visible indication of such aesthetics as a key concept that is to be manifested in the environment, demeanor, language, and content of the profession. This visible aesthetic should be apparent in general education curricula in addition to the specialized fields of interior design or textiles and clothing in family and consumer sciences. Thus, an aesthetic philosophy should be seen as the underpinning concept similar to that originally tied to the foundations of education. It is this search for an aesthetics philosophy as the foundation of moral principles that prompted my interest in this topic. As phenomenological hermeneutics explicitly attempts to draw inferences from the context of the communication, whether in art or written or verbal communication, and the "essence" of meanings, and apply these meanings to self and others, the observer/interpreter becomes a medium through which the communication and intersubjectivity should occur. Such a position allows persons to operate from their own perspectives in interpretation and value judgment and remains a given as observed by Jung (Kohak, 1978).

There is intertwined a meaning of communication within the context of the times and traditions that is yet beyond and above tradition (Carr, 1999). The "notion that philosophy can only be done historically" requires an historical hermeneutics in the discussion of aesthetics and beauty from within the context of beauty and theology over a course of time (Roberts, 1987):

Yet, "confronted by certain problems, such as the

discrepancy between traditional religion and science" even during the time of Descartes, there is something missing without historical hermeneutics. The discourse presented attempts to make the reader aware of the tendency of the past. Thus one of the standard features of historical *narrative*—attending to and accounting for human actions—that has traditionally applied to the history of ideas as much as to the history of other human activities is completely missing from Heidegger's account. (Roberts, 1987, p. 13)

From the perspective of historical hermeneutics and phenomenology, I present some of the themes which have evolved in the course of the literature review and the presence of aesthetics themes that are revealed consistently, up to the period of events being analyzed. Although it may seem a duality of process to follow the modified historical hermeneutic phenomenology with critical theory, I believe this interplay and sequential consideration is necessary, not only for new knowledge but also to present a rationale for any actions which would seem appropriate to the present condition, as well as for critical thinking in the methodological approaches to ethical reasoning from a Kantian perspective of ethics (Wall, 2005).

There follows a detailed analysis using an arts-based portrayal of the hermeneutic reasoning about the various art workshop experiences. The researcher is also a participant and an observer in art and music workshops in Glasgow, Scotland, as well as a student and artist at Iowa State University. The aesthetic conflicts are considered from the perspective of phenomenology, psychology, and critical thinking. The significance of this participation in an actual creative process, at locations so important to the context of the Scottish Enlightenment, makes the use of historical hermeneutics and phenomenology all the more exciting. The reader should also be reminded that at one time Iowa State University was considered one of the most architecturally beautiful campuses in the world. The incidents that are described are far from that tradition of aesthetic physical beauty and demonstrate the conflict in the spiritual world. The process of expressionism is less formalized, yet multilayered in it presentation of concepts simultaneously. Despair experienced in this conflict is expressed in art works. "Pope Paul and Two Fatimas" though painted by the researcher in Holland, demonstrates similar emotions as expressed in our introductory poem, "Artist as Philosopher, " specifically, in the images created in the poems lines "to kiss the roof of heaven/to confirm that this is hell" (Hinterland, 1990). These artistic expressions reflect the same despair experienced by William Wundt, the founding father of experimental psychology, during his university studies. Wundt has described his experiences at Bruchsal, for example, as a "school of suffering" (Bringmann & Tweney, 1980). Regretfully, I will always remember Iowa State University as "a school of suffering" as well.

The more traditional impressionist artworks present an interpretation of aesthetics and beauty in the tradition of the sublime. For example, I have added a small charcoal drawing purchased in Bosnia Herzegovina to demonstrate the concept of experiencing the sublime through simplicity in line and shape. This little drawing by an unknown artist in Bosnia, "Angelico," demonstrates the use of the simplest lines to express the contrast of beauty and purity of "the Christ" with a backdrop of "the maddening crowd" and a mob mentality of violence. It is this interplay between extreme opposites that creates the aesthetic response of the sublime.

The presentation of the major overall themes in relation to the topic, and my own interpretations as to what I find significant in this search for meaning in order to understand conflict is achieved through the world of art. To do this I must provide an explanation of my own worldview and life experience. This expanded dialogue about my personal viewpoint is consistent with phenomenology (Kalsi, 1978) and its goal of expanded perception and an intersubjective interpretation. I will attempt to present the multidimensional meaning of symbols in paintings, music, and historical documents previously mentioned, and some not yet elucidated within the consideration of the total experience. The interpretation, thus, from my own life world, and the interpretations by the reader and art critique may differ. There should be a core of universal symbols and understanding that remains common to all by virtue of our shared humanity. For intersubjectivity to occur, there should be some common experiential ground. This is the tradition of truly great art and the goal of universal communication and language and development of the global "Christ-consciousness" in the "new world" (Wundt, 1921).

The significance of music and art within the domain of language is an extension of Gadamer's explanation of meaning embedded within the communications of cultures. The idea of "transcending" personal biases in interpretation by virtue of experience with other *horizons* of time and culture does not fully explain the notion of simultaneity (Roberts, 1987). This requires a synthesis of description and its significance to my own personal experience in the development of meaning. Thus, "the researcher as instrument" and "as subject," interacting with the various forms of human communication, books, music, spoken communication, painting, and environments, are the aesthetic phenomenological process under consideration. It is also somewhat similar to the *Volkerpsychologie* of Wundt's experimental psychology in interpretation of cycles of universal history (Wundt, 1921). It is Wundt's *Volkerpsychologie* that some may argue framed the later development of Jung's triadic analytical psychology, and his notions of personal, collective (or archetype), and becoming (potential) meaning in art.

Jung's hermeneutic of doctrine is simply an interpretation of the levels of meaning in dreams or paintings which hold the key to individual and collective meaning. Drob (2010) has examined extensive evidence that in his later years, Jung finalized his theory of the collective unconscious as taken from the study of the ancient Kabbalah, a Jewish mystical tradition and world view reemerging in the modern world. Thus, the reflection of the self in the being process is hierarchical in its presentation of reality within the hermeneutic phenomenology. Jung provides an explanation for this collective notion that each of us is part of a bigger being, the collective unconscious, the cultural collective conscious where we are all one. A somewhat similar example taken from Heidegger addresses the notion of being and a being:

> If we follow this indication of being in all beings, we immediately find that being is encountered in every being uniformly and without difference. Being is common to all beings and thus is the most common. The most common is without every distinction: the stone is, the tree is, the animal is, and man is, the "world" is, and God "is." Against this thoroughly "uniform is," and in contrast to this uniformity and leveling of being, many levels and ranks show themselves within beings, which themselves allow the most diverse arrangements. We can progress from the lifeless, from dust and sand and the motionless of stone, to the "living" of plants and animals, beyond this to free men, and yet beyond this to demigods and gods. We could also reverse the order of rank among beings

and declare what one ordinarily calls "spirit" and the "spiritual" to being a discharge of electrical phenomena and an excretion of materials whose composition, to be sure, chemistry has not yet discovered but will discover one day. (Heidegger, 1993, pp. 43–44)

To begin, I must provide the reader (now a participant in the phenomenological hermeneutics process of communication) with a better understanding of why I have chosen this topic. Why have beauty and aesthetics become such central realities in my life? As presented in the introduction of the paper, my background as a singer, painter, political scientist, and law enforcement professor, a professor of ethics, philosophy, psychology, and political science, corrections counselor, family counselor, art teacher, and writer, may seem somewhat perplexing in relation to my interest in beauty. In addition, I am also the mother of six children (two natural and four stepchildren), a widow, a divorcee, and a wife in later years. I mention these things because they become fundamental to my own search for beauty in response to the realities of life.

Life presents all of us with many challenges, much pain, and great beauty. I find pain and chaos to be the counterpoint to beauty (chaos and destruction versus harmony and balance), necessary in the balance of perception. To know beauty, it is necessary to know its opposite. The same is true with pain and happiness. Some of us do seem to be dealt more pain than others. Wundt describes his own experience in the "school of suffering" as not only an experience of his life, but a central point in the development of his later psychological theories and his lifelong response to the cruelty of his world. Yet, in the course of my own life, I have found that the more severe the pain, the more vital the drive to find beauty, as a counterbalance. This is a logical outcome in response to the reality of pain in life, not a denial of that pain. Perhaps my religious philosophy and guidance have been the primary influences in the formation of this perspective. Christian and Kabbalistic traditions instruct that the suffering of Christ and the fellowship of His suffering help modify the weight of such things that fall beyond our control. Jungian psychologists instruct in the spiritual ancient traditions common to all humans (Shamdasani, 2009). This religious belief system reflects not only a personal philosophy, but a spiritual tradition of the culture in which it was formed. The personal, the individual becomes more significant as we consider the examples of "uncivil discourse" and non-traditional behavior as relevant not only to the individuals demonstrating such behavior, but to the culture in which such behavior occurs. This is the basis of Baldwin's argument for reflection and critical thinking in searching for meaning and response to what she terms "the adolescent crisis" and social anomie in the fragmentation of society (Baldwin, 1989).

There is no logical circle of reason that can reduce the reality of suffering. This is one purpose for the use of the circle of hermeneutic phenomenology to assess one's perspective and discern the accuracy of the experience and communication in relation to one's own perspective and that of others. For my own clarification process, religious guides had presented long ago a rational explanation of life's pain in connection with the suffering of Christ and the refinement of the soul. The very need for such pain has meaning, then, as a component in revealing the great joys of life, and is a natural part of the higher order of things. Some might say one can only know great joy if one has also known great suffering. Whether this belief is accepted as valid by all is not within the scope of this research. It explains my own perception of a relationship between the two phenomena, pain and the desire for beauty. Beauty and aesthetic experiences have become then a cathartic necessity in responding to life sorrows and pain, both physical and experiential.

In the search for beauty over a lifetime, I find this particular place, Iowa, among the most beautiful. Though it is said environmental beauty can be found anywhere, there is a natural flow and rhythm in the gentle hills and valleys of Iowa that I find reflected in the temperament of the people. Somewhat similar to Jung's notion of "connectedness" between people and places, and Wundt's *Volkerpsychologie* (1961), I perceive such gentleness of spirit easily evident among the people in this place (Jacobi & Hull, 1970; Jung, 1966; Jung, 1992; Jung, 1995). In fact, at times the people may be seen as too passive from the political scientist's perspective, allowing themselves to be taken advantage of and led astray by those of suspect and less than honorable intentions.

Perception becomes more important within the phenomenological methodology necessary for this study and the ultimate analysis of the greater meaning in the challenge of the traditional white male culture as exemplified in what I consider examples of uncivil discourse and a challenge of one of the most traditional concepts of educational philosophy, aesthetics as a theology of beauty. That those persons demonstrating such "uncivil discourse" were not citizens of the state or the nation creates concern as to the challenge of Western culture and civilization. As the only American in my first of two doctoral programs, this targeting and observed challenge to aesthetics and its relevance to Dewey's global democratization is more suspect.

The process of existing in the course of writing cannot be easily separated without conscious effort, which is contrary to the act of reflective analysis. Thus, to reflect upon one's past brings the most significant experiences to the forefront of consciousness in the phenomenological process of exposition. In addition, the process of historical discovery and sensitivity to synergistic effect is relevant to the aesthetic experience in this search. "The task of hermeneutics, according to Schleiermacher (2000), is that of penetrating the mind and heart of the author in the moment of the act of creation, putting one's own frame of mind into that of the author" (Seidel, 2000, p. 13). The reading of an unconscious motivation into the text of a "behavior pattern" does not necessarily reflect the text of its author, "rather, that of the psychologist and his theory" (Seidel, 2000, p. 15).

> When Freud would read da Vinci's relationship to his mother into the ambiguous smile of La Giocanda, the unconscious motivations that are being interpreted need not necessarily be those of the painter but, rather, a "text" read through Freudian spectacles. ... It may seem trivial to say that it is necessary to bring a philosophical mind to the study of a philosophical text, a legal mind to the study of law, a musical ear to hearing music, and so on, but the point is far from trivial. (p.15)

Perhaps my own experience of victimization and the pain that followed makes me more intolerant when I identify attempts to disrupt the natural flow of things in a beautiful place. Yet, if my perception is correct that people manifest this passive and gentle spirit, the destruction of that "beauty" of temperament and environment seems senseless. For, if the presentation of a philosophy of beauty as connection to the soul is true, it would only follow that its opposite would struggle for dominance, the constant interplay of yen and yang, good and evil, in the world of everyday existence, or as the kabbalists would say, between chaos and the light. Do the actions and communications within the context of natural and manmade beauty make sense (Baldwin, 1989)? For example, when

I find situations totally contrary to what seems the essence of the people and place, a dichotomous interaction, a conflict as to truth as well as the causes?

This same experiential challenge in "life as experience," as described in Dewey's aesthetics philosophy of being (1959), seems more relevant within this current context. His discussion of the challenge of overcoming conflict, modifying the perception of it may result in becoming a stronger being. Unsuccessfully dealing with the ambiguity and conflict may, however, result in death. This, too, seems relevant to the current discussion of the aesthetic existence of life and the world around us (Dewey, 1926).

Schubert Kalsi (1978) has explained this experience clearly in his introduction to *Alexius Meinong: On Objects of Higher Order and Husserl's Phenomenology.* In the following statement, Kalsi presents the levels of experiencing from a phenomenological perspective where "[a]n idea presents the property blue, but a feeling presents the property beautiful" (p. 9):

> Feelings, then, are dependent upon ideas or judgments or assumptions as their "psychological presuppositions." The Pieta, or the Ninth Symphony, or any such things must be known before the feeling of beautiful can be had. And values, in order to be, are also dependent upon objects or objectives which have value. (Kalsi, 1978, p. 9)

I would then interpret Kalsi to mean that without these values, and "psychological presuppositions" in relation to beauty and aesthetics, the feeling of beauty cannot be had. In this, the main point may be found. Without a systematic analysis and reflection as to the existence or absence of such sensitivity, the current condition of social evolution may not be determined. The meaning of "blue" and a "feeling of the property of beautiful" is both experienced within the current culture and its meaning defined by the context of the times.

"A kinder gentler America" (Bush, 1992) will never happen, without some sort of assessment as to where we are in developing such potential in educational curriculum. The evolution of the human spirit is my own interpretation of the meaning of this statement. The tradition of developing "tact" and "sensitivity" as part of the pedagogic responsibility in teaching (Van Manen, 1991) was met with a counter-movement of mean-spirited "uncivil discourse" as a challenge to that evolving universal psychology as part of the dominant traditional white male culture of Western civilization. The need or lack of need for such sensitivity becomes more evident if we think of our own response to mean-spirited people. I would doubt any of us would choose to be in the presence of such company if we had another option. Yet, the development of this aspect of sensibility is central to aesthetic intelligence, and fundamental in developing the sort of communications skills necessary in a complex society. The ultimate goal, then, of hermeneutics is the more sensitive tack of thoughtfulness in human interaction and teaching (Van Manen, 1990). The goals of education for the new millennium are from "individual to collective intelligence" (Costa & Liebmann, 1997, p. 31). This requires the "paradigm of process" and teaching "the creative process" in thinking skills, problem-solving process, and communication skills (Strickland & Coulson, 1997).

The hermeneutic process of reflecting upon "feelings" includes, then, as a basic assumption, that "the communication is honest" *and* "appropriate" for all persons participating (Baldwin, 1989). The habit of this sensitivity of mind then becomes basic in all patterns of communication. In educational curriculum, this habit, or principle of sensitivity in communication of aesthetic sensibility, becomes incorporated into the method of teaching. "[T]here is a technique of teaching, just as there is a technique of piano-playing. The technique, if it is to be educationally effective, is dependent upon principles" (Dewey, 1904, p. 9).

The principles discussed in the method of hermeneutics phenomenology are those based upon a theory of beauty and a philosophy of aesthetics, thus not greatly different from principles of ethics (Dewey, 1939; Santayana, 1896, 1955). Much like Dewey's rationale for observation in general education, the purpose of the initial meeting that prompted this research was not for simple criticism of the profession.

> This observation, moreover, would not be for the sake of seeing how good teachers teach, or for getting "points" which may be employed in one's own teaching, but to get material for psychological observation and reflection, and some conception of the educational movement of the school as a whole. (Dewey, 1904, p. 19)

It was with a spirit of observation that I attempted to search for the meaning as to the current presence or absence of aesthetics in the family and consumer sciences curriculum content. The concept was not only no longer being taught in any formal course, but the key concept of aesthetics (and thereby beauty) was challenged as to its applicability for the entire college curriculum. That "theological aesthetics" is said to begin with the term "beauty," using some "nonsecular logic" as justification for the separation of aesthetics and beauty from current discourse, seemed as disastrous as Von Balthsar (as cited in Roberts, 1987) noted occurred during the Middle Ages. During that time, the nature of beauty and theology was foundational and later transferred to a theology of beauty:

> His conviction is built on his insight into the nature of beauty an insight which he would argue was the foundation of the myths, philosophy, art, and literature of the classical world and was carried over by the Fathers into a theology of the church. (Roberts, 1987, p. 2)

Historical investigation revealed the profession of family and consumer sciences with origins clearly focused on aesthetics and the connection to a moral value base. The profession's past traditions clearly stood for ethics, values, and aesthetics as grounded in a theology of beauty and concepts of the soul. Negative comments concerning aesthetics and beauty in the curriculum committee meetings were felt to be personally and professionally offensive, as if someone had insulted my home and my family—my home of academic study in family and consumer sciences education and my professional family. Consistent with the critical thinking process, I was faced with choices. It was necessary to explore my own perceptions of the *trigger events* and current status of aesthetics. The presenting situations, the past, present, and future of the profession in regard to this personally important issue limited options: modify my own perception of the situation; accept the situation as too bad but not important; or attempt to identify a change in process, with its manifesting stages of confusion prior to a possible higher resolution. The incidents reflected a larger conflict than the incidents at Iowa State University, for example, conflict in all areas of higher education over the place of moral critique and its various manifestations, such as aesthetics and a theology of beauty.

What was I about and how would this conflict impact my place in academia? A search for the core of a profession and my own value base became the mobilizing force for the study. In the search for a place and idealism, similar to that of Husserl (Kalsi, 1978), the importance of developing "psychic phenomena or 'consciousness' needed to be examined in the method of phenomenology" (p. 39). In an attempt to evaluate the perception of experiences surrounding me, it also became an attempt to understand the perceptions of persons communicating with me. This communication could be in the form of words, music, art, or demeanor. In the tradition of Husserl's notion of "pure consciousness," not only observation, but response to the communication was necessary for analysis of meaning:

> Reflected experiences in interactions, observations, or interpretations of symbols as *a priori*, then became not the object, nor the communication, but the responses as relevant to phenomenology. The summations of themes in relation to aesthetics and beauty form a group of elements which form similarity in context and a unity of thought. (Kalsi, 1978, p. 57)

In this case, the overwhelmingly negative responses to concepts of aesthetics and beauty were contrary to national trends in education and incorporation of "aesthetic cognition," " aesthetic knowing," creativity and problem solving techniques, and the larger "norm" of an evolving sensitivity in teaching pedagogy (Costa & Leibemann, 1997). Through the search for subtle nuances for meaning in communication, the initial trigger events were far from subtle. Stated challenge and loud contentious ridicule in regard to civil conduct and beauty were shocking. The normal standard of civil conduct, like all traditional definitions of civil conduct, was another manifestation of challenge of traditional norms and standards of Western civilization.

Van Manen tells us the process of reflecting upon perception of the most subtle of nuances assists in development of a refined sensibility as to our total existence. In the development of curriculum in particular, this behavior demonstrated the need "of vitalizing and illuminating *intellectual* methods" in teaching and aesthetics theory (Dewey, 1904; Van Manen, 1990).

That such sensibility was often lacking in the university art studio was difficult to understand. I had not experienced such blatant disrespect and mean-spirited ridicule in any other studio in America nor overseas (until Scotland). This was something different from anything I had experienced in my many years in higher education and many classrooms. The focus was on the "beauty of garbage," literally, seeking beauty in dump sites. The students were painting "monsters," like subterranean forms from some primordial ooze. The paint pallets were muddied as well, reflecting the tone of the studio gestalt. A Jungian would have identified unresolved conflict and persons on the edge of psychotic breakdown (Jung, 1966). What was going on? It became increasingly impossible to be in the studio. I was literally driven out. I painted in a side room separate from the other students, painting icons and religious subjects to counter the "cult" phenomenon. When I sought investigative assistance from the psychology department for persons better trained in Jungian concepts, I was told "you will have to go to California for that" (Anderson, 1997). During these initial confrontations with conflicting values and views, I felt Jungian trained analysts could best identify an archetypal complex in play and in escalating severity. I found the claim that there were no Jungian trained analysts at this major university shocking. Later, Federal Bureau of Investigations research into "cult" activity at the university would reveal this "worship of death" as standard in satanic and other forms of "cult" activity occurring on Iowa State University's campus and worldwide (Gunderson, 1997). Seidel explains the need for civil discourse in communication:

> Finally, there is the *inspiration* of the society—language. Again this is not simply communication, the language within which the society thinks and expresses itself, since it also implies the language of thought and of play (poetry and song), the epics and myths in which, and through which, the values and ideals of the society are preserved and communicated to its members. (Seidel, 2000, p. 91)

This communication and language revealed fragmentation of society at the highest level of education. The dominance of such an attitude in a teacher preparation program could be indicating not just a local but a state and national trend. This evaluation and search for meaning was the next step in the critical thinking analysis and philosophical inquiry.

Development of a Concept of Simultaneity and Multidimensionality in Aesthetic Cognition

The introduction to the study presented consideration of the current scientific identification with aesthetic knowing and truth and aesthetic intuition (Sorokin, 1928; Wechsler, 1978). In the process of searching for a specific meaning and relevance of beauty and aesthetics, a simultaneity and multidimensionality in aesthetics cognition was considered. The entire notion of cognition, or thought processes, being an aesthetic experience was found to be central to scientists such as Einstein (Weschsler, 1978). Yet, some hermeneutic phenomenologists seem to wish to "bring together the intellectual elite ... without an ethic" (Wild, 1972, p. xii). I will present thoughts about a core elite of movers and shakers, but remind the reader that we will see this concept as "an accusation" in examples of conflict at the university. Returning to considerations as presented by Edie (1971) who alerts us as to this darker potentiality in his introduction to Berger (1972), who had died in a car crash in 1960:

> He (Berger) organized the Fulbright Scholarship program in France and presided over the Institute International de Philosophie as well as numerous other national and international philosophical societies; and, in 1957, he founded the Centre International de Prospective, whose purpose was to bring together the intellectual elite, the inventors, the creators from all the professions (high government administrators, industrialists, managers, economists, doctors, psychologists, university professors, writers, and scientists) in order to foresee and to influence, if not to plan, the future development of human societies. It was because of his irrepressible social consciousness ("without an ethics ... metaphysics loses all interest") and his own primarily spiritual interest that most of his later work ... took the form of ... ethical subjects. (Berger, 1972, p.xii)

We find similar concern about ethical dilemmas expressed by Paul (1991) in a challenge to his inclusion of moral critique as a vital component in the teaching of critical thinking. There is a continual struggle for a balance of thought and ethical action that goes further than a single dimension, in this example, what is known as Paul's third dimension or moral critique. As we begin to search for the past traditions and definitions of beauty and aesthetics for a theory and philosophy, we find layers through not only *time*-relevant examples, but hidden "glyphs" of multilayered aesthetic *meaning* (Jauss, 1982). Like the artichoke, the more we search for a simple answer, the more complex the connection between basic aesthetics concepts of balance, truth, patterns in nature, and process as process begin to evolve.

> Examples of universal meaning in the specific are presented in: "Buildings and the Ordering of Minds and Bodies" in *Philosophy and Science in the Scottish Enlightenment* (Jones, 1988). In this essay on the aesthetics of the architectural design by Stark for the Hunterian Museum (1803–1804), we find layers of structural hierarchy in the location of collections and articles. Jones explains that art and knowledge (paintings and books) are found much farther within inner architectural design of the museum than are nature and medicine (natural history and anatomy) (p. 217).

The two-dimensional design of the structure resembles more a pattern in a Mackintosh natural plant painting than a schematic for a floor plan of spatial structure and staircases. Like a spiral from the cosmos to the underworld, the "glyph" presents an oblong progression from the outer cosmos, spiraling to the underworld in an obtuse sort of pattern, less than balanced (Jauss, 1982;). Yet both Bacon and Mackintosh (Hofstadter, 1965) advised, that in observing nature, we will find this same irregular structure intended to communicate symbolically. The same is true in art and aesthetic antiquities and artistic expression. This requires observations of change and irregularity of pattern to better identify a new communication. This irregularity of pattern prompts observation for "new knowledge" (Baldwin, 1989). Conforti (1999) examines the significance of patterns in mind, nature, and psyche in his development of a field theory approach to analysis of archetypal fields and potentially harmful complexes that may extend to the greater culture.

For example, I feel there was an archetypal field in process while I was conducting research into the Aesthetic Movement in Scotland. While in Scotland, I was drawn from my painter's studio to a small bookstore near the Royal Academy of Art. For no apparent reason, I wandered to a small basement area and found a nearly hidden text on Rosslyn Chapel, built in 1446, in Roslin, Scotland, not far from Edinburgh. Some of the Templar Knights had escaped burning during the thirteenth century and had built this most unusual and amazing chapel, now claimed to house not only the tombs of some of these knights, but also the Holy Grail. The beauty of the structure was beyond description. The incorporation of similar concepts of the ordering of minds and bodies as at the Hunterian, discussed earlier, was evident in Rosslyn Chapel. This structure, however, was built, again, in 1446, not during the last Enlightenment.

It was initially surprisingly difficult to find persons in Glasgow who knew what Rosslyn Chapel was, where Roslin village was located, and how to get there. This hidden place, like its contents, required determination beyond the casual interest in passing. Finally, by chance, a Scottish maid helped me find a train route to the tiny rural community. Besides the wonderful chapel, a castle is present as well. Such notables of the Scottish Enlightenment as Sir Walter Scott, Samuel Johnson, Robert Burns, William and Dorothy Wordsworth, and James Boswell had frequented the village during this last Enlightenment. Again, how and why such an important place, central to the activity of the last Enlightenment, should be relatively unknown to the local people seemed confusing. This particular Templar chapel is said to be the seventh in a series of Templar initiatory chapels that fall under the Milky Way and form chakras of a sort on the earth. The chapel chakras are said to be like those in the body, which create a path of enlightenment and spiritual illumination. The architectural symbolism of the temple is identical to that of the Temple of Solomon in Israel. The "Star of Solomon" within a circle also forms the path and location of the chakra temples, the earth being the temple of God. Once again the concept of the ordering of minds and bodies of the cosmos are evident in the literary and architectural symbolism of Rosslyn Chapel. In addition, the locations of these temples under the Milky Way are said to direct one to the symbolic date of apocalyptic transformation in the earth's "heartbeat" and "new world" and cosmic "Christ consciousness" (Wallace-Murphy & Hopkins, 1999).

The aesthetic experience of Rosslyn Chapel went beyond a sensory perception and critical appreciation for the most ornate stone interior that I have ever seen. The experience, which was sublime, was similar to what I had experienced in the tomb of the Holy Sepulchre in the Holy Land of Israel. To find later the text describing the path of Enlightenment and the arch under the Milky Way, so similar to the unusual description of "Buildings and the Ordering of Minds and Bodies" in Jones' (1988) text is one example of the simultaneity of a multidimensional reality in the written communication and the symbols in the stones of structures. This experience is also an example of what Jung described as synchronicity and the shift in conscious knowing and interconnection of all things (1970); the shift in Schumann Resonance from 8 cycles to 13 cycles; and a shift in the code or patterns of life in the Fibonacci Series (Henry, 2000). The ever-present reality of a complex matrix of a webbing of interconnected realities and levels is like the artichoke of hidden meanings within a meaning also exemplified by Jauss's concept of "literary evolution" (1982, p. 32).

There are dual pillars in Rosslyn Chapel, representing the pillars of Boaz and Joachim, which stood at the inner entry way of Solomon's Temple in Jerusalem. One of Rosslyn's pillars is called the Apprentice Pillar. The name is derived from the apprentice who died, like the builder before him in Jerusalem, in the building of the pillar. The death sequence and parallel historical events between Hiram Abif in Israel and the apprentice mason in Roslin are identical. There was a reflected duality of time (Rosslyn, 1997, p. 56). But, more than the duality of time in this example, the Apprentice Pillar of Rosslyn also presents in the form of the "glyph" the double helix for the now-controversial cloning of Dolly, the sheep, in Roslin, by scientists from the University of Edinburgh. The symbolic representations in Rosslyn Chapel are said to house the secret code of the Holy Grail in the tradition of arcane knowledge known to the initiated and the "blood line of the Holy Grail, the Stuarts" (Wallace-Murphy & Hopkins, 2000).

Bacon's comments regarding the hidden secrets of all of creation within nature, the observation of irregularity revealing "new knowledge," became clearer after observation of this most unusual place and the even more unusual process of finding the Rosslyn Chapel. The significance of the Templars as guardians of the Holy Grail, the Stuarts as the "blood line of the Holy Grail and descendants of Christ" and "peacemakers" and "missionaries of the cosmos;" the Rex Deus families as supporters of the Stuart bloodline, with all that may imply (especially in relation to global economies), may be debated. However, the aesthetic beauty and tradition of a universal symbolic language dating back to earliest antiquity, even before the Temple of Solomon, presents quite a collective of concepts to experience and interpret through historical hermeneutics of doctrine and transcendental phenomenology. That all these observations and events were the result of a "dirty" studio, resulting in the finding of this treasure, does challenge and yet substantiate the tradition of Jung's notion of synchronicity.

The balance of systematic observations of beauty based on an inner truth reveals an intricate pattern of connections in all life, past and presents (Jung, 1970). The "conversations" with the past, which were beginning to manifest themselves more clearly as a synergistic networking of intricate threads of delicate weaving, were simultaneous with their explanations. The questions also held the answers. Black holes leading like worm holes to white holes in space (now believed to be holes in time) bring a beautiful logic to the nature of the cycles of questions regarding space and time. Art and architecture reveal this perception of the multidimensionality of the concepts of time folding over upon itself in layers of reality (Hawking, 1993; Hawking, 1998; Henry, 2000).

The spiritual communication from another layer upon layer began to unfold like the artichoke. The phenomenological hermeneutic "circle" or "spiral" was "bootstrapping" new meaning and updated relevance based upon communication from antiquity (Mallery et al., 1987; Sokal, 1996). The artichoke tops the Caithness tomb, where the fourth Earl of Caithness and great-grandson of the founder, Sir William St. Clair, third and last St. Clair and Prince of Orkney, is now buried. Around the tomb and chapel are blue angels, scrolls, and books with "themes" from, for example, Revelations: 20:12: "I could see the dead, great and small, standing before the throne: and books were opened. Then another book was opened: the roll of the living. Interpreted from what was written in these books, the dead were judged upon the record of their deeds" (Rosslyn, 1997, p. 15). The inscriptions also contained *the seven virtues and the seven deadly sins*. As I continued to search the intricate carvings, more extraordinary observations followed.

The aesthetician looks for subtle irregularities. A pattern analyst in fields of psychology and aesthetics seems quite like the scientist in search of contrast or a change of pattern. Another creative irony evolved in Rosslyn Chapel and may be found in the architrave above the south aisle from the lower stairs leading from the tomb, or sepulchre, where some of the Templars are buried. A series of carvings on two sections contain what are known as *the seven virtues and the seven deadly sins*. The virtues are on one stone and the deadly sins are carved on a separate stone. However, the stone carving of Avarice—a man with bags of money clasped to his chest—and Charity are misplaced in their order and are actually reversed. Charity is among the seven deadly sins and Avarice among the virtues (Rosslyn, 1997). Could there be such mistakes in a building that took hundreds of years to carve? It would seem reasonable to argue such mistakes are not likely and do not occur. Like the Apprentice Stone, only recently to be "interpreted" to contain the double helix, might this stone symbolize a reversal of some significance in the spiral of communication which transcendental hermeneutics may "reveal"? The hidden is ever present, waiting for interpretation, like nature, to unfold, like the flower, its inner secrets (Bacon, 1968).

Somewhat similar to Mackintosh's 1901 pencil and watercolor painting of "Holy Island," which is no island at all but tiny fragile connections of Stork's-bill plants, the attraction to the *seven virtues* was immediate and compelling. In Mackintosh's tiny drawing are patterns of obtuse irregular regularity of design, not at all representational of the actual plant from a botanical perspective, but from a strange combination of dimensionally, hidden within the simple structure of the outlines of the plant and placement of patterns which evoke impressions of deeper meaning. Mackintosh's theory of space and relation of aesthetics experience with time and space is consistent with the mind and ordered bodies of the earlier architectural structural hierarchy of the Hunterian Museum. Mackintosh describes his art and himself as a botanical artist:

> In nature you may go mad over some great landscape but nevertheless every tree—aye every leaf—every blade of grass and even "every wee modest crimson tipped flower" demands and I hope receives its share of admiration. (Mackintosh, 1893, cited in Robertson, 1995, p. 39)

A "dynamic unity of minds" (Siler, 1990) exists within the ever-present language of art, nature, and some architecture, when those who create do so within the concept and confinement of the symbol:

> We cannot approach the neurocosmology without mentioning the study of the unconscious as a course of self-knowing ... The covert language of the human

> psyche … the processes of creative thought most visible
> in the privacy of our dreams, Jung helped many turn their
> minds inside out to see the symbolic contents of their
> thoughts. (Siler, 1990, p. 335)

For Jung (1966), art was the largest seaport and gateway to the psyche. His search of symbolic art forms attempted to unfold how all forms of art are a rich source material for understanding something of the inner language and intentions of the thinker. Siler (1990) clarifies the relevance of symbolic representation in and of nature and art:

> Art speaks to the whole of human creation—including
> physics, chemistry, biology, and the social sciences … Art
> *bridges* these separate aspects of material and metaphysical
> reality through its symbolism, its processes, its forms,
> and its meanings. Art is nature interpreting itself.
> Understanding the psyche is the key to understanding the
> art of nature. More broadly, it is the door through which
> we enter other planes of consciousness—one of which is
> scientific. (Siler, 1990, p. 335)

As we travel down into deeper layers of the unconscious, like the artichoke, we find "autonomous functional systems" which become collective and "universalized." At the bottom of "the psyche is simply 'world' " (Mauron, 1935/1970, p. 335). The world of universal truth, the philosopher's stone, the Holy Grail, the paths of Enlightenment—this is the world of the Scottish aesthetic experience in Rosslyn. What prompted that unexpected journey was pain. Why artists must suffer for their vocation is not understood. Art chooses the artists, they do not choose it. The artist as philosopher becomes the bard, the poet, speaking the language of the birds, like the Song of Solomon, and workers of words.

Mauron (1970) explains that "[e]xpressive art, in my opinion, flourishes most happily apart from or rather on the edge of the great eddies of the human soul" (p. 68). The "wretched cruelty of creativity" is the price of the gift of creativity. Yet, for those able to read the language of symbolism, the hidden meaning to the "initiate of the arcane," there is no return. Once able to read, one does not return to illiteracy (Jung, 1964).

The Phenomenological Studio and Evoking a State of Mind

Psychological pain prompted a search ... escape ... escape from what? The studio experiences prompted what Dewey, Jung, Wundt, or even Huntington (1996) could have described as presentation of some conflict. There was to be present a nude model. I have done paintings of nude models before. This was a non-issue, within the experience of why people do paint nude models or at least my perception and past understanding of the goal of painting live models. A symmetrical body without "sophistication" is quite beautiful, like the country girl going to town in her mother's dress. So, what was the problem creating a Deweyian or Jungian crisis (Dewey, 1966; Jung, 1963; Jung, 1993)? The subtlety of nuance and the essence of the environment are critical to the sensitivity of a painter. What constitutes a negative exemplar, a negative aesthetic experience, or just a mess, really is not the issue. Some would say a dirty, ill-kept studio is not this issue. Some are able to create in any environment. An aesthetician would not be. Aesthetics is not only art. Here lies the conflict.

Some artists produce social statements that have nothing to do with aesthetics, and, like the Iowa State University studio scenario and the San Francisco Art Institute's performing art work, again, the defecating on stage as performing art (Chronicle, 2000), have questionable relation to art or aesthetics. The nude was not aesthetic. In fact, she was grotesque. Like an intentional attempt to drop one of Degas's chorus girls or Van Gogh's night life characters in the middle of the aesthetics of the Scottish Enlightenment, the subject did not reflect the theme of the sublime aesthetic: balance, form, and unity.

Thus, the artist as aesthetician was burned like a Templar Knight. Running from the studio, I sought *any* escape from the horrid reality in front of me. With my "friends," I usually seek books. Books are an escape from reality, to a supra-reality, because "books are our friends." And, as always, a beautiful world awaited me, unlike that in front of me: my "window friends," the Ann of Green Gables and the beauty of the country girl going to town in her mother's dress ... books, a window into the world of Jung's collective mind ... into the land of French *Blue* ... and a European Unification ... a Theory of Everything.

Fortunately, my traveling companion was a passive Iowa farm boy, along as a witness to this synergistic misadventure. In all naiveté and blindness to the potential dangers of an overseas tour de jour, off we went, looking for the Rosslyn Chapel. This was not such an easy task. One would have thought we had asked directions to the end of the world. Finally, again, a very shy blonde young girl who would check my room saw my journal and book, and saw that I was looking for Rosslyn Chapel. A beautiful young woman, a country girl in her mother's dress, without pretense or sophistication, only honesty, presented a presence of knowing. She would come in to tidy up the very lovely and sophisticated room of the Thistle Inn. She approached with a shaking voice, as young girls do to those women they don't know quite what to make of. She was pale, light-haired, with milky white skin, and the flushed cheeks so often seen in the lovely little children of Scotland. She evoked the ideal of pure innocence in contrast to the vulgar studio nasty. She did not present false statements, like the linguistics of aesthetics within the context of hierarchy, but direct truth, like Victoria and her obsession for the Highlander. Her essence was of the air which passed as she opened the hotel window of my room. She told me how to take a train to the tiny town of Roslin, inhabited by less than two thousand people.

The village was originally built by the first prince to house the Masons as they copied their master designs into Balkan wood before making this most remarkable place. Our Apprentice Stone, The Stones of Virtue and Deadly Sin, the last initiation in a chain of events was unexpected, but so vital. Every major participant in the Scottish Enlightenment had visited this chapel. The stone ceiling, like the "roof of heaven," reveals to the initiated the cosmic calendar in the green language of the alchemist. Though so unlike the empiricist men of science who attempted to follow the Grail during the last enlightenment, the bards, the poets, of this enlightenment have translated the apprentice pillar in the decoding of the DNA structure of life. Thus, our twenty-first century journalists speak of the Lamb of God beside the creation of man, Dolly, our cloned little sheep.

You can catch the train into Edinburgh, she told me. The young woman added the specifics of the rail connections from there. One is struck by the quiet of the people and the countryside. Such a difference from the hostile America I had just left. A little girl, about four, sat quietly in front of me with butterfly pins and pigtails with her young mother in pink.

Watching the window ... Iron works, Victorian grate works, like gates to another world ... finally to Rosslyn Chapel.

The landscape ... the rolling green hills ... the haze. The village is composed of a tiny row of shops; one Indian grocer, a doctor of medicine, an inn, where we had coffee and spoke to the local people. Home ... a country girl going to town in her mother's dress. So we enter the Chapel, the stars and lilies on the stone ceiling. I've never seen anything like this. I doubt anything else exists like this place. To say it is beautiful seems so inadequate. As in a trance, I feel a pulling to a staircase to something ... a lower level, very different from the Chapel main. A treacherous walk followed down a dimly lit set of stairs into an ill-kept room. Blue angels line the walls. A tomb holds a Templar Knight ... I knew they were here somewhere. A stone misplaced ... A fleur-de-lis. Um ... so ... I sit in the cold, cold room and sketch the fleur-de-lis and think of Wales and the cold, cold lake of Snowdonia, a red glove on the fence post of the hide, and about the country girl going to town in her mother's dress. The afternoon light begins to fail ... and we return to Glasgow.

The Music

I went to a concert at the Royal Academy. Actually, I went to a number of concerts per evening at the Royal Academy of Art in Glasgow, Scotland, during the international arts workshop. The finest musicians from around the world presented solo and chamber pieces. Piano and violin, viola, and the pipes were most frequent. Music is "the language of emotion," a "peculiar semantics of self-referring symbol ... tonal form representing only itself" (Kaelin, 1970, p. 194). Like patterns in nature and art, "variations in tonal intensities and effects of rhythm and accent" create sensations of the mind, outside, yet within the context of the music (p. 192). Musical experiences become a virtual reality of the mind, life lived for a few brief moments outside the context the present, a state of multiplicity. I wondered how many persons present were in pain—artists suffering for their art. "And the engineer or doctor who knows that his work increases the health or comfort of hundreds, will always be amazed to see a genius like Beethoven gravely putting down in his notebook this result of prolonged observations: 'The bigger the stream the deeper the note'" (Mauron, 1935/1970, p. 70). Music, this language of emotion, is well described by Kaelin (1970):

> Musical significance is internal to the psychological stimulus, and is fully controlled by our perception of the music's structural relations. On second thought, then, "language of the emotions—yes; but emotions removed from the sphere of bodily sensation and presented to the listening ear through the sensuous medium of moving, meaningless, wondrous sounds. (Kaelin, 1970, p. 191)

The "qualities of shapes" of music and art create a process of transport from the local, while still preserving "the similarity of melodies and figures in spite of general changes of key or locality" (Kalsi, 1978, p. 57). The transport is from the "feeling" depth of emotion. The communication, to be transcendent through time and space, yet remain relevant, must be based upon the most similar of human nature. It is in this expression of feeling the difference in temperament between artists and the duality of mind (Mauron, 1970).

There are two attitudes of mind, one active (always thinking of the future) and the other contemplative. Roger Fry identified the contemplative attitude as the "distinguishing mark of the artist" and the "man of science" (Dewey, 1926; Heidegger, 1989; Heidegger, 1992; Mauron, 1970, p. 28). Yet, the active mind always moves toward some future, while the contemplative lives in the present. By implementing Fry's notion of experiencing the present in emotional response to art, we may share in the perspective or the vantage point of the artist's contemplative attitude. Fry further clarifies why these emotions may be evoked:

> There is in art, I think, an affective quality which lies outside that [intellectual construction]. It is not a mere recognition of order and interrelation; every part, as well as the whole, becomes suffused with an emotional tone. Now, from our definition of pure beauty, the emotional tone is not due to any recognizable reminiscence or suggestion of the emotional experiences of life; but I sometimes wonder if it nevertheless does not get its force from arousing some very deep, very vague, and immensely generalized reminiscences. It looks as though art had

got access to the substratum of all emotional colours of life, to something which underlies all the particular and specialized emotions of actual life … Most artists seem in this way to remain voluntarily on the edge of great human emotions. (Mauron, 1935/1970, pp. 26–27, 69)

Although Fry dropped this theory as a result of the scientific rationalism at the time, it developed a logical difference between human emotion and aesthetic emotion. The two-minded attitude of active and contemplative required the observer to join the artist in his state of present feeling to appreciate the contemplative mind set, one of passive experiencing. As Fry later points out, the artist by natural predisposition cannot or does not normally act upon aggressive human emotion. The artist is a passive transmitter of deep human emotion and reveals through his art the intensity of emotion common to all humankind (Kaelin, 1970):

The aesthetic enactment is like pregnancy: there cannot be a "little" of it; it is there or it is not … It is as if there were no alternative model for the explanation of aesthetic communication to that afforded by speech: idea-expression-idea. (Kaelin, 1970, p. 65)

The possibility of being self-in-its-world-together-with-other-selves, which constitutes the aesthetic world, is, in philosophy, somehow proposed as the possibility that is becoming actualized as life-in-the-world (Kaelin, 1970, pp. 67–88). Thus, the artist is in and of the world in an active yet passive way. The *Gestalt* "tonal shape" begins to manifest in its own intuitive *anschaulich* reality (Kaelin, 1970; Schubert Kalsi, 1978, p. 58).

We as participants in the total reality create an emotional field, a force within the world in which we participate (Sokal, 1996). The "tonal shape" of that world becomes self-reinforcing. We may thus become more sensitive to the subtle nuances of variations in this force and field of existence. Music, especially, will move directly into evoking emotional "shape" and "form" in its vibratory field of being, the heartbeat of the world (Hozeski, 1994; Wundt, 1921).

In other words, a melody is like a journey in the land of music. Any combination will assure us a ramble without disaster, and the sum-total of combinations, if we could follow its design, would correspond roughly to a road map. But the reader must be careful. Any composer has the power to create a large—theoretically an infinite—number of tunes all in C major, all based on the initial rhythm of "God Save the King," all forming acceptable combinations. (Mauron, 1935/1970, p. 81)

In considering the potential for a simultaneity thesis, in that "a melody cannot precede the idea of the last note, but that it can follow it," I would argue that simultaneity is more similar to "the perceptibility of things past, psychic actual time," a sort of "stretched time" (Kalsi, 1978, p. 188). Further, I would argue, a melody may indeed precede the idea of the last note. Like Beethoven's "wide stream and deep note," the acts of creating and participating in that creativity as an informed observer allow the lapse or modification of dimensions of the perception of time. At minimum, the transcendental phenomenon of "bootstrapping," again, would indicate the creating of "new knowledge," and thus not replication or repetition of exact consciousness. This is the Schuber Kalsi (1978) "stretched" or "compressed" time. If artificial intelligence is based upon the phenomenological hermeneutic structure, process, and rationale, our own cognition must be capable of "compression."

Berger (1972) explains: "At the transcendental level the notion of essence, like that of fact, has only an analogical meaning" (p. 60). Like the computer, the compressed essence is represented by some other symbol; in the computer this may be numbers, voltages, etc. Yet, the ego does not line up meaning of essence alongside each other, but interprets the "root" of the value and recreates a composite (p. 60). Three types of scientific fact and logic of essence coexist, according to Husserl, and are "unveiled" through the transcendental realities of hermeneutics (p. 60). Eco's discussion of the palimpsest debate of meaning (1992) and Rosslyn's artichokes both demonstrate concepts about the simultaneity of time and meaning, creating a compressed reality. The hermeneutic spiral in search of the underlying truth and aesthetic theology of beauty of the soul as core is thus the process and the content of aesthetic knowing.

The significance of aesthetics in the contemplation of such notions as "new knowledge" or "successive layers of the human mind" seems more within the domain of the expanding of the potentiality of perception. Jung created the notion of synchronicity to describe such simultaneousness of events and happenings. This human psychic process is similar to the artificial intelligence of computers and "bootstrapping," where the previous is replaced by a revised or updated version of the past experience.

> The significance of the *gestalt* as it forms or evanesces before the subject's vision is the tension felt in its perception; and as such, it constitutes a modification of the perceiver's bodily schema or basic spatiality, which is defined by a range of the controlled responses of the living organism. (Kaelin, 1970, p. 71)

Like art, music manifests layers, or "thickness" and "thinning" of compressed experiencing which cannot be ignored. Kaelin (1970) helps us understand this "thickness" and "thinning" of meaning as it relates to aesthetic terms, such as superficial surface, and in hermeneutics, depth analysis. To do so, to ignore manifestations and layers of compressed meaning would be like attempting to ignore

> imaginal values of representational works of art at the expense of the perceptual values of their sensuous surfaces, is to ignore an important fact of aesthetic creation: that the meaning of a representational painting, literary work, and the like, is controlled by the manner of presenting an idea or image on the surface of the work. [L]inking the intuition of a form with the significance of its organization goes a long way to answer some of the lingering questions of aesthetics—especially questions as to the relative values of material, form, and expression. (Kaelin, 1970, p. 71)

Music presents the outline—of a story, a journey, which flows like the underlying energy of the world (Cairns-Smith, 1999). The story and journey come from underground tunnels, beneath the surface, like the London underground. The underground world, Jung's inner core (1964), holds and creates the pool of potentiality and constant movement in process, "the artist on the edge of emotion" (Kaelin, 1970). Ever refining sensitivity in the process of experience, fine tuning the perception of subtle changes of patterns and movement, becomes the process of the mind of the aesthetician. The search for the irregularity where and in which the "new knowledge" lies in nature and experience is the process of not only creative discovery, but also recreation of a new potentiality. The artist as creator recreates the process of the evoking of potentiality. The creative/

critical thinking process is the process as content of aesthetic knowing (Costa & Liebermann, 1997; Wilks, 1995).

Just as the surgeon's knife "fragilely" opens the life force of his patient, the artist draws his thin line of reality across a page to begin to reveal the reality within the canvas. His hand becomes the medium of transport from the essence of the potentiality of the transcendental phenomenon. He releases through his own process of creation the multidimensional glyph of "any essence whatever to the transcendental subjectivity which is implied by all essences and which constitutes them all," to a core reality, by "the process of ideation" (Kaelin, 1970, p. 60).

While listening to these master musicians, the luxury of "aesthetic vision" could take place. I could "observe this inner landscape with the same contemplative detachment as if it were a part of the outer world." I could become the "double-minded" artist (Mauron, 1935/1970, p. 61). "Biologically, human pleasure is a luxury, a surplus, a point in our curve above the perfect zero which represents the absence of pain. Art is part of this luxury" (p. 70). The musicians provide the "safety" for the pilgrimage to the "Holy Land" of the sublime truth, the "process of ideation," in search of the mind of God. As the bell tolls and the heart beats, the pulse and rhythms of this potentiality in the mind of God manifests the essence of the flow of life. The artist and the surgeon hold life in their hands for a brief time and know the hand of God.

To create, the artist must be "carried away by a movement of feeling" on this inner journey of the mind (Mauron, 1935/1970, p. 61). "For if the artist does not let himself go enough, feeling becomes thin and dies, and the very stuff of expressive art is lost" (p. 61). Yet, "expressive art can only hope to remain art by evoking states of mind which are rather placid and already tinged with contemplation" (p. 71). This state of meaning, interpretation, and architecture of the language of nature returns the artist to the historical roots of the hermeneutic process through transcendental phenomenology. Thus, we have reached the relevance of aesthetics to the philosophy of life and education.

The Appendix is a collective of works of art that are, for the most part, straightforward. One piece, "Expressionist Art: The Lover" presents a multidimensional compression of emotions evoked via music, experience, tradition, and evocation. Whether a "break-through" experience or one of "revelation," the intent is the layering of realities to present and represent, again, the dichotomy of the sublime. Ashfield and De Bolla describe this sublime as shock and astonishment of the soul. "Astonishment is that state of the soul in which all its motions are suspended, with some degree of horror" (1996, p. 132).

The music of the concerts promoted this state of contemplation, separated from pain. Thus, it cannot be argued that all art and music evokes aesthetic "placid" states of "contemplation" where luxury from pain may be manifested. This certainly was the source of happy anticipation in retreat from a negative studio to the luxury of the concert hall. Although it may be argued that interpretations of verbal and nonverbal behaviors during human contact may or may not be valid (Galloway, 1976, p. 9), the experience prompted the avoidance of the pain it created.

> Nonverbal communication is present in every face-to-face conversation.
>
> A person instinctively watches those he talks with to determine whether they are interested in and understand the spoken word ... The listener is "hearing" not only the words chosen by the speaker but also the inflections in his voice, the movement of his eyes, and his stance. (Galloway, 1976, p. 8)

Sometimes, the communication is not so subtle, but quite "in-your-face" for full effect. If this were not an aesthetics workshop, any sort of experience that promoted a creative act might be considered acceptable. However, the environment, or place of creating, was of less consequence than the communication taking place, which created its own "energy." I found this situation too similar to previous experiences in a studio at Iowa State University. Statements like "some people like things dirty" (Rizzolo, 1999) further clarify a dual reality and mission in process for both. So aesthetic sensibility required painting in my room, very similar to the storeroom at Iowa State University, separate and in isolation from the group studio.

I found isolation a "luxury from pain" at the evening concerts. This world was far removed from that being created in the studio—two languages, two missions. The worlds were folding over upon themselves once more. The pain, which drove me from the Iowa studio to family and consumer sciences, also drove me to isolation and the beautiful world of Rosslyn and the evening concerts at the Royal Academy. Some "otherness," some interplay for dominion over the physical and essential environment of both places, was in process.

> The battle-lines for the forthcoming epic struggle between faith and science are being drawn in a small Scottish community where Roslin's cloned lamb of science lies down uneasily with Rosslyn's Holy Lamb of God. The two are cohabiting for the time being—but in the long run this town ain't big enough for both of them. Maybe that's what the Templars were trying to tell us. (Pender, 1999)

The phenomenological experience itself does not allow determination as to cause and effect of anything, only the actuality of perception of experiences. Understanding is the phenomenological goal, not challenge of the internal experience (Berger, 1972, p. 12). Berger (1972) explains: "[T]ruth supposes intelligence capable of truth. Absolute reason is the correlative of absolute truth" (Berger, 1972, p. 18). Thus, how can one speak of truth to an audience who does not hear, who takes concepts like aesthetics and education as "not necessary" for family and consumer sciences education? To attempt to consider beauty and aesthetics outside the context of religion is not possible because of its early connection to theology (Roberts, 1987):

> Just as the Spirit of God the Father had to be made explicit in the "Son of Man" in and through his crucifixion, so the perfection of the religious community can only be attained when eternal love is made explicit as an essential aspect conceptually woven into the makeup of the social life of the "adopted sons of God," and not just a contingency subject to the vagaries of feeling. But this final explication is hindered by the fact that the actual world which the religious self-consciousness confronts is divided and disintegrated [*gebrochen*] (Kainz, 1983, p. 170).

Once again, the relevance of a sort of "bootstrapping" of historical phenomenological hermeneutics is quite appropriate. "A reasonable aesthetic is then possible, and we see it being constituted under our eyes precisely on the model of the science of religion. Like that, it will consist first of an external and historical study of the relevant acts" (Mauron, 1935/1970, p. 8). To consider aesthetics outside the context of value is to modify its very essence. Thus it is quite appropriate that the college of art and design separated from home economics and became something other than the study of beauty and aesthetics at Iowa State University. The history of our Western civilization is tied to the religious history of our culture (Huntington, 1996). Our culture, now under attack, is founded on the "attitude of mind and a condition of the soul that fosters a capacity to perceive the reality of the world" (Pieper, 1963, p. 1).

The original truth and purpose of aesthetics in relation to a theology of beauty have been lost. Now the goal is not to modify what is left in family and consumer sciences into this changed thing. We will become something other than what we originally stated our goal to be. The modification may not be evolutionary. Some people like things dirty (Rizzolo, 1999), and some people do not. To remove the choice is to dictate the underlying philosophy of the profession. Our future educators will only be allowed "to like things dirty" in public education. The pedagogy, which "may thus become the impetus for political thought and action" is presented by Van Manen (1991). In his text, Van Manen addresses the "pedagogical tact that requires of us certain worldliness and the moral fiber to stand up for political views in which we believe" (p. 213):

> Modern education has lost much of its moral currency. The passion and struggle for teaching excellence has been inhibited by a variety of social forces including bureaucratic rationality. Current calls for "participative management" and "shared governance" are a step in the right direction; however, this type of terminology still lacks the vital moral element which this text addresses. (Van Manen, 1991)

The ethics of Dewey and Hunt have become "old hat" in a branch of aesthetics philosophy as the foundation of a core value in educational philosophy (Ryan, 1995). Aesthetics will become a modified experience of superficial sensation, rather than a search for universal truth, with beauty meaning truth. Thus, the college of art and design may do art, but not aesthetics. The San Francisco Art Institute may claim to do art, but not aesthetics. "This branch is already fully developed. Not only is the art of recent times studied with systematic minuteness with the result sometimes of veritable discoveries (in music, for example), but vast explorations pushed in every direction reveal to our astonished eyes the creations of men the most remote from us in time and space" (Mauron, 1935/1970, pp. 8–9).

The process of transcendental phenomenological hermeneutics allows us to explore this core nature of beauty and aesthetics along with the core of truth and value in being. Husserl (Kalsi, 1978) has shown that one cannot elicit the logical from the psychological. He does not seek to derive from a world of pure logical essences the reality of experienced facts. Husserl states, "[I]t is impossible to reduce fact to essence or vice versa" (p. 60).

> One route alone remains possible: the one which, starting from logic and from psychology, will lead us to a basic discipline. The psychology of Jung differs at once from both, in that it seeks archetypes and core identities, in which they will have their common origin, their final justification and the foundation of their reciprocal relationships. The "neutral" investigations of this new domain will constitute the "phenomenology" … Phenomenology thus presents itself to us as a purely descriptive [study] of the experiences of thought and of knowledge. (Berger, 1972, pp. 20–21)

Reason, in "time, tempi, and temporality," takes the psychological experience out of the context of being (Kaelin, 1970). Music, then, creates a "black hole" where a "white hole" experience occurs. The choice of experience, then, by selection of sublime melody or chaos, may create heaven or hell. I went to a concert at the Royal Academy. Actually, I went to two concerts each evening while at the Royal Academy of Art. Beauty becomes a cathartic for pain. Its potential is the ability to transport through music, language, the arts, to a world transcendent, to the mind of God. Thus, the choice to transport, method, and means will in part dictate the final focal point for experiencing:

> Whenever we have any experience which might be called "aesthetic," that is whenever we are enjoying, contemplating, admiring or appreciating an object, there are plainly different parts of the situation on which emphasis can be laid. (Ogden, Richards, & Wood, 1929, p. 18)

Let us consider one particular aesthetic experience in the music concert hall. One experience which stood out at the International Workshop was the piano concerto by Claude Frank. The Danzas Argentinas, by Ginastera (1916–1983), followed Chopin's (1810–1849) Fantasy in F Minor, Op. 49, and preceded Beethoven's (1770–1827) Sonata in C major, Op. 5 (Waldstein). Mr. Frank debuted with Bernstein and the New York Philharmonic in 1959. Mr. Frank was from a family of distinguished musicians; his wife, pianist Lillian Kallir, and his daughter, violinist Pamela Frank, joined Frank at his concert. Whether it was the demeanor and subtle perfection of age and experience or the execution of his art, I do not really know. At a series of concerts where all the participants were the best in the world, why one stands out and prompts a little watercolor is the business of the "aesthetic experience."

Perhaps the lighting at the concert, the time of day, and/or the persons in the audience participating with the musical performance created a collective field of a unifying reality—a sublime aesthetic. At any rate, the aesthetic field of sound set the mind to wander. Or, perhaps it was the execution of an intentional journey, as the conductor presented his "map" for a self-guided journey of the "luxury." Or perhaps, after such an intensive concentration of music, the aesthetic sensibility begins to expand and grow, as a child learning to walk. This would be more in my own thinking, which is consistent with the rationale for teaching aesthetics to begin with—hope of an expanded and increased sensitivity and sensibility. Regretfully, this sublime aesthetic was not to last. Shortly I would return to Iowa State University and the reality of the times. This was not a unified field of an aesthetic sublime, or even a marginally positive field experience. The next section will discuss in some detail examples of a field of a different sort, a field of aesthetic conflict that led to the evolution of a riot.

Mobbing at Iowa State University

The purpose of this study was to examine aesthetics in educational curriculum planning. The book considers a number of questions related to aesthetic education: For example, what do we mean by aesthetics, what is aesthetic knowing, and why is aesthetics a core concept in education? Further, can an observed aesthetic conflict be better understood with the psychological approach of field theory? Buescher (1986) presented a brief statement after an interview with Elliot Eisner and pedagogic efforts to better serve the needs of education for gifted children:

> The ability to experience, to imagine, to represent … is a fundamental process of human intelligence. The process as well as the product that grows from it can have a deep, moving, and aesthetic character to it. Being able to experience what is subtle, to imagine what is interesting or useful, and to be able to adequately represent what has been experienced are each influenced by the conditions in which one lives … Why do we have music or dance or poetry or stories? Because it is only through these modes and others that particular kinds of human experience can be communicated. We have to do this as a people. Human beings invented the forms that can meet that need to imagine and communicate. (Costa & Liebmann 1997, p. 108)

Conforti (1999) examines how matter is the outcome of the creative process:

> Fields alone are real. They are the substance of the universe. Matter (particles) is simply the momentary manifestation of interacting fields which intangible and insubstantial as they are, are the only real things in the universe (*Dancing Wu Li Masters,* 219).

> A significant implication of this hypothesis—that form and substance are the by-products of intangible interacting fields—supported by Jung's ideas about archetypal reality, ideas which were once perceived as mystical, Jung described the archetypes as the psychological correlates of the instincts because they force an image generated by the archetypes as the primordial, universal thought of humanity, which exist independent of consciousness and the will. (Conforti, 1999, p. 50)

Abbs (1994) considers communication from the perspective of Socratic and aesthetic learning that is a similar communication link found in aesthetic creativity necessary to understanding and images, as described by

Conforti (1999). After we consider Abbs's definition of art, we will examine a number of related concepts specific to this discussion:

> Art embodies the invisible logic of the life of feeling and sentience and, in so doing, brings it to conception and consciousness. Once this is clearly recognized the common education distinctions between cognition and affect, between meaning and expression, between objective and subjective, between public and private break down and give way to what would seem a more valid differentiation between kinds of knowledge, between kinds of intelligence, between kinds of symbolic forms, between kinds of public language. (Costa & Liebermann, 1997, 109)

Defining Aesthetics

Why art is and is not aesthetic:

After consideration of the content of the dissertation, we find aesthetics to contain primary components of unity, harmony, and balance. These components may or may not be present in various individual works of art and art pieces. As noted by Brown (1981), "Though beauty has value it is not value."

Considering aesthetics and art as part of the history of Iowa State University and home economics:

Mary Welsch began the college of home economics in 1871. Introduction of art courses began in 1885. By 1970, the department had grown to four majors: interior design, art education, advertising design, and general and applied arts and crafts, art history, drawing, and painting. By 1970, 564 men and women were enrolled. Thus, aesthetics as a core concept in education, which included general educational course work for home economics, was a given. Like general public educational programs, aesthetics philosophy was central to a good liberal arts education (Sherman-Eppright & Strorm-Fergusson, 1971, p. 275). Some might argue that when art separated itself from home economics, it also separated itself from aesthetics.

Kenyon, in his 1998 dissertation on Aesthetics and Leadership identifies the processes for the education of leaders as the same as is found in aesthetic education, "an art of problem framing, an art of implementation, and an art of improvisation." (Kenyon, 1998, p. 76).The notion of a unified whole in the aesthetic process of creation of what was termed "the good life" was central during the Scottish Enlightenment. During and after that Enlightenment, the International Arts and Crafts Movement developed, with concern for synthesis of "head, heart, and hand." Thus, the incorporation of such concern for aesthetics was transferred to the United States in the educational reform schemes of John Dewey and Caroline Hunt. As members of a universal Enlightenment movement, these key educational developers brought with them their understanding of an evolving consciousness of human dignity and value founded in creativity and individualism.

Restating the Problem

The curriculum committee challenge of aesthetics as a core concept in education and in Family and Consumer Sciences began shortly after my admittance into the doctoral program at Iowa State University's Department of Family and Consumer Sciences Education. At that time I was assigned to the Department Curriculum Committee as part of my graduate assistantship. The role provided me with great insight into the duties, issues, and process of curriculum development in a profession in flux. Not long after identifying my topic and proposed methodology of aesthetics in Family and Consumer Sciences Education and hermeneutics as a methodology, I found written memos presented in that committee challenging the topic and the need for Family and Consumer Sciences Education. This challenge was not by members of the Department of Family and Consumer Sciences, but by the College of Family and Consumer Sciences Curriculum Committee. My initial response was confusion and disbelief. Why would such a traditional core concept, dating to the earliest history of philosophy in education, be challenged? This made my mind wander to earlier incidents in the Iowa State University Art Studio, which were what I have later been advised were incidents of "mobbing" and what I term "uncivil discourse" toward those demonstrating various forms of "traditional" orientation in art and personal philosophy, most especially, theological philosophy.

> *Costa & Liebmann (1997) further clarify the significance of creativity and aesthetic in the modern educational curriculum: "The creative process as the content is vital in the creation of future thinker, for the future belongs to those who can think. This thinking process has been termed critical thinking, creative thinking, and/or philosophical inquiry."*

Dr. Richard Paul, one of the foremost experts in the teaching and assessment of critical and creative thinking, has noted the significance of creative thinking and values in his three dimensions of critical thinking and moral critique: skills, disposition, and morals. We will discuss the relevance of Dr. Paul's proposal, "A Proposal for the National Assessment of Higher-Order Thinking at the Community College, College, and University Levels."

Costa and Liebmann continue in identifying the paradigm shift in cognition and science, similar to our consideration of the last Enlightenment process: "Because of increased knowledge about how the brain learns, because of paradigm shifts from the new sciences, and because of societal needs to engage in systems of thinking, the time has come to shift our focus from the *what* of knowledge (content) to the *how* of learning (processes)—as Seymour Papert (1991) states, "instructionalism to constructionism" (Costa and Liebmann, 1997, p. xxii).

Consistent with our charge to "empower individuals, families, and communities," we as Family and Consumer Sciences Education professionals were expected to educate the public and our fellow professionals as to the renaissance currently in process in general and Family and Consumer Sciences Education. Csikszentmihalyi (1990) states: "The most promising faith for the future might be based on the realization that the entire universe is a system related by common laws and that it makes no sense to impose our dreams and desires on nature without taking them into account …We need to equip every member of society with the skills to survive in and contribute to a chaotic universe that is in constant change. All members need the strength and courage to live their lives to the fullest by giving their unique gifts back to the universe. According to Costa and Liebmann (1997), perhaps it is time that we as educators found the courage to open Pandora's Box and release the butterfly inside" (p. xviii–xix). This dissertation is the opening of that Pandora's Box at Iowa State University. The implementation of creative thinking, critical thinking, and philosophical inquiry which includes phenomenology and hermeneutics, is the process as content in the ongoing analytical process.

Initial Conclusions and Interpretation of Facts:

The art studios reflected core conflicts, as did the challenge to traditional educational core concepts in higher education curricula, such as Family and Consumer Sciences Education. The most overt manifestation of a conflict in core values was the appearance of what I term "freak" posters, isolation from other students, student newspaper articles published at the university on topics of perverse "cult" figures and blood sacrifices, incidents in the graduate dorms of posters of women in underwear advertising the college philosophy club, students attempting to appear to be masturbating in front of porn websites in the computer labs in the graduate living unit, sites of women being burned on crosses, lined up naked with numbers for sale or identification, challenges to the access of disabled in the classroom by foreign students, and overall hostile environments.

It appears that about every traditional standard of educational pedagogy and "civil behavior" was being challenged. Though this may be identified as a personal "mobbing" by fellow students, there was also a more widespread concern about the basic values being presented. This challenge necessitated the use of an analytical process to verify and interpret the meaning of a complex web of inappropriate communications and an interaction to determine not only what was happening, but why. Critical thinking and its various analytical processes seemed the only appropriate method which would also allow for recommendations and tentative solutions. That this phenomenon was being observed not only in education but in society in general in various forms of "cult" activity necessitated a process-driven orientation, consistent with the current challenges in educational curriculum development. This would also be consistent with curriculum development in higher education and the role of the family and consumer science education profession as a social change agent.

How do we make sense of this?

The fragmentation process and its impact on modern education has been examined extensively by Brown and Baldwin (1995), foremost philosophical and theoretical researchers in Family and Consumer Sciences Education regarding critical thinking. They find consistency of observations of a challenge to traditional norms in process, requiring philosophical inquiry through qualitative methods of research. Costa & Liebmann (1997) state:

> The disciplines as educators have known them and taught them no longer exist. Rather they are being replaced by human activities that draw on vast, generalized, and trans-disciplinary bodies of knowledge and relationships applied to unique, domain-specific settings ... We are shifting our metaphor from compartments and clocklike mechanisms toward more complex ecosystems—decentralized interactions and feedback spirals. Today, researchers work together to find and forge connections and themes as they search for universal similarities in the behaviors of minds, machines, animal, and societies. The study of self-organizing systems is, in some ways, the "related opposite" of the study of chaos. In self-organizing systems, orderly patterns emerge from lower-level randomness. When one studies a flock of birds, for example, there really is not a lead bird. Each bird flies freely, yet together, they create an exquisite pattern. In chaotic systems, unpredictable behavior emerges from lower-level deterministic rules ... knowledge is constantly being constructed and reconstructed." (p. 24)

> There is underlying unity ... one that would encompass not just physics and chemistry, but biology, information processing, economics, and political science, and every other aspect of human affairs. If this unity were real ... it would be a way of knowing the world that made little distinction between biological science and physical science—or between either of those sciences and history or philosophy. Once, the whole intellectual fabric was seamless. And maybe it could be that way again. (Cited

in Waldrop, 1997, p. 67; from page 25 of Costa and Liebmann, 1997)

Further, Daniel Dennett (1991) proposes a multiple-drafts model of consciousness, arguing that there is no single stream of consciousness in the mind. Rather, multiple narratives are simultaneously created and edited in parts of the mind/brain (Costa and Liebmann, 1997, p. 25). It is through the qualitative process of a merging of hermeneutics and phenomenology as subcategories of critical, creative thinking that a field theory approach is best understood. Life as experience and the interpretation of aesthetics or lack of aesthetics in that life process and the attitude of mind and the condition of the soul in the perfection of the human society is the driving force of this analysis. As Pieper (1963) states, "education concerns the whole man; an educated man is a man with a point of view from which he takes in the whole world. Education concerns the whole man, man *capax universi*, capable of grasping the totality of existing things. (p. 36).

A method of analysis that is comprehensive must be both qualitative and psychological in nature and merge the hermeneutic phenomenological approach with critical thinking and psychological field theory. For the present discussion, a brief list of terms and definitions is provided. More extensive definitions are found in totality in other chapters.

Aesthetics: A philosophy of art and beauty where balance, form, ethics, and virtue are the harmonious balance of life as experienced (Heidegger, 1981/1993).

Artificial Intelligence: Hermeneutics research and artificial intelligence has been examined by researchers at MIT (Mallery, Hurwitz, and Duffy, 1987), who further clarify the relevance of hermeneutic thought when these researchers describe various "naïve hermeneutics of early modern Europe and Dilthey's more historically conscious, nineteenth-century *methodological hermeneutics* which sought to produce systematic and scientific interpretations by situating a text in the context of its production. In the twentieth century, Heidegger's and Gadamer's *philosophical hermeneutics—* shifted the focus from interpretation to existential understanding, which was treated more as a direct, non-mediated, authentic way of being in the world than as a way of knowing. Reacting to the relativism position, Apel and Habermas introduced *critical hermeneutics—*a methodologically self-reflective and comprehensive reconstruction of the social foundations of discourse and inter-subjective understanding. Finally, Ricoeur in his *phenomenological hermeneutics*, attempted to synthesize the various hermeneutic currents with structuralism and phenomenology" (Mallery, Hurwitz, & Duffy, 1987).

Critical Thinking: An active, purposeful, organized cognitive process we use to carefully examine our thinking and the thinking of others, to clarify and improve our understanding (Paul, 1995; Topp, 1999).

Hermeneutics: Hermeneutics grounds the meaning of texts in the intentions and histories of their authors and/or in their relevance for readers. Unlike analytic philosophy, which usually identifies meaning with the external referents of texts and structuralism and finds meaning in the arrangement of their words, hermeneutics regards texts as means for transmitting experience, beliefs, and judgments from one subject or community to another.

Jungian Field Theory in Analytical Psychology: More specifically, the complex, for example, Wotan archetype. This archetype, which found a physical and human manifestation in the personage of Adolph Hitler, took over an entire country, in fact, the entire world, compelling individuals to engage in activities otherwise unthinkable. The archetype's power to entrain and draw individuals and entire nations into its orbit suggests the need to reassert and reinvestigate Jung's findings regarding the strength and autonomy of the psyche. In much the same manner as an attractor site—be it magnetic or archetypal—serves to draw the trajectory of a system into a specific region (or, as it is termed in chaos theory, a basin of attraction), so too does the archetype work through the creation of an attractor. The attractor is the complex.

The Complex: The complex is defined by Jungian analyst Yoram Kaufmann as a quanta of energy organized around a certain theme—for instance, a mother complex, a father complex, a sexual complex, etc. The complex, like the attractor, functions as a magnetic epicenter creating the convergence of archetypal potentialities into a singularity, a highly patterned behavioral tendency, drawing to it one specific facet of an archetype.

Phenomenology: A twentieth-century philosophical movement dedicated to describing the structures of experience as they present themselves to consciousness, without recourse to theory, deduction, or assumptions of science. Experiencing the world through its essence as expounded upon by such philosophers as Husserl, Heidegger, Ricoeur, and Gadamer.

Jungian Analytical Psychology as Hermeneutic of Doctrine in Phenomenological Research

Costa and Liebmann reference Carl Jung and his four psychological ways of knowing and process perception: sensation, feeling, thinking, and, intuition (Costa & Liebmann, 1997). From Carl Jung's three methods of analysis in analytical psychology (personal, amplification, and actualization), symbolic expression moves to and through hermeneutic interpretation. Thus, phenomenological experience is interpreted through hermeneutic circles and spirals of experience. "Jung is seen to address himself to motifs and realities that theology and theology alone is presumed capable of dealing with" (Brown, 1977, p. 18). It is not possible nor intended, as expounded by Brown, that "psychology is equipped only to speak of the soul or psyche of man, and should accordingly leave to theology and theology alone the task of speaking of God" (p. 19). Thus, Jung's method is a hermeneutic of doctrine. Jung was considered to be "an avowed empiricist and phenomenologist" as described by the Analytical Psychology Club of New York in 1962:

> [Jung] distinguishes between symbols and archetypes. Symbols are the infinitely variable expressions of the underlying, comparatively static archetypes ... That [the archetypes] are performed in the unconscious as potentialities makes understandable both the wide range of their variability and the traits of a definite structure which limit the possibilities of variation. (pp. 29–30)

Examples of Arts-Based Genre in Jung's Three Components of Analysis

Brown (1977) examines the symbolic expression in hermeneutic interpretation in his text, *Jung's Hermeneutic of Doctrine: Its Theological Significance*:

> *That Jung is a hermeneutic peculiarly suited to disclose these components of meaning, specifically, that when a hermeneutic of secular man's lived experience—attempt to bring light and inter-relate the patterns of symbolic meaning of that experience—gives way to an attempt to conceptualize the religious horizon or dimension disclosed in these patterns and to theistically ground this horizon, for example, gives way to what we would designate "philosophy of religion" ... that this its chief hallmark, is also its chief theological value. (Brown, 1977, pp. 164–165)*

A "cognitive revolution" also includes examples of how aesthetics and visualization in science are "part of a trajectory of thinking in art and architecture that rises about the highest planes of analytic reasoning" (Siler, 1990). The "planes of analytic reasoning" discussed in the new science are compared to the transformation of "various degrees of enlightenment." Like Buddha, the neurocosmological practice involves phases of initiation "from the passive viewing of familiar objects and images (the known and the pictured) to the gradual, active letting-go of all recognizable forms (the act of embracing the unknown and the un-pictured)" (Siler, 1990). This process does not seem that much different from Francis Bacon's earlier process of induction, with the now exclusion of the divine, nor Dewey's "habits of the mind" and visual organizations, and "organizational habits," which must be challenged by creative thinking and "aesthetic knowing." Habits and will, like ends and means, are a process of conscious ordering. For new knowledge, there must then be a change of habit of mind or ordering of the pattern of the known. Thus, our final chapter discusses critical thinking, also known as creative thinking, or philosophical inquiry which challenges the known and unknown by formal process of philosophical analysis. Next, we will consider the Socratic Questioning process of Paul's form of Creative and Critical Thinking.

Through the processes of reflective thinking and moral critique, the family and consumer sciences education professional is to observe and evaluate social situations and conditions and determine what action, if any, is most appropriate. Our current investigation of social anomie and conflict as reflected in the college classroom and graduate living units is one specific example of this anomie. The degree of social confusion spans the society and the culture from "uncivil discourse" to acts of extreme violence, for example, my own published research (Brady, 2000), titled "America in Crisis: Mind Control, Ritual Abuse, Battered Woman Syndrome, and Family Violence," published in volume 92 (5) of our professional journal, *The Journal of Family and Consumer Sciences*. Regretfully, that research continues to be timely and relevant to our discussion of "uncivil discourse" and the challenge of traditional norms in college classrooms at all levels.

Again, the most traditional of foundation core concepts of Dewey's aesthetic philosophy in public education, and Hunt's grounding work in home economics were challenged in very specific incidents. Whether this activity might be considered "mobbing," consistent with current research by adjunct professor Davenport here at Iowa State University, or what I term "targeting and uncivil discourse of a cult nature" may be interpreted by degree and intent. With respect to our current consideration about the research, a challenge was in process, requiring consideration of past traditions and reflective consideration of current conditions and future actions necessary. For example, examination of patterns during the last enlightenment, the Scottish Enlightenment, where aesthetics is said to have been born, and philosophical connections between science, aesthetics, beauty, and the soul were considered.

Hospers (1969) states, "The idea of a fount of wisdom became the fount of the universe and cosmology, psychology, and "techne" (purposive human action), that forced the emergence of aesthetics as a metaphysics of beauty and the soul's response to the process of creation of the beautiful. For example, extensive research on the connection between science and aesthetics was commissioned by King Maximilian II in the 1800s. This research helped clarify the meaning of aesthetics and beauty as a state of process as well as content. Lotze (1885) explains:

> But we are told that the beautiful is not given to man in
> the form of a concrete intuition, or of a finished concept
> whose marks may be distinguished and read off in order

by aid of logical processes. The beautiful is rather given to man in the form of the Idea. No individual, therefore, can fully compass it; can have more than a share in the understanding of it—according to the degree of his attainment in the culture of its appreciation. (Lotze, 1885, p. viii)

Hunt defined aesthetics as the philosophy of beauty where "[a] broader and better conception brings into its province all beauties, including those of lives in harmony with their physical surrounding and their social environment" (East, 1982, p. 126). Redfern (1989) tells us that there has been a tendency in science to oppress the historical connection of aesthetic imagination from historical, scientific, or philosophical imagination that has led to much confusion (p. 22–26). Psychology, too, considers aesthetics from the perspective of unity and wholeness. For example, Conforti (1999) describes the destiny and patterns in relationship to identification of synchronistic experiences and intuitive abilities as examined by Edward Whitmont:

Relevant events in a patient's past history, which we have been in the habit of viewing as causes of current psychopathology, may now perhaps be seen as manifestations of the beginning life-pattern. Traumatic events of childhood ... may perhaps be seen as essential landmarks in the actualization of a pattern of wholeness, as the necessary "suffering of the soul" which engenders present and future psychological advance. (Conforti, 1999, p. 55)

From this initial consideration of Jungian pattern analysis we find a methodology closely linked to hermeneutics and critical thinking in that there is a holistic approach to understanding the events in relationship to incidents and a larger pattern toward a big picture or archetypal field. Yet, Conforti continues to explain how, by the identification of the specific archetypal field complex in process, persons may better understand how they may, by diverting the trajectory of a complex field, modify outcome:

Regardless of which field is activated, whether it involves children of alcoholic parents, orphans, etc., change is clearly possible. While the deep archetypal, morphological core of the orphan archetype will remain a central constellation within the individual's life, what can change is that he or she can establish and individual, highly differentiated response to it. In so doing, he or she can learn about the archetype's objective features and tendencies. For example, orphans, through the experience of having the security of the parental archetype shattered at birth, are more children of the Self and the deep unconscious than the material, mother world. This often translates to their experiencing a high number of synchronistic experiences and having uncanny intuitive abilities. (Conforti, 1999, p. 55)

Dreams, symbols, and patterns of behavior are considered in analytical psychology as a method of analysis to determine what archetypal complex might be in play personally and universally, in order to determine what intervention is necessary to redirect the trajectory that is already an established pattern that is in process and will escalate. Thus, when we look at the individual incidents described in this document, we must also consider what the essence of the underlying archetypal field is, what the personality and traits of the complex in play are. If we can identify the complex in play, we can suggest the necessary intervention to halt further suffering. The initial considerations of archetypal fields will be considered in the interpretation of these events. The archetypal field theory may be considered an alternative perspective in analytical thinking that builds upon the traditions of hermeneutics and critical thinking. In fact, Drob (2000) and Wolfson (1995) present facts that substantiate their thesis that Jung developed his theory of analytical psychology and archetypal fields from studies in kabbalistic myth, symbolism, and hermeneutics.

Therefore, the analysis process of critical thinking that calls for developing alternative perspectives mandates consideration of a *global verstehen*, or what Wundt (Jung's predecessor in development of psychological theories) would possibly term *Volkerpsychologie* toward the development of a "universal code of conduct." For example, as we move toward a global society and possibly a global archetypal field, regretfully, a continued lack of acknowledgment of the current crisis in America in regard to the effects of social fragmentation could more likely lead to acts of global violence. Thus, even the "celebratory riots" at some of the major universities must be considered in relationship to a larger global movement.

Once this source of conflict is identified, and it was my aim to do so in the dissertation discussion of aesthetics and a return to a theology of beauty, reflective courses of potential action may be pursued. At the present time, with conditions being what they are, the choices are quite limited. That this conflict is occurring at all levels of education may be seen by the examples presented and the critique of Dr. Richard Paul's proposal to the U. S. Department of Education, in the challenge of the need for his third dimension, moral critique in critical thinking. In the conclusions and consequences of the text, I will present recommendations for actions taken from the initial interpretations of the essence of the activities described. I remind the reader that all of the incidents mentioned were formally reported to security personnel at Iowa State University, the Governor's Office of Iowa, and Iowa State Senator Tom Harkin of Iowa, as well as local police officers in Ames, Iowa. Only the local Ames Police Department offered recommendations and solutions as to how to stop the "mobbing" and incidents.

I have offered one possible course of action, school reform and the use of school vouchers. That is only one course of action. The assumption that there are rules and regulations for civil conduct in public universities has been proven to be erroneous. The growing call for international OSHA regulations for private industries facing similar "mobbing" activities as presented in the text titled, *Mobbing: Emotional Abuse in the American Workplace*, by Dr. Noa Davenport, Ruth Distler Schwarts, and Gail Pursell Ellliott, published in 1999 at the time of these reported incidents at Iowa State University. The research on "mobbing" is a growing body of research reflecting the challenge of more than traditional mores. The challenge of our Western Civilization and the root of that civilization, "the traditional white male culture," are reflected in the disrespect of the spiritual tradition of Western education. In closing, I would call attention to the final reflection in a call for return to aesthetics and a theology of beauty:

Summary Reflections

It is the process of aesthetic cognition and the aesthetic experience, which allows a reflective process to retain and modify its original essence of reality beyond its time (Hultgren & Croomer, 1989). Though this analysis is approached as an aesthetic analysis, the use of critical thinking, hermeneutics, and field theory are critical to understanding the larger picture, the archetypal complex, the field in relationship to the big picture. The individual incidents give us a pattern of activity and thought, to include the incorporation of an entire college campus, a profession, and law enforcement officials. Even the fact that the incidents reported were met with the turning of a blind eye is a pattern. The fact hat the most conservative of the educational schools, Family and Consumer Sciences Education, was eliminated is evidence of a pattern. The incidents that demonstrated a "total violation of all boundaries" (Jungian Analysts, Assisi Institute, 2010) are part of a pattern. Like art of ancient cultures, we may as observers re-experience the "feeling" dominant in the creation of the artist within the context of the meaning then and now. We are pulled into the hermeneutic history of the conflict of the past and present. It is this transcendent "feeling" which separates us from animals (Findlay, 1981). We search not for the experience of loss of hunger without taste, but another dimension of experiencing life around us.

Fundamental ideas of phenomenology, such as reduction and the theory of constitution, have been presented. The first, reduction, allows the mind to discover its own nature and to elicit from it the forms under which it appears to itself in the world as a determined being, as man:

> Its sole task is to elucidate the *sense* of this world, the "productive action," the constitution, of clarifying the *sense*. The transcendental subject does not "make" anything, strictly speaking. All action unfolds in the world; it is, consequently, a constituted structure ... Every phenomenological discourse sees its sense completely transformed to the very extent that it employs natural language ... The mind creates its own intuition and "intellectual vision creates its own object—not the semblance, the copy, the image of the object, but the object itself ... It is between a doctrine of the *world* and a doctrine

> of *another world* that transcendental phenomenology must
> find its own path. It continually risks—and this it must
> remember—falling back into nature or vanishing in the
> ineffable. It is in no way a comfortable doctrine where one
> could contentedly settle in; a continual effort is required
> in order to balance oneself on the narrow ridge, which is
> its proper domain. (Berger, 1972, pp. 76–77, 79, 91)

Thus, the artist ever remains "on the edge of emotion" (Kaelin, 1970) in *another world* of transcendental phenomenology, searching for his own path. This is not a world of psychological idealism, but of phenomenological transcendentalism (Berger, 1972, p. 91). I would argue this may be, for some artists, a search for "a world of psychological idealism" lying below the layers of "dirt" to reveal a higher order of ultimate reality and truth.

> The curious Husserlian idea of "primary givens" which
> are not psychological facts or subjective constructions, or
> irrational elements, or absurd things-in-themselves can
> be clarified by a study of the relations between Husserl
> and Hume. If phenomenology is to set in opposition to
> Hume's philosophy, it is because it has passed through
> Hume and because it too has known how to push doubt
> to its farthest limits. (Berger, 1972, p. 128)

This may be a reference to Hume's notion of "sensible thing to sensations," which Green interpreted to mean "not as a sensation, but a compound of feelings."

"He (Hume) makes space (extension) a compound of which the ultimate parts are not extended (spaces), but are sensations of colour or hardness" (Nettleship, 1906/1969, p. 239), with the notion of sensation being akin to perception or intuition.

Our musical experience then must include the awareness of the "thickness" or "thinness" of this "form" of space experience. Like the "width of the stream" comparing to the "depth of the note," music becomes a map for "fearlessly exploring the cosmos" (Markowsky, 1994). "We can say, then, 'our mind reaches the thing itself'" (Berger, 1972, p. 61). It is what Husserl calls the *cogito*. It is also what Jung calls *the inner child* (1963; 1964). Although he did not expound upon this notion more than to allude to a concept of *ideas*, "up to each of us to see for himself:

145

if we do not see 'ideas,' for example, it is because we are affected 'with a kind of spiritual blindness' due to our own prejudices" (1964, p. 40). Transcendental phenomenology is to Husserl a "purely descriptive [study] of the experiences of thought and of knowledge" (p. 21).

Thus, a judge, in determining what constitutes pornography or "art," might ask, "What is the intent?" Like language, art is a statement, "an intention is at work in his (the artists) [*sic*] speaking, guiding it toward an end" (Hofstadter, 1965). Depending upon the "intention" or environment of communication, the language, art, and "communication" may be judged. This judgment may be called a critique. In the field of education, and more specifically, family and consumer sciences education, we have set standards in the past to determine value and worth. These standards were established in the Lake Placid Conferences, which formed the structural base for our mission and key concepts of the profession. If we are currently re-examining our key concepts and value base, there must be a standard to consider "intention."

The next chapter examines the historical transcendental phenomenological hermeneutic experiences along with conclusions and consequences from an ethical perspective. The critique or criticism is based upon the concept of "truth of statements." "Intentional, purposive entities are subject to criticism; they can be judged as right or wrong, good or bad, valid or invalid, successful or unsuccessful" (Hofstadter, 1965, p. 87). The process of critical thinking provides a systematic evaluative mechanism for the method of historical transcendental phenomenological hermeneutics employed in this study as well as a structure for the consideration of the need for a more in-depth archetypal field pattern analysis in regard to these events and other "celebratory riots" (Hacker, 2005) across the United States.

CHAPTER 5. CONCLUSIONS AND IMPLICATIONS: A CRITICAL THEORY AND FIELD THEORY APPROACH

To my mind, the laws which nature obeys are less suggestive of those, which a machine obeys in its motion than those a musician obeys in writing a fugue, or a poet in composing a sonnet ... If the universe is a universe of thought, then its creation must have been an act of thought

—Sir James Jeans,
The Mysterious Universe (Siler, 1990)

Introduction

The purpose of the current chapter is to present consideration of what I have come to term "uncivil discourse" in the college classroom and its indicatons in relationship to the bigger picture. The term "uncivil discourse" evolved during the process of this hermeneutic phenomenological investigation and its relationship to aesthetics and beauty as core concepts in educational philosophy in past teacher education programs, the arts, and family and consumer sciences education (home economics). The term reflects the current status of a profession in a state of "transient situational disorder." The manifesting of "uncivil discourse" in the most traditional of American professions was analyzed along with other incidents that occurred at Iowa State University during a doctoral degree program in higher education.

In this chapter I will consider these incidents of verbal and physical acts of aggression as symptoms of a larger disorder—an archetypal complex that was in the process of escalation toward riotous and destructive behavior. Jungians might term the collective destructive acts that culminated in riots as a collective psychosis—resulting from the archetypal complex manifesting in a field. However, the initial red flag was the phenomenon of "uncivil discourse." This presenting "disorder" was found to be the result, in part, of an imbalance in educational philosophy toward empirical scientific methodology in research. Baldwin (1989) feels the imbalance in education philosophy toward empirical methodology has left society in a state of lost moral values. However, the choice of this loss of social values and formlessness also manifests the current "clash between civilizations" to which Huntington speaks (Huntington, 1997). This normlessness and ambiguity has left a void which is being filled by experimental communication (Jauss, 1982) of a less than honest nature, serving as a veiled method of insult and slander in the college classroom and general society of America.

Regretfully, this "covert communication" is also occurring in middle school classrooms, in an attempt to conceal interaction of a cult nature. One example, the Mary Kay Letourneau case (Kurtis, 2000), in which Letourneau communicated with her pre-teen lover in the classroom by references to scenarios and wording within videos and CD lyrics. This recent example, in addition to its presence in the teacher education classrooms at Iowa State University, makes more serious the debate in process. America is in crisis. That crisis and conflict of civilizations is manifested in the arts, and "uncivil discourse" as a challenge of Western civilization and thus, the traditional white male culture (Huntington, 1997).

A cultural crisis is driving the debate regarding public education and its future direction. An assessment of the actual social situations experienced (described in this document) and the presence of this "uncivil discourse" has been explicated through hermeneutics and phenomenology. These processes lead to the final critique through critical theory and critical thinking (Berger, 1972; Berleant, 1992; Brown, 1983; Brown, 1993; Carr, 1999; Dewey, 1946; Dewey, 1979; Dolan, 1999; Gadamar, 1976).

It is one goal of the current analysis to present a cause for social action through critical theory (Baldwin & Brown, 1995). The significance of interpretation of both verbal and nonverbal communication has been well established by experts in curriculum and instruction (Galloway, 1976):

"Just as a pattern on nonverbal messages of exclusion can eventually lead the student to feelings of alienation from the school, so the same pattern can lead to a feeling that no one cares" (p. 15). That no one cares seems too frequently the acceptable norm in classrooms and social situations, where "caring" as a value issue is also being challenged. The core of underlying value issues surrounding aesthetics as the central core concept associated with a spiritual and/or theological underpinning is then naturally excluded. Galloway continues:

> No matter what his philosophy of education, the student of nonverbal communication will be inescapably drawn to the humanistic approach. After examining the variables that influence nonverbal understanding, he will see the frailty of the human condition and the powerlessness of many persons to be understood well, if at all. He begins to see that many nonverbal messages, including some cloaked in inappropriate behaviors, are the cries and calls to fellow human beings who cannot make an unperceptive and insensitive world aware that they need to be recognized and given a chance to live an existence with meaning. (Galloway, 1976, p. 15)

Historical hermeneutics and phenomenology have been used in presenting considerations of the significance of aesthetics in experiencing human interaction through various forms of communication. Yet, some consideration of the assumptions outside hermeneutics and phenomenology is necessary for the development of possible conclusions and recommendations. Critical theory will be presented as a viable critique process, with critical thinking and philosophical inquiry as the method of cognitive analysis.

A concern for reflection and interpretations of experiences are not seen as valid methods for inquiry and critique by all. This is especially the case noted in the introduction in regard to a current culture of a dominant empirical scientific method of analysis. Dewey found himself in a similar situation nearly fifty years ago; the developer and an observer of science, yet believing in values as fundamental to philosophy in art and the act of creating, seems possibly less understood today. In the poststructuralist and postmodern era, there is a challenge to traditions and values to an even greater extent.

Although it has been suggested that values as assumptions are not susceptible to objective inquiry, and that to allow natural scientific investigation to be influenced by "the socially controlling" activity, will "result in its corruption" (Sim, 1992), critical theory does provide a procedural structure for reflection and social action. The act of making choices as simple as what topic to research and what issues to allow to be examined is a process of critical thinking. First I will define critical thinking as it is used in this study. Although different authors have developed complex attitudes and assumptions, Halpern (1984) simplifies the initial concept as follows: "Critical thought is a rational and purposeful attempt to use thought in moving toward a future goal" (Brookfield, 1987, p. 12).

Gentzler clarifies the terms critical theory and critical science in the definitions presented in the first chapter. Again, critical theory "represents the outcome, while critical science includes the means toward that end" (Gentzler, 1999, p. 23). Further, critical science is not only the process of critical theory for a specific project, such as this dissertation, but, "an integrated process to be carried out through professional practice" (p. 23). As family and consumer science professionals, then, we are to identify problems and issues, such as our trigger event, and determine "a morally defensible outcome, as opposed to simply making a decision" (p. 25).

The use of critical science is a process of identifying three types of interests "central to our formulation of knowledge." The three types of interests are: technical, practical or communicative, and emancipative (Gentzler, 1999, p. 27). The first is concerned with environment, the second with formulation of character, and the third with freeing self-formative constraints and development of autonomy. The constraints are exposed through critical science, critical thinking or philosophical inquiry, and self-reflection.

The use of critical thinking is defined by Topp (1999): "An active, purposeful, organized cognitive process we use to carefully examine our thinking and the thinking of others, in order to clarify and improve our understanding" (p. 156). Thus, this analysis was conducted using the method of critical thinking in the research and writing process, critical science in the formulation of a rational reflective process for a cause for action, and critical theory in the final end result of the recommendations for possible actions to be initiated as an ongoing professional process.

Therefore, analysis should be ongoing to ensure a proper understanding of the forces in play and the potential archetypal complex formation.

The major points of critical theory and its implementation are required in the practice of family and consumer sciences education. Because [family and consumer sciences] is a critical science, its professionals have an obligation to critically analyze social forces which affect individuals and families. It is not enough to work within systems that simply perpetuate the status quo, especially if individuals and families are being exploited by those systems. It becomes the responsibility of [family and consumer sciences] teachers to prepare their students in building systems of action that lead to their freedom from dominant forces obstructing possibilities for an improved quality of living. By doing so, we employ two components of critical science as proposed by Fay (1987), including "the education of its audience [or client], and their empowerment" (Gentzler, 1999, p. 28).

The initial purpose of this paper was to research the meaning of what appeared to be a challenge to the relevance of aesthetics in family and consumer sciences and general education as it related to the global progressive movement initiated by Dewey some fifty years ago. However, as events escalated in psychological and physical destructive tendencies, the analysis moved toward Jungian analytical field theory. This was necessary to better understand the meaning of the conflicts in process. Through the process of hermeneutics and phenomenology, we have examined the significance of aesthetics to a higher order thinking and connection to a theology of beauty. The education of the public and our members as to the need to reorient our focus on a value-based profession becomes a matter of choice. This choice has been impacted by the unexpected negative exemplars encountered via "uncivil discourse." This "uncivil discourse" currently manifesting itself in the most traditional of American professions has now been analyzed and examined as to meaning and need for action.

That this manifestation has been identified at the global level as a "clash of civilizations" by Huntington (1997) and "Western civilization versus the rest" helps us understand its manifestation at the micro level within the college classroom. It could be argued that subsequent events (listed in the previous chapters) were an outward manifestation of inward complexes escalating to an outward trajectory of the archetypal complex in a field of actions. That these outward actions have been identified by Jungian-trained analysts as "a complete violation of all boundaries" is indicative of not only a pattern of verbal challenge, and content challenge, but behavioral challenges to accepted norms on a college campus.

The initial identification of potential archetypal complex characteristics was presented after conversation about events that took place at Iowa State University during a conference at the Assisi Institute on May 14–16, 2010. The escalation of outward manifestation of an archetypal complex in play culminated in riots at Iowa State University and Southern Illinois University, among others. In November of 2005, Iowa State University in Ames, Iowa hosted a National Summit on Preventing Civil Disturbances. The major speakers, McCarthy and Clark McPhail, sociology professors at Penn State University andthe University of Illinois, Urbana-Champaign, reviewed 384 campus disturbances between 1985 and 2002 (Hacker, 2005). Initial results of the study suggest that between 1998 and 2002, campuses with over 20,000 students were twice as likely to experience celebratory riots. Most riot participants are likely to throw things, fewer than 15 percent make verbal threats, and only 17 to 23 percent engage in physical attacks. Though these statistics are informative, the analysis does not address the underlying cause of the riots, nor do the statistics consider the implications of a potential trajectory of further escalation of riots outside the campus community. Escalation of riotous events in frequency and intensity has been experienced in recent years at Southern Illinois University, Carbondale, where over 2000 students have consistently participated in Halloween riots (McCann, 2005), and Madison, Wisconsin, where over 20,000 students participated in riots. These large campuses have been termed the modern "animal houses" of college campuses (Thompson, 2010). If one were to accept this term as the modern reality of campus life, what does it mean?

Animalistic Paganism or Puer Aeternus

Identification of the actual archetypal complex that could be in process and escalating at university campuses across the country and possibly the nation is beyond the scope of this study. However, consideration of field theory as a component of hermeneutic analysis of initial aesthetic conflicts at one university and how these incidents continued to escalate can best be understood from a Jungian analytical psychological approach and archetypal patterns. Whether a conflict between civilizations, from a political scientist's perspective, or an archetypal complex in trajectory, from a psychologist's, the incidents described and discussed in this study present a dilemma for educators in higher education, campus security personnel, and city law enforcement officials, to name only a few of the stakeholders affected by an aesthetic conflict and the evolution of riots.

When comments identify this destructive behavior as "Animal House," we must also consider what that actually means from a psychological perspective. If students who participate in such riots could be caught up in the archetypal field of the *puer aeternus* (the eternal youth) they will manifest identification with this "god of vegetation and resurrection of the god of divine youth. Their behavior will then align with corresponding complexes, such as the oriental gods as Tammus, Attis and Adonis" (Von Franz, 2000, p. 7). The *puer aeternus* literally means eternal youth. This juvenile thinking leads to what Marie-Louise von Franz (2000) calls a "provisional life," in which there is a strange attitude that the individual is not yet in real life. Campus life could most surely be described as unreal—an ivory tower (Lovitts, 2001). In this state of mind, the individual and the group find that they refuse to commit to the moment. The *puer aeternus* consistently attempts to fly high and be above the reality of earth, where flying high symbolizes attempts to "get away from reality, from earth and ordinary life" (Von Franz, 2000, p. 8). We must consider the potential for danger and harm in a collective of such adolescent psychosis demonstrated on the campuses described and the escalation toward a social psychosis. A trajectory of high-risk behavior and "flying high" establishes an archetypal field with attraction to the *puer aeternus*. This initial diagnosis is tentative and provided as an example of how an archetypal complex may create a field of activity where individuals and organizations are drawn into the abnormal field of energy—the social psychosis.

I began the discussion with the description of what I considered a strange series of challenges to traditional norms in higher education theory. The discipline most impacted by this challenge seemed to be the most traditional field of study, Family and Consumer Sciences Education. In the beginning of the profession of home economics and public education, there was no doubt as to the relevance and indeed the mandate of education in teaching civil conduct and moral community standards. Today, the moral mandate and responsibility for the formation of student character for the future seem to have become muddied with a clever language of freedom that disguises a more sinister agenda. Baldwin explains (1989) that too often the only choice in public education is normlessness and anomie, a choice made by government officials and elected leaders as to the use of funds for such normlessness and perpetuation of the adolescent crisis. Role models are often advocates for consumerism, models, strippers, and drugged-up athletes. This was not the reality of public education and the republican tradition of Madison that was defined "by assimilation of interest and feeling, by a sense of common country, common political family, common character, fortune and destiny" (O'Reilly, 1999, p. 343).

> The indoctrination of the public school pupil with the moral and civic virtues of the society was the goal of the schools. The principles of morality were as thoroughly taught as the principles of science. This assumed that there was some common morality within society that all pupils would be taught ... Republicans required schools to produce citizens imbued with civic and moral virtues and sufficiently educated so that they could avoid bias and narrow self-interest when voting and governing ... Sandel documents the rulings of American courts in this century in which value questions and any notion of the public good are systematicallydeleted from the arguments of the courts. (O'Reilly, 1999, p. 344)

This systematic negation of civil virtue and moral fiber has resulted in the loss of notions of aesthetics as more closely related to the soul and beauty as theology. The "good life" now is more an optimum level of income for maximum hedonistic consumption and self-focus. The loss of central value orientation has left beauty of spirit and person as absent as balance and unity in traditional art and applied art in the home. As the society becomes more focused on consumerism, the profession, too, becomes lost in the worship of idols of materialism. Without the prayer to life forces and the spirit, children and adults pray to their gods of lifeless mass production. Because of the lack of life force in these gods, their prayers and their focus are useless. Not surprisingly, their gods cannot serve the needs of the spirit and the soul. Children and adults become lost and misdirected in search of what is missing in their lives. Weaver (1984) describes this loss of civility and custom and the resultant debauchery:

Every group regarding itself as emancipated is convinced

that its predecessors were fearful of reality. It looks upon euphemisms and all the veils of decency with which things were previously draped as obstructions which it, with superior wisdom and praiseworthy courage, will now strip away ... but one consequence of this debauchery, as we shall see, is that man loses discrimination. For, when these veils are stripped aside, we find no reality behind them, or, at best, we find a reality of such commonplaceness that we would willingly undo our little act of brashness ... Barbarism and Philistinism cannot see that knowledge of material reality is knowledge of death ... Our age provides many examples of the ravages of immediacy, the clearest of which is the failure of the modern mind to recognize obscenity. (Weaver, 1984, pp. 26–27)

We as education professionals, who claim concern for the well-being and empowerment of individuals, families, and communities, must first recognize this anomaly. Use of critical theory and the process of critical science through critical thinking helps us to identify the source of our misery and the disease process—the collective psychosis—in order to propose solutions. This analysis identifies the source of the problem and misery, a loss of soul of the profession. Weaver (1984) clarifies:

What happens finally is that socialism, whose goal is materialism, meets the condition by turning authoritarian; that is to say, it is willing to institute control by dictation in order to raise living standards and not disappoint the consumptive soul. And as there is no limit to appetite or animal desire to consume, the majority without capital necessarily eats up the capital of the minority, and the civilization steadily decays ... The false world picture in the withering-away of religious beliefs, the conviction that all fighting faiths are due to be supplanted ... Society pauses before a fateful question: Where can it find a source of discipline? (Weaver, 1984, pp. 125, 127, 128–129)

The solutions must be considered by a collective of informed individuals. First, persons must be made aware of the root source of the problem before they may consider their options and potential solutions. The lack of clear identification of the causes of the current crisis, manifested in a growing "uncivil discourse," results in the repressive mandate of forced public education. An argument in favor of school vouchers is presented along these lines of reasoning. For example, along with this forced education come the philosophies of social liberalism or republicanism. In both cases, whether by virtue of the liberal theory of a market economy or the republican mandate of a social virtue, the need for school vouchers may be justified. Whether one takes one's voucher and purchases the best education for one's money, private or public, or accepts the status quo in public education, the individual citizen retains the power of choice.

Until either public education embraces the issues of morality again, or vouchers allow persons to purchase alternative sources of education where values are identified, the normlessness and violence too often present in our classrooms today will continue (Brady, 1997; Cohen, 1998). Family and consumer sciences professionals could have taken the lead in making the public aware of the major issues addressed, initiated public discourse; and allowed a forum for informed individuals and voters to confront their elected officials as to their desires. That is empowerment. That is our charge.

The "translating of human situations through hermeneutic phenomenology to ascertain what steps are necessary to provide possible solutions or actions" requires the critical analysis presented in this dialogue. "In essence, educators are called to 'understand how the considerations of power undergird, frame, and distort educational processes and interactions'" (Brookfield, 1995, p. 8, Gentzler, 1999, p. 28). Shall we stick our fingers outside and see which way the wind is blowing before we make a stand on educational reform? Shall we begin by reforming our own profession?

The core concept of aesthetics in college curriculum development in family and consumer sciences education became central to educational philosophy in the formation of the profession. I believe that answer became self-evident in the search for a theology of beauty. A simple concept of beauty of person, soul, and spirit takes on more than decorative shallowness; like an iceberg, it is the tip of the movement beneath its "sensuous surface" (Farrar, 1989; Heidegger, 1993). The profession was founded upon concepts of service to others rather than service to self. The loss of consideration of a moral critique is also a conflict of Western civilization and its historic connection to Judeo-Christian faith (Huntington, 1996/1997).The use of critical theory as the end result requires the process not only of critical science but the component of critical thinking as part of the larger whole of critical theory.

Elements of Critical Thinking

The categories, characteristics, and assumptions of critical thinking have been developed in a variety of ways by different authors. In this study I examine those elements and components of critical thinking presented by Jernstedt, Paul, Bloom, and Beyer (Gocsik, 1997). Jernstedt presents what he terms seven "discrete activities": observations, facts, inferences, assumptions, opinions, arguments, and, finally, critical analysis. The process of critical reflection presents an opportunity to assess and differentiate between inference and opinion, premises and biases. In formal ethical reasoning, critical thinking is practiced in order to lead to a reasoned judgment (Wall, 205).

In addition to the elements of critical thinking, Jernstedt presents Bloom's six processes of critical thinking: knowledge, comprehension, application, analysis, synthesis, and evaluation (Gocsik, 1997, p. 5). The elements presented in Bloom's Taxonomy will be modified somewhat to incorporate more current critical thinking in the critical science elements. Therefore, essential elements presented by Beyer (1995) will be incorporated. Brookfield (1987) presents five phases of critical thinking that contain the elements of the process toward a conclusion and action: trigger event, appraisal, exploration, developing alternative perspectives, and integration. The process and elements of critical thinking will be applied to the presenting trigger events that prompted this study and a synthesis of the elements explicated above. Paul (2006) presents eight elements of critical thinking: Purpose, Issue/Question, Facts, Assumptions, Viewpoint, Concepts/Terms, Conclusions, and Consequences of the Conclusions. A detailed consideration of each of these elements will lead the thinker to more ethical, fair-minded reasoning toward an ethical decision or reasoned judgment.

Examples of the application of critical thinking in the questioning phase may be framed as follows (Gocsik, 1997): What information about aesthetics and education are most important to our argument? What could or should be left out of the presentation of critical analysis? What do I really think about the subject of aesthetics in education and family and consumer sciences education curricula in higher education? Why do I feel this way? What is the transcendental phenomenological hermeneutics that led to feelings about aesthetics in education? What are the underlying assumptions regarding aesthetics and an anti-intellectual counter movement (Jauss, 1982) to be considered in presenting my argument? Are these assumptions valid? If so or if not, why? How can I present my argument by facts, observations, and inferences, in order to convince others of the force of my argument?

Process of Critical Thinking

Brookfield (1987) identified the development of a process for critical thinking through various stages:

> The beginnings of critical thinking are frequently seen in people perceiving a contradiction between how the world is supposed to work (according to assumptions acquired and trusted up to that point) and their own experiences of reality ... This perception of anomalies or contradictions is seen as the first stage in various conceptualizations of critical thinking, realizing that something is wrong, that there is a certain discomfort in one's life, that a societal situation could be different, and that certain policies are not working properly. (p. 24)

The challenge to our underlying beliefs and behaviors is fundamental to the critical thinking process. Thus, the initial discomfort in the studio situations and the curriculum committee meetings, the assaultive behavior of students in the dormitories (Reitmeyer, 1999) all presented a challenge to my own personal value system and social norms experienced over many years in classrooms in higher education. The conflicts were in the classroom, the committee planning meetings, the living dorms, and the larger campus community. Thus, examining the validity of the situation as a social norm or a transitional social stage in process became the initial reflective questioning as to my place in the profession of family and consumer sciences education.

Had I fallen into a black hole overnight and had the world changed values from Illinois to Iowa? Had educational theory changed between states, or between professions of political science and family and consumer sciences? Had established norms been relevant only to that location, or was there some other explanation for this discomfort? Absolute puzzlement was what I felt while sitting in an educational curriculum meeting and not believing what I was reading.

Phases of Critical Thinking

The first of a series of phases in what Brookfield (1987) identified as patterns of process in critical thinking had been identified. The first phase, the *trigger event* had occurred. Although usually negative, a positive trigger is said to be possible. This was not a positive trigger. This transitional stage felt just as Brookfield described: "Hopson and Adams (1977), for example, write of this transitional stage as one of shock and immobilization" (Brookfield, 1987, p. 26). That reflection and change usually emphasize negative events is quite similar to Dewey's concept of "experience" and the organism being faced with a challenge of sorts. Although not as severe as a "fight or flight" response, I would say it was close. This initial shock was to be followed by the next phase of critical thinking, *appraisal* (p. 26). "We identify and clarify the concern (Boyd & Fales, 1983), engage in self-examination (Mezirow, 1977), and begin looking for those confronting a similar contradiction" (Brookfield, 1987, p. 26).

The self-appraisal became one of challenge to my own values and beliefs. Yet, as I attempted to find a tolerable and acceptable limit, I found I could not physically be in the presence of what I believed to be a deeper problem, the intellectualization of damaging social situations which were demeaning to all participants and their human value. The art studios became "dens of filth" with veiled communication disguised by an intellectual cloak of justifications for perversion. The students were uncomfortable and so was I. In trying to discern others who did or did not share my perspective, I was advised to "rise above it." I felt these issues were more critical than a messy studio or use of a nude model. This was another level of essence in the process, disguised in a double-talk in which the speakers felt they provided themselves protection against accountability. An example of this type of double-talk is the following, given at a conference to specifically clarify this problem. The statement was made to a man regarding his wife: "Your wife is the prettiest woman to walk the streets." A clever disguise for insult, the response to this statement, as to its intended meaning was, "Prove it."

The environment dictates the intention. Like the judge attempting to differentiate between pornography and art, by virtue of intention the situation and the location also determine the appropriateness of the observed behavior. One would expect comments such as the above in a bar, or on the street corner in a red-light zone. One does not expect this sort of communication in a place of higher learning, or in "civilized" company. In a civil society, the "community standards" determine the social norms. If these were the standards accepted by all, the appraisal would be complete. I was not so sure this was the case. It seemed more apparent that traditional social norms were being held in a state of reprehensible oppression by a minority of persons who wished to force their perspective upon the majority. If such comments were to be allowed as simple jest, so much the worse. Although explicated by Von Bingen sometime between 1158 and 1163 in *Liber vitae meritorum (The book of the Rewards of Life)*, the relevance of her words ring true today in our example of double-talk and veiled insults (Campbell, 1991):

> Through his squalid ways a jester makes me play, just as they want and choose to do. The evil spirits want to mock the heavenly harmony, but they will not prevail. Therefore, through a jester they mock and assault various people; they mock them with lies when they cannot make them play games with the truth. Harmonious praise, which is proper to God, cannot, however, end since it is unfailing in the fullness of truth. A jester questions his own soul to see where he can soar and what he can do. When he looks at himself in the mirror of knowledge, he becomes vain and lies. The sound he makes while on earth pleases him no matter where he goes. (Hozeski, 1994, p. 52)

The *appraisal phase* of critical thinking became more pressing because of the potential for harm to others if the social situation were not clarified and, if need be, remedied. A twentieth-century term for such behavior has been defined by Davenport and Purell Elliott (2001) as "mobbing." This updated definition, developed by industrial psychologists, reflects a change in terminology, not a change in human behavior or relevance to the dignity of persons. The "mobbing" phenomenon, like "uncivil discourse," may progress to a mobbing syndrome. This syndrome is defined by Davenport, Distler Schwartz, and Pursell Elliott (1999) as "an emotional assault. It begins when an individual becomes the target of disrespectful and harmful behavior ... These actions escalate into abusive and terrorizing behavior" (p. 33).

Because of the policies and the hierarchical nature of higher education, especially teacher education, upon all levels of the society, the manifestation of this conflict was a red flag. Concern for the next generation and the children of teachers prepared within this mindset made the issue of value and social norms more pressing. If concepts of morality and human value issues integrated in a natural theology of beauty and aesthetics in educational philosophy were removed, only sensory hedonistic self-gratification would be taught to those most impressionable. The power of the position dictated the conversation of educational philosophy. "Critical reason that tries to unmask the irrationality of others as unreasonable is a struggle for power ... The logic of the example not only pays attention to what is being said or written, but also and especially to what one does and what the source is from whence one acts" (Van Manen, 1991, p. 217).

A pattern of consistency in the manifestation of a basic value conflict began to become evident in most of the experiences that followed. The consistent evidence was most obvious in overt expression of a total lack of regard for the dignity of the other person(s) being offended by the predators' behaviors. Removing any consideration of what constituted loveliness of person or being in effect removed civility as a necessary component of teacher preparation. The only acceptable solution for one who did not "feel comfortable" in a questionable situation was to remove the objecting party. Silence those who did not share the "value" or lack of values, thereby setting the standard. I was forced from the artists' studio to family and consumer sciences education.

Thinking I had escaped a situation that could not be changed by one person, I found the same conflict in process in the questioning of value-based terms and concepts within the most traditional profession in higher education, family and consumer sciences education. What was going on? If concepts of values could not be discussed in this profession, were we in the process of total anarchy in higher education? Was every traditional value of centuries of learning to be cast aside as not appropriate for public education? Were the people who could not afford private schools to be held hostage to funding of the dismantling of all of their social norms? What would replace traditional concepts of civility and decency? I am reminded of Weaver's discussion of piety and justice (1948/1984):

> It is highly significant to learn that when Plato undertakes a discussion of the nature of piety and impiety, he chooses as interlocutor a youth who is actually bent upon parricide. Euthyphro, a youth filled with arrogant knowledge and certain that he understands "what is dear to the gods," has come to Athens to prosecute his father for murder. Struck by the originality of the proceeding, Socrates questions him in the usual fashion. His conclusion is that piety, which consists of cooperation with the gods in the kind of order they have instituted, is part of the larger concept of justice. It can be added that the outcome of the dialectic does not encourage the prosecution. The implication is that Euthyphro has no right, out of his partial and immature knowledge, to proceed contemptuously against an ancient relationship. In our contemporary setting the young man stands for science and technology, and the father for the order of nature. (Weaver, 1948/1984, pp. 170–171)

Like Brookfield (1987), alternating between denial and minimization and "brooding on the exact nature of our perplexing contradiction," I found those of similar mind silent and "shocked." Whether they were young men trying to study Italian Renaissance painters, Korean students in search of a cosmic balance of colors, or older women like me, all seemed in shock, silent, and powerless. This commonality of a demeanor of passivity struck me most, as if a temperament, normally the stereotypical "artist's" nature of timidity, like butterflies scattered with the first sudden movement. Their world was invaded by brutal statements of intolerance in word and work. There was also the double-talk.

The ambiguity of the appraisal stage can be exemplified by another scenario from the Scotland studio. A young American woman was reproducing sheep in a pastoral scene. I asked her where she had found the sketches, noticing graphic tracings that were unusual for a fine art studio. She had a newspaper clipping of sheep in a pasture. Her comment was, "We just keep blowing them up until we get the one we want." It would be a harmless comment if it were not for the situation, newspaper articles discussing the recent tragedy of the airplane crash of young John Kennedy. I left Scotland.

The significance of historical transcendental phenomenological hermeneutics for the appraisal stage of critical thinking becomes self-evident. Brookfield (1987) states: "Moral conduct is recognizable in any society by certain innate features" (p. 13). My understanding of my society meant abusive, defamatory, speech as well as conduct was not "socially acceptable." If there were a dialectic change in reality in process, as evidenced by veiled intent, where would this future direction lead us? Rather than a "kinder, gentler America" I was finding a "mean-spirited" force being released, without any specific target, but upon whomever or wherever the unrestrained impulse occurred; anyone in the path would become a victim. "And after all if 'hypocrisy is the homage which vice pays to virtue' it may be better to be a hypocrite than to pay no homage to virtue at all" (Temple, 1951, p. 62).

> If it is reasonable, as it surely is, to be guided here by the standards of those who are ethically most sensitive, as in the sphere of beauty by those who are aesthetically most sensitive, there can be no doubt about the intimation of their experience. To fail in duty is felt by them not only as an injury to a neighbor, not only as a degradation of self, not only a breach of Moral Law on conformity to which all the welfare of man depends, but as the flouting of what justly claims our reverence. This feeling is the most constant, no doubt, in those who believe that the Moral Law is the content of the Mind of God; and it is one of the chief practical advantages of a theistic belief in the moral sphere, that it enables people not especially sensitive to ethical matters by natural endowment, to feel toward the claims of duty as the most sensitive feel towards them without added stimulus. (Temple, 1951, p. 254)

The escalation of licentious behavior was not limited to the artists' studio, though some argue art is first to reflect a change in social reality. The campus suffered many sexual assaults, investigation of faculty misconduct with students, and a long-term problem with the exploitation of students in the filming of young students in the showers without their knowledge (White, 2002). The lack of restraint of any kind evidenced an absence civility, rejection of early historical hermeneutics concepts such as beauty and aesthetics aligned with soul and religiosity and ethics in a theology and an educational philosophy of beauty. This manifestation of a lack of core concepts of beauty and aesthetics became self-fulfilling in revealing the consequences of a loss of values in society. Hearts were hardened to the tragedy of the loss of young souls and empathy for the feelings of our fellows. Perhaps it is the shock of such a loss that is required for a society to take stock of its current situation and critically evaluate whether or not this is a direction in which it (society) wishes to continue. The *triggering events* lead naturally to the next phase of critical thinking, *appraisal*, followed by *exploration*.

In the appraisal of the trigger situation, self-appraisal and historical review of the social norms for higher education need to be considered. The earliest history of the profession of family and consumer sciences education began as home economics under the tradition of Dewey. The core link to the early history of aesthetics as central to an educational philosophy, not merely home economics, has been discussed in the literature review. In addition, the separation of values from the context of education since the 1950s and a subsequent return of Dewey's progressive education movement must be considered. The special relevance of critical thinking in evaluating this trigger situation follows along the same lines as Dewey's concern for community (Dewey, 1904).

Proficiency in critical thinking is especially relevant to the progressive educational movement, as a distinctly American process. As Beyer (1995) points out in his Phi Delta Kappa Educational Foundation publication, *Critical Thinking*, "A democracy cannot survive unthinking citizens. Being a thinking citizen in a democracy and in a rapidly changing world requires the ability to make judgments about information related to personal, social, economic, and political issues. To do this well requires critical thinking" (p. 28). As value systems and behavioral codes are socially constructed, they are "provisional, relative, and contextual" (p. 28). Brookfield (1987) identifies the following examples of contextual awareness:

> Workers who understand that the "normal" ways of
> working or organizing production at the workplace

reflect the personal philosophy of their chief executive officer. Citizens who realize that what a government defines as "normal" unemployment or inflation reflects a particular political philosophy and set of part manifesto priorities. Adult sons or daughters who are aware that their parents' opposition to their marital or career choices is often grounded in cultural rules and expectations assimilated when these parents were themselves growing up. (Brookfield, 1987, p. 17)

The moral and value codes that have been culturally induced are challenged by amoral or valueless behavior. In this case it was the lack of civility and respect for individual rights and right actions as well as for any cultural custom. There seemed to be an attempt to destroy tradition without a well-thought-out alternative proposal, or a simple attempt to negate anything which represented the "White Anglo-Saxon Male" tradition and Western culture. What is to replace it is still in the formative or combative states. The chaos and confusion were typical manifestations of the change process. If the alternative norm is this "chaos culture," it does not appear to be a positive move toward a social evolution. Other *trigger events* seemed to be the lack of tolerance for disabled persons and an attempt to recruit a "multicultural master race."

All of these events were centered on the demeanor of uncivil and mean-spirited communication and destructive action. Echoes of a past pre-Nazi mentality were beginning to be manifested. How ironic that we see Dewey's (1937) resurrection simultaneously, with his own past history fighting these issues in the Leo Trotsky case in the 1930s. Was it the circle of time, perhaps? Again, the appropriateness of the historical transcendental phenomenological hermeneutics for this particular analysis is critical.

Relevance of Past Historical Perspectives

Considering the relevance of past historical perspectives of aesthetics within the context of its place in a value-based educational system is necessary if the current lack of such a place in educational philosophy is a possible explanation for what is perceived as a lack of civility which blocks open communication and learning. Knowledge, comprehension, application, analysis, synthesis, and evaluation as processes of critical thinking are not simply steps in a single general procedure. The assertions made must be probed and implications as well as consequences as to a number of alternative explanations must be considered. I will attempt to probe the assertions made via Socratic questioning.

In establishing criteria for analyzing the validity of assumptions, I will turn to Hultgren's analysis of Habermas's four types of validity assumptions in critical theory. The criteria become evident with an initial review of these very basic assumptions of validity and rational discourse. The question of validity arises with the speaker's intentions as true and appropriate, and in the right of each to participate in equal opportunity. The example of both the American and Scottish artists' studios are a case in point. Not only were the speaker's intentions questionable and likely untrue and inappropriate, the right to participate had been denied, leading to isolation from the groups. With some of the basic assumptions of validity in question, the process of the standards of critical thinking has been breached.

Credibility of an Observation

The observations and the denial of access to participation in the studios in America and Scotland were the triggers that prompted this analysis and investigation. The issues were reported immediately to the directors, security personnel, and instructors. The only offered resolution was for the reporter to be isolated from participation. Attempts at minimal inference in the initial stages of the appraisal have been difficult. The abrupt disruption of basic value orientation in civil rights compounded the impact of the *trigger events*.

In an attempt to remain as objective as possible, I reverted to past practice and a long history as an investigator in corrections administration, special investigations, and procedures which would stand the test of court cross-examination. As a past policy and procedure developer, and program planner in a maximum security prison, I am especially sensitive to potential litigation issues in human rights violations. As chair of a number of special investigations in not only correctional prison settings, but on university campuses, I found these situations beyond belief in their blatancy. I felt someone had changed the rules of civil society and forgotten to tell the courts and law enforcement officials, or this university campus was "beyond the law" of order of other universities.

I observed this same sense of shock in the expressions of other observers of this strange phenomenon. The cycles of disbelief, denial, and shock, continues. The rationale for basic standards of human interaction and civility has been challenged. Was this an intergenerational problem? It did not seem to be. Was it a regional problem? Was there a breakdown in the development of adequate communication skills somewhere before coming to the university or was this a problem within the campus community? As the persons participating in this sort of behavior overseas were not the young students, but the older participants, inference could be that any participation by the young was a result of negative role models. With mass communication further complicating the development of national standards and norms, could there be a change in mass communication that could be misdirecting the standards of conduct? If this were the case, this behavior should be observable outside the campus community.

If this larger social problem existed, what are the implications for accountability for teacher educators? What would be the role of family and consumer science educators? Would teachers and professors become the moral conscience of the society? Would they be allowed to present concepts of value and the rationale for civil conduct? Was this a clear call to teach critical thinking in the classroom among teacher educators? Would we be allowed to do so?

There is a problem with the initial assumption for validity in critical thinking, that people will behave in an appropriate and honest manner. In past traditional settings of higher education, the standards were well established and conduct was clearly defined. There were no gray areas or vague and unidentified standards of conduct. Violation of those standards resulted in social rejection. Social rejection results if one does not choose to participate (at least in the context of experiences analyzed in the case study) in lewd and degrading appreciation of a "worship of garbage" and "pornography." That the observations were correct has not been disputed. This lewd behavior was repeated in the graduate living hall in a number of incidents in the public computer lab. For example, a student was reported to be masturbating in front of a pornographic web page where nude women held numbers, or another where women were being burned on crosses. Though this and all incidents were reported to campus security, no action was taken. The hall director overheard the perpetrator giving a justification for his actions with the statement, "She thinks she is superior because she is whiter than the rest." I don't know what that was intended to mean. However, this and many incident reports fell on deaf ears. That anyone cares has not been established. When students attempted to constrain these actions, they were most often met with no action. In fact, the standard response to shock is, "So what, who cares?" Is this new callousness an indication of the future? What will be the result of such insensitivity to "uncivil discourse"? How can teaching or learning occur in such hostile environments? That the campus security personnel did not respond is another indication of a disease process, an archetypal complex and field where all are pulled into the power of the collective psychosis. Conforti (1999) explains:

> To illustrate the overwhelming power of the archetype to consume and absorb the individual and the collective consciousness, consider the atrocities in Nazi Germany, which occurred under the sway of the Wotan archetype. This archetype, which found a physical and human manifestation in the personage of Adolph Hitler, took over an entire county, in fact, the entire world, compelling individuals to engage in activities otherwise unthinkable. (Conforti, 1999, pp. 23–24)

The professional journal for family and consumer sciences education has identified this new standard of intimidation in the classroom. Classes in conflict resolution, sensitivity training, and mutual respect have been implemented in the lower grades. Is it time to learn from these children and teach civil propriety in the university classroom? Are deportment and civil conduct too "old hat?"

As this reflective analysis of the concerns revealed in the original question of the role of aesthetics in family and consumer sciences education, distinguishing verifiable facts, value claims, and reasoned opinions becomes critical. The necessity to do such assessment through critical thinking has been clarified by Baldwin in Hultgren's (1989) essay titled: "A Critique of

Home Economics Curriculum in Secondary Schools." Further, Baldwin has provided an appropriate definition of curriculum with which to consider these larger issues and concepts, such as aesthetics in education.

> The curriculum translates specified educational goals into processes of teaching and learning; it describes the teaching methods to be used and the subject matter to be taught. The curriculum is essentially political-moral in its influence as the beliefs and practices it generates intervene in the lives of people to bring about change; thus, it has implications for the student, the culture, and the society. Viewed in this light, curriculum theory should provide a rationally and morally defensible explanation of why certain content should be taught and why certain methodology should be used. (Hultgren, 1989, pp. 236–237)

The aims of curriculum in Hultgren's critique are "categories of action," to promote the goals identified by the curriculum as "means-end or purposive-rationale action, symbolic interaction or communicative action, and purposive rational action" (Hultgren, 1989, p. 237). The significance of the "beliefs and practices" curriculum content and methods teachers generate are relevant to the present argument. The significance of aesthetics as a core concept of family and consumer sciences and general education must be distinguished from the term art. Although aesthetics can be a component of art, as we have seen, in its theological perspective, art does not necessarily need to contain aesthetic virtue. The change in the relevance of a value component to the definition of aesthetics has resulted in its loss of status as a concept in educational philosophy.

Political-moral and value-based concepts have been repressed at the expense of the society and cultural standards. The current loss of a sense of cultural identity, as an attempt to reject the traditional male-dominated culture has resulted in anomie and confusion as members search for a new identity. The youth have lost their role models and a traditional core to question and challenge as they attempt to form their own sense of identity (Baldwin, 1989). The void in traditional role models is being filled by the dominant mass culture, which meets the needs of expediency. The considerations of the mass culture being manifested in art were presented in the literature review. As art is a communication of cultural identity, its honesty is often shocking. It reflects this mass culture's search for some identity to replace the traditional culture. Thus, if art has its fingers on the pulse of society, it is revealing a weak and sick culture in need of attention.

The Management Process

Baldwin (1989) identifies three steps in "decision making" (p. 237). In this situation, what to do about a loss of value base and a loss of aesthetic content in educational philosophy is the first step in "recognizing the need for a decision." The next step, "identifying and weighing alternatives," is begun by identifying past practice and the incorporation of aesthetics values in educational curriculum today in general higher education, and to identify aesthetics in other educational movements, such as in the revitalization of Dewey's progressive philosophy, aesthetics in science, and technology. The final step, a call to social action, is discussed in the process of critical thinking.

Credibility of a Written Source

In this case, the review of aesthetics as a philosophical principal in general educational philosophy and family and consumer sciences educational philosophy was undertaken in the literature review. The identification of aesthetics concepts in other areas of higher education indicates a growing movement of its relevance in other fields (Costa & Liebemann, 1997). Family and consumer scientists must re-examine their own priorities within the context of other specialties in education. Does the profession want to eliminate a fundamental concept while others are incorporating what was used initially? Is the profession becoming something other than that which it began as? Is the role of home economics as a moral conscience with educators of skills and ethical influence in policy and curriculum no longer a goal? Jax (1989) sees similar social crises and a parallel of need between 1909 and 1999. Social change, skyrocketing divorce rates, and children believed to be reckless, lawless, and irresponsible were the key concerns in 1909. How much has changed today? The now post-industrial revolution has disrupted and displaced people and families, resulting in their loss of orientation.

> But persons who carry out their tasks in life by teaching others according to the command of almighty God resound, so to speak, on flutes on sanctity. For by the voice of reason they chant justice right into the hearts of men and women. Thus says the Word, and that sound resounds once more. The Word is heard by means of sound, and it is also disseminated so that it can be heard. Just as a flute can strengthen the human voice, the teacher's voice can be strengthened among other human beings through the fear and love of God. Thus that voice can bring believers together and drive off unbelievers. (Campbell, 1991, p. 24)

Did the prophecies of a twelfth-century religious mystic presage such intentional exclusion of those of religious faith from public education? Will the only voices heard from the teachers of teachers be those of the agnostics or the Satanists? Is this the reason for the questioning of a place for aesthetic values and the educational core of a profession and its relevance in higher education? Such a conflict is consistent with research by Huntington (1996/1997), one of the foremost experts in comparative politics and international relations. He addresses this conflict in a quote from Bernard Lewis's analysis of "The Roots of Muslim Rage:"

> It should now be clear that we are facing a mood and a movement far transcending the level of issues and policies and the governments that pursue them. This is no less than a clash of civilizations—that perhaps irrational but surely historic reaction of an ancient rival against our Judeo-Christian heritage, our secular present, and the worldwide expansion of both. It is crucially important that we on our side should not be provoked into an equally historic but also equally irrational reaction against that rival. (Huntington, 1997, p. 213)

Our current "uncivil discourse" is thus more than a challenge to a traditional white male culture; it is a challenge of the core, the Judeo-Christian foundation of Western civilization. That challenge is being evidenced at the micro level within the college classroom in the Western cultures by the triggers examined in this dissertation. The profession of family and consumer sciences education had as its foundation in its early history soundly placed upon a value base, teaching critical thinking and questioning social situations which pose a danger to the society and the democracy. That profession is now in question as a result of its questioning the relevance of or absence of these traditional core values. The teachers of teachers are to express no faith, no value orientation, and no curriculum development as to how to best maintain order in the classroom, nor specific taxonomies as to how to best teach critical thinking. They have been silenced. Why? It is harder "to be alone in a crowd than to be alone in the desert" (Eckart, 1991, p. 83).

Choosing or Resolving Available Alternatives

The final step requires first an examination as to what alternatives are available for restoring aesthetics or expanding the concepts into the curriculum. After appraising the trigger events, the critical thinker moves into the next two phases, *exploration* and *developing alternative perspectives*. In these stages, examinations of role models, identities, and educational philosophical assumptions, as well as satisfactory and congruent relationships, have been presented. If complaints by beginning teachers are correct regarding such issues as classroom control, teaching citizenship, and respect for other students and teachers, what does this mean and what can be done? Is it an indication, as has been posited, that the loss of value orientation has resulted in these and other social problems? If so, is there time to reverse this degradation of tactful structure of thoughtful action? Is this being done through thoughtful reflection in public education or only private? If so, does this have meaning in a desire by some to disallow vouchers for private schools, leaving parents with no choice? What are the real educational policies and agendas for the twenty-first century?

How does the silencing of a value base impact this agenda? A profession whose history was founded on social reform and attention to the needs of families is in danger of being eliminated, if a lack of funding is any indication of priority. It is probable the profession will survive only in private schools. Why is this occurring simultaneously with a supposed call by government officials for more attention to family policy issues? Is there a larger agenda, a hidden force that promotes social disorder and the continued destruction of families? Why would we want to prepare a next generation without moral conscience? Why would we want to promote by our curriculum and educational policies a decadent and amoral society that will, through its lack of restraint and civil discourse, result in its destruction? These are the questions family and consumer science professionals must ask as critical science theorists, but they will be silenced if the profession does not address its own internal situation. The "gentle child" of academia speaks: Pedagogical action calls for thoughtful reflection and action in this matter. "Thoughtful reflection discovers where unreflective action was 'thoughtless,' without tact" (Van Manen, 1991, p. 205):

> To those, however, who shine with a little light, he will speak softly because if he surrounds them with bitterness, they will be destroyed completely and will become even more evil than they were before (Hozeski, 1991, p. 256).

The thoughtful reflective discourse, like the traditional values of our civilization and the Judeo-Christian values of the Western world, are, like the hermeneutic heritage grounded in metaphysics, being thrown to the wind. All about our Western tradition is in question. The collective *verstehen* and social fragmentation reveal this conflict in process.

Dimensions of *Verstehen*

It is necessary to consider the previous arguments now, within a hermeneutics research perspective, before the final phase of critical thinking, *integration*, may be concluded. For this purpose, *verstehen* will be generally understood to mean "understanding" through the hermeneutics process. Daines has presented the use of *verstehen* as a means to a more comprehensive understanding along with hermeneutics. Comprehension of the three forms of understanding through this process is given as follows: *verstehen* as understanding the meaning of an action; *verstehen* as understanding the motivation of action, and, *verstehen* as understanding of a particular action (Daines, 1989, p, 74–75). In hermeneutics, this *verstehen* of an action occurs when "Meanings are created through one's lived experience and being in the social world." In understanding motivation of actions, "[m]eanings are experienced and constructed in their moral or value-oriented dimensions." Finally, *verstehen* is intended to mean the understanding of a specific meaning of a particular action; "[m]eanings of 'actions of being' within the human life context of the social world are built through critical self-reflections, dialogue, and examination" (Daines, 1989, pp. 74–75).

In Daines's (1989) discourse, *verstehen* in critical thinking is "inextricably linked to the process of interpretations" through one's own language and life experiences. As meaning is constructed by the individual, based upon life experiences, these experiences are not collective but interactive with other individuals' individual meaning constructs (Daines, 1989, p. 77). In the argument presented thus far, the interpretation of meaning without the influence of moral dimensions would thus be quite different from those who have presented education within a framework of such. The perspective and meaning would be blinded to any value or moral base.

The significance of *verstehen* in the development of cultural patterns within a society and a collective meaning may result from the process of interaction in critical thinking and the *integration* phase, if, as discussed earlier, the basic assumptions for validity are present. The individual's participation in the collective society will thus be modified by the collective *verstehen* regarding these issues. If the collective *verstehen* does not include dimensions of value and moral reasoning within the development of educational curriculum, the collective *verstehen* will manifest those dimensions, as some could interpret the example *trigger event* for this study. My own individual *verstehen* has been developed over a different generational context than many (certainly not all) of the individuals with whom I was interacting. That the collective *verstehen*, or understanding or "consciousness" of a people, may be intentionally manipulated to exclude certain concepts, such as aesthetics and education within the philosophical domain, becomes the primary issue under investigation.

As we move toward a global educational system, the collective *verstehen* will require consideration of the complex interpretive nature of human existence. This experience of being in the global community is "formed through interpretation of the world (Daines, 1989, p. 45). The process of "encountering phenomena ... must become phenomenology as it turns to the processes of understanding and interpretation through which things appear as human existence is revealed" (Daines, 1989, p. 45). The method of hermeneutics in this case is ontological, or the argument for the existence of God based upon the meaning of God (Mish, 1994).

Daines (1989) further clarifies the process of *verstehen* in this hermeneutic consciousness and the "art of asking questions" for openness and thinking. "Understanding is viewed as an event (the placing of oneself within the process of tradition) in which the past, present, and future are constantly mediated through language" (p. 47). That some would argue the global community retains a more open acceptance to the possibility of a supreme being requires serious consideration of the limitation of such a concept in the curriculum of higher education in America. The global community could be said to operate upon a foundation of basic standards relevant to all human conduct, such as the Ten Commandments or global human rights. The issue of the universality of religion then lies in the rules of human communication and meaning in a *global verstehen*.

Gadamer developed the major concepts of a philosophical hermeneutics, underlying conditions of historical and interaction common to human understanding based upon an ontology of language (Hultgren, 1989):

> Philosophic hermeneutics takes as its task the opening up of the hermeneutic dimension in its full scope, showing its fundamental significance for our entire understanding of the world and thus for all the various forms in which understanding manifests itself: from interhuman communication to manipulation of society; from personal experience by the individual in society to the way he encounters society; and from the tradition as it is built of religion and law, art and philosophy, to the revolutionary consciousness that unhinges the tradition through emancipatory reflection. (Hultgren, 1989, p. 46)

It is from this "tradition as it is built of religion and law, art and philosophy" the foundations for the revitalization of Dewey's progressive education movement have been reestablished. Brookfield (1987) stated in his presentation of the phase of *developing alternative perspectives,* "Leaving behind a familiar but now inappropriate assumption or behavior is a wrenching experience" (p. 27). I would suggest that insensitive and abusive disregard to the differences of others is a major "wrenching experience" for those who must now learn a new method of interaction founded on respect and civil communication, and based on universal values and standards in a global society. The lack of such sensitivity breaks down communication, which is vital for interaction in this New World environment. Although a student code of conduct normally exists on university campuses, there appears to be a need to reevaluate the context within the scope of a "universal code of conduct," as the number of foreign students with varying cultural and religious backgrounds increases.

Consistent with the phase in critical thinking of *developing alternative perspectives,* the process of testing and exploring ways of thinking and acting that "make sense" in the situation (Brookfield, 1987), the transition into a global awareness of universal norms requires consideration of phenomenological aesthetics. Ecker (1998) has addressed this process in a paper published in the *Journal of Aesthetic Education,* "Navigating Global Cultures: A Phenomenological Aesthetics for Well-Being in the Twenty-First Century." Another example of global aesthetics in the college classroom is presented in this same issue by Farrar (1998), "Phenomenology as a Tool for Aesthetic Education in the Multicultural College Classroom" (Cohen, 1998). Thus, what is termed a global aesthetics is fundamental in the multicultural world and a *global verstehen.*

Establishing the significance of aesthetics as a method of not only interpreting the phenomenological hermeneutics of the art work, but also as an alternative means of understanding and communication, is best achieved by setting universal standards and norms in the multicultural classroom. The uniqueness of aesthetics in the process of teaching this universalism is grounded in a respect for diversity and differences, rather than intimidation and insult to those revealing feelings outside the ethnocentric "mean-spiritedness" of "unruly children" in the college classroom. Further, veiling such attempts in double-talk does not escape the phenomenological hermeneutics process of critical analysis of intent. A clever manipulation and disrespect is quickly disclosed in this total process.

The underlying structure of aesthetic education with phenomenology as a tool transforms consciousness (Farrar, 1998). It seeks universal truth and identifies elements, such as balance, form, rhythm, and shape, which fall outside the minute details of any specific language or hidden meaning. Transparency takes on new meaning of intent, not merely lack of corruption, as from the language of political science. The universal core is truth, as it is manifested in a multitude of ways in various cultures and religions. Through the "steps" of Kaelin's formal analysis, the primary ground for a phenomenological, structured pedagogy are presented (Farrar, 1989). I would add, however, that the number and specificity of the methodology in this pedagogy is of less importance than the underlying attempt at universal truth through interpretation of human commonality of emotions and feelings.

This is the strength of phenomenology. The common aspects of our humanness in experiencing fear, love, hate, and sorrow are best presented in art. In art, unlike other forms of communication, there is immediate truth; emotions are presented "on the sleeve" of the artists, without ability to disguise the inner emotions being expressed. Thus, the art works in the *Appendix* reflect my own inner world as I experience the outer world and my self-expressed reaction and interaction with it.

Unlike the underlying truth of religious parables, double-talk disguises insult and contempt for the dignity of its target. It walks in a shallow film of transparent civility, while moving toward degradation via its underlying reality. It is in this reality at the core of a search for meaning that phenomenology discloses truth. Hildegard von Bingen's parable of a millstone and wheel in the changeable nature of humanity exemplifies this process of degradation and social fragmentation (1994):

> Customary actions of men in the pursuit of pleasure …
> makes men … restless so that they now have these customs
> and then those, and now do these actions and then those.
> This image turns the wheel because changeableness does
> not remain in any particular position but is always unstable.
> It fans itself with the winds so that it chooses by measure
> these things and then neglects them, so that it holds onto
> by measure the old customs of men and then seizes all
> the new customs. … This image, however, has curly black
> hair because this fault leads me to thinking they have
> a lot of knowledge in their minds, which, nevertheless,

they do not, since they are not made strong with the fullness of righteousness but instead choose the blackness of perversity with tortuous vanity. Its hands are like those of the forefeet of a monkey because all of man's works are more foolish than they are truly prudent. Whenever man thinks he has the beauty of prudence, he walks in foolishness. It has feet like those of a hawk because man shows bitterness when he wants to do only what is for his own pleasure; what he wants, he does for himself and does not think about whether it is useful to others. Its garment has black and white stripes on it because sometimes man adorns himself in justice while he is actually surrounded with scandals and insults; other times he hides himself on the path of deception when he makes himself appear holy while he is actually wicked. He does not follow the glory and honor of the wise and disciplined but rather follows the despair of those who do not love wisdom and who actually consider it to be a pestilence. People who are consistently honest and upright do not choose or venerate those who are changeable in their words and actions ... This fault, however, values its own motives and thinks those who refuse to follow it are foolish. ... Steadiness responds to changeableness and shows that it is foolish and empty and that it will descend with its followers ... (Hozeski, 1994, p. 193)

For the philosopher in search of truth quoted by Hozeski above, in the mystical parable of Hildegard von Bingen of the eleventh century, truth does not change with time or place, but remains relevant throughout time (Hozeski, 1994). So too, does the process of a transformation of consciousness in phenomenologically structured aesthetics (Farrar, 1998). Farrar describes the transformation of consciousness and suggests that the "defanaticized states of consciousness are the goal of aesthetic education." The intersubjectivity of an emotional response to the common elements of art, to a historical review of social meaning, to an updated consideration of the meaning within the context of current society is educational aesthetics. Like the process of critical thinking, a critical analysis of any artwork must take place within the context of meaning.

The communicability of meaning and notions of "universal values" are currently being challenged (Farrar, 1998). "The goal of communicative intersubjectivity as a primary objective of aesthetic education is particularly urgent today. As notions of 'universal value' and a Eurocentric canon of 'humanistic education' lie expiring at our feet, it is time to look up and around and to engage creatively the contemporary realities of higher education" (p. 47). It is hard to say if this is a transient rebellion against tradition. It does reflect the strange chaos culture experienced in the Iowa State University studio. Farrar does not explicate her exact meaning in this article, but references Dissanayake (1995). There is some inconsistency in Farrar's quotes from Dissanayake (1992). The following is one example of the confusion in her discussion of the chaotic state of the arts today:

> Certainly, intimations of sacredness, beauty, privilege, refinement, and imperturbability continue to cling to the idea of art like wisps of mist shrouding a tree's higher reaches. More evident, however, is the trashy clutter at ground level, the less estimable associations of co modification, provocation, charlatanry, fickleness, and vulgarity. ... Repudiating the whole of Western civilization is a harsh and rash response to admitted social inequities, so that postmodernist remedies that recommend flushing away the baby with the bath water can well seem even more misguided than the malady. (Dissanayake, 1992, pp. xiv–xvi)

While artists and art teachers might especially welcome a biological justification for the intrinsic importance of their vocation, everyone, particularly those who feel a loss or absence of beauty, form, meaning, value, and quality in modern life, should find this biological argument interesting and relevant. Ironically, today words such as *beauty* and *quality* may be almost too embarrassing to employ. They can sound empty or false, from their overuse in self-help and feel-good manuals, or tainted by association with now-repudiated aristocratic and elitist systems in which ordinary people were considered "common" for not having the opportunity to cultivate appreciation of these features. Nevertheless, the fact remains that even when we are told that "beauty" and "meaning" are socially constructed and relative terms insofar as they have been used by the elite to exclude or belittle others, most of us still yearn for them. What the species-centered view contributes to our understanding of the matter is the knowledge that humans require these things. Simply eliminating them creates a serious psychological deprivation. (Dissanayake, 1992, p. xix)

Ferry, a professor at the Sorbonne and the University of Caen, transcends this time-specific altercation and addresses the "somewhat fragile chain of 'a history of democratic individualism or modern subjectivity'" in the field of aesthetics. There are the formulation of the definitions of subjectivity, based on philosophy (which most people are unaware) and the interpretation of a discipline, aesthetics, within the concrete history of art (Ferry, 1993, p. vii). Ferry's presentation of the "quarrel between heart and reason—and end of this history" best exemplifies what I have been attempting to explicate in my historical phenomenological hermeneutics experiences in these art studios and the "quarrel" in curriculum development. Ferry (1993) discusses a question of reason or emotion:

Within the discourse, Ferry (1993) offers the core of my present discussion and critical analysis of a loss of traditional value orientation. A dominant belief by educators is that learning is essentially a scientific field of study where what are most important are the basic facts and empirical knowledge produced by scientific inquiry (Van Manen, 1991, p. 41). As we have seen in our examples, this is a false logic leading to social destruction:

> And if it's true that the crumbling of traditions leads us to the era of indefinite questioning, the latter in turn contributes mightily to their erosion: the more that questions come up, the less comfortable are we in answering them, bereft as we are of all reestablished criteria; the more these criteria fade away, the more numerous are the aspects of intellectual—but also daily—life which enter the field of individual questioning ... If we are secular humans—as the end of theological-political thought constrains the immense majority of Christians to be, at least in the public sphere—we have to admit that in the next decades it will be in ourselves, therefore—in, by, and for humanity—that we shall have to find the answers to these questions that the progress of science and technology will certainly force us to raise ... the intimidating question of the limits that must be imposed on the power of man over man. ... On this path the history of cosmologies or

of the great religions can no longer serve as guide; nor can that of modern political philosophy, although, obviously, both must remain present in the mind as the negative of another history, that of aesthetics, in which are inscribed in a positive fashion not only the various conceptions of subjectivity that constitute modern times, but also their sharpest tensions—that with the question, repressed but always underlying, of the individual's relation to the collective. (Van Manen, 1991, pp. 4–5)

What has been termed *global verstehen* requires a universal aesthetics theory and value orientation. A habit of mind, as Dewey would have called it, makes universal respect reciprocal. The problem that was difficult to resolve in the American studio was the disrespect for one's fellow, not a cultural miscommunication. The anti-European contempt of historical context of painting exercises, which demanded not a collective but a sublimation or elimination from the arena of higher education is completely void of any reference to or artistic expression of that faith. If it had been any other than Judeo-Christian, it is doubtful the contentious mean-spiritedness would have followed. This is consistent with Huntington's thesis (1997), first explicated in print in 1993.

How do we answer any of these questions "bereft as we are of all pre-established criteria," from the perspective Ferry (1993) has pointed out, as they relate to family and consumer sciences education in the Western civilization? Ferry further identifies and answers his own individual questions in regard to this phenomenon in his chapter entitled "The Problem of Ethics in an Age of Aesthetics": "It is simply the case that cohesion must from now on lie in inter-individuality (to avoid saying intersubjectivity), and not in the transcendence provided by a cosmic reality that would be humanity's shared lot" (Ferry, 1993, p. 246).

As the withdrawal of limits, of boundaries, results in anomie, we are tempted to return to a more secure reality in traditions. Thus, we must know our history before we can assess and evaluate, by critical thinking, those traditional beliefs that no longer apply in today's world. Yet, without limits, the potential for misdirection is great. In addition, the responsibility of the individual for great historical analysis as part of mature reasoning is questionable. Lacking traditional foundation, the potential for brute force becomes a potential for the return to barbarism. The loss of socially accepted limits for appropriate social conduct through traditional forces, modified by constraints, results in violence and intimidation. The lowest common denominator in the human drive for the "greedy self" requires the use of force of language and conduct in demanding its own way.

I do not believe the problem is in a lack of tolerance for differing cultures or religious values. As discussed previously, the commonality of all these traditions is evident. This is not the conflict being manifested by overt confrontational behavior. Physical and linguistic assault is veiled in the language of freedom of speech that is disrupting the social order and forces the will of the most dominant upon the most passive.

Though the practice or specifics may vary, traditions function on a system of universal truths which guides their continued existence in the non-secular world. The problem arises when the laws of a common universal faith no longer are applied to civil discourse. The problem does not lie with the faithful; rather it is the repression of the faithful by the faithless. The movement toward using the critical thinking process to justify the transmittal of a tradition is as absurd as Ferry's (1993) argument to the contrary:

> Confronted with the withdrawal of the world, the temptation to restore lost traditions becomes strong, and the nostalgia for the past that is the most frequent companion of the ideologies of decline seems to be the obligatory concomitant to the anguish created by the disappearance of well-established reference points. It alone can permit us to understand the seductive aspect of the project to reactivate lost tradition—but also its absurd and dangerous aspects. (Ferry, 1993, pp. 247–248)

This line of reasoning does not allow the possibility of validity to universal truth, or the cycles of civilizations and change processes. The timeless truths of various faiths, which are clarified in times of transition, span more than a few decades within a specific culture or political system. The fickleness of man, who believes he is the interpreter of his own destiny without a guiding force, is like Hildegard's parable of the wheel. These are not transient truths spanning a decade, but continue to be truths after millennia. The names of the messengers may change, but not the message.

When a critical analysis of the meaning of this superficial justification for not facing the reality of a transition into a more hedonistic, self-focused culture is made with surety of purpose, the "seductive aspect of the project" is in the temptation to follow the crowd over the edge into the abyss. The path of least resistance is too often the path of self-destruction. Logic directs humans in a society to develop laws to promote the best potential for the survival of the largest number of its members. This Nietzschean nonsense seduces the logic toward its own destruction. The only absurdity is the abyss of the abstract.

> The soul strives to live itself out untrammeled in the world of imagination it has fashioned. ... [W]hen considering the artistic man, we shall be shown most impressively that suffering is the very state which heightens the value of personality. I might almost say that suffering really creates this value for the first time. Through the mode of his suffering man become really what he is called to be, and no guilt which leads to suffering can rob him of his humanity. If it is trivialities, we smile at his despair ... if it concerns the things that make life worth living, we sympathize. (Dessoir, 1970, p. 164)

Balthasar's method further explicates the relationship to the positive value of moral critique for the world. He combines the aesthetic and religious parts of reality. Although we have been "knocked about by both structuralists and deconstructionists ... the theological aesthetics of Han Urs von Balthasar constitute a promising combination of the old and new for the future direction" (Roberts, 1987, p. l):

> The initial thrust involved walking a tightrope between aestheticism in the narrow sense and a puritan rejection of art: "Who affirms the higher does not have to reject the lower." He added, "Art moves from the concrete and is, if one will, a process of abstraction (if not logical). Religion on the other hand is concerned with the concrete *katexochen*; namely, fate and decision of the unique person." (Roberts, 1987, p. 36)

That these two philosophies will never unite is a given. The philosophies pit hedonistic self-pleasure at the expense of everything against the survival of the greatest number of humanity. The argument is not between faiths, but between the faiths and the faithless. The argument against vouchers in America is not to separate church and state, but to eliminate a church from the state completely. The religious will be forced underground, as has been the history in other oppressive states, when the government became "the religion" of the people. The current "religion of the state" is empirical science.

If it is not a tradition of faith that is in question here, what part of tradition is no longer applicable? What part of tradition do we wish to challenge? What are the traditions that no longer apply which are a carryover from the "Eurocentric humanism," or do they mean to say, "the white man's' culture"? Why all this veiled deception of intent? What is the issue here, a white man's religion as core of Western civilization, or any religion at all?

1. There must be respect for life, respect for life as it comes into existence and for handicapped, suffering, and dying life.

2. Unlimited individualism and autonomy threaten to turn into egotism. This threatens the foundations of human society in matters great and small.

3. Freedom can be abused by a mentality of "Whatever gives pleasure is permissible." In the long run, this must prove destructive, not only for human relationships and society, but also for the ongoing happiness of individuals themselves. (Kung, 1995, p. 114)

The dignity of life and the implications for a value centrality are further explicated by Ogden, Richard, and Wood (1929) in *The Foundations of Aesthetics*. While art became a pastime, its role was largely influenced by the Freudian preoccupation with trivializing the female position within a sexual context. That art became play rather than a form of accessing the unconscious, as Jung would have argued against Freud at the time, its place within the *verstahen* becomes obvious in the following passage:

> The definition of art in terms of psychological effect came particularly into prominence with the evolutionary theories of the seventies [1870s] which occupied themselves chiefly in discovering the survival value in everything which had

succeeded in making its right to survive. The evolutionists of those days regarded pleasure as a feeling which could be correlated with physiological function, and since Art seemed a form of activity with little apparent utility it was considered wise to relate it closely to Play which (*vide* kittens) involved the very practical idea of Exercise … and in Art a method of harmlessly expending superfluous energy … This sort of treatment became known, and still known on the continent as the "English aesthetic." (Ogden et al., 1929, pp. 49–50)

The strange connection of art to the right to survive within the explanation of play and expending energy is difficult to totally understand with today's changeable meaning of art and its purpose. The definition of terms becomes modified to fit the context of the times. For example, the term "culture," initially tied to concepts of contemplation and meditation necessary for reflection upon God, as meaning "schooling" and "learning," was tied also to theology. It now has been disassociated from "schooling" and theology (Pieper, 1963).

High art may produce cathartic results but, as examined earlier, a "true" artist, attempting not to replicate what is observed as an imitator, but as a creator, suffers in that creative process. The change of the role of art and aesthetics today places it in the center of conflict, as a messenger of the social situation, in open communication. This communication is found in the conflict for even a definition of aesthetics and Eurocentric versus other interpretations of reality. The challenge of traditional values, like the meaning of aesthetics, demonstrates the complex situation in which academicians and citizens find themselves in the global society. Further, there seems to be some ambiguity in the interpretation of Dissanayake's position on aesthetics as presented by Farrar (1989). Dissanayake presents her cumulative views in the conclusion of her text:

Not only the National Endowment for the Arts, but federal, state, and local departments of education and community development should, in my view, be exploring ways to enable all people to make their individual and collective lives more significant through art—making things special— rather than acquiring, consuming, interpreting, disputing, destroying, or cynically repudiating them, which seem to be the entrenched if ultimately humanly unsatisfying responses to our postmodern world. (Dissanayake, 1992, p. 225)

Will the "new tradition" implement equality in a more equitable way, or merely replace one oppressor for another? Man over man was Ferry's concern with individualism. Man is to find reason outside of any past tradition, within himself, without counsel except among those who reject past practice. This sounds like a Utopian non-reality based upon a theory of the blind leading the blind, like the family trying to do family counseling and finding a pile of feces in their living room. Nobody knows how it got there, but because they cannot believe it is there, they try to ignore it and pretend it does stink. In the meantime everyone is getting sick. So the family goes to the government for help, and is told there is nothing wrong with having a pile of feces in the living room. It's just their imagination and past tradition from some white man's world that you shouldn't be able to live with a pile of feces in your living room. You should use critical thinking and come to a new thinking about it. Your intolerance is simply a result of your past traditions, because "some people like things dirty."

Somewhere between the blind leading the blind lies what De Man (1971/1983) terms in his title *Blindness and Insight: Essays in the Rhetoric of Contemporary Criticism*. Speaking of a period around 1970, he states that at "that time, the main auxiliary discipline for literary criticism was undoubtedly philosophy" (p. 4). De Man speaks of a period of cooperation between phenomenology and literary critics:

> These philosophers were themselves engaged in working out a difficult synthesis between the vitalism of Bergson and the phenomenological method of Husserl; this tendency proved quite congenial to the combined use of the categories of sensation, consciousness and temporality that is prevalent among the literary critics of this group ... Philosophy, in the classical form of which phenomenology was, in France, the most recent manifestation, is out of fashion and has been replaced by the social sciences. (De Man, 1971/1983, p. 4)

Jung tells us the unconscious is the deposit of all human experiences, back to the most remote beginning (1966). Hidden in the symbolic representations of dreams, artworks, and direct communication are the core historical "archetypal" truths which transcend time. The third eye of revelation, or contemplation, is not accepted by all. "Der Knoig Oiedipus hat ein Auge Zuviel vielleicht [King Oedipus has one eye too many perhaps]" (De Man, 1996, p. 246). Curreri-Alibrandi (1996) follows the symbolic tradition of Jung in analysis of human history through visualization and epochs with the following observations:

> [There are] three single moments in the whole history of Western Art and, as it appears, of mans civilization, in which Visual Perspective (VP) seems to have made its earliest appearances. An arc of possibly 50,000 years, from the last Paleolithic Ice Age to our days ... The conscious and unconscious states of the mind, appearances and disappearances of works in tridimensional Visual Perspective (VP) through the ages from a precise and coincident graph delineation ... These and other data have led me to consider possible the development of a congruous theory concerning the unconscious origin and the essentially symbolic expression of VP in art. (Curreri-Alibrandi, 1996, pp. xxvl–xxvii)

Similarly, for the Greek poet, word imagery made feasible the creation of discrete space around pivotal characters, whose personalities assumed a dimensional, sculptural quality. Curreri-Alibrandi (1996) presents a theory by Usner:

> Usner described the evolutionary process of verbal expression that took place in early developmental eras, primarily in response to the need to identify and categorize the forces of nature. The use of symbols was noted by the scholar in relation to mental evolution of mankind through expression and ideation: There have been long periods in mental evolution, when the human mind was slowly laboring towards thought and conception and was following quite different laws of ideation and speech ... The need to explain the mythical world of the primitives and that: The link between language and myth is metaphor ... Cassirer stresses the magical nature of the metaphor that is imbued with "unconscious powers" bust because of

the myth that it expresses. Echoing Cassirer, Jung stated that: "An archetypal content expresses itself, first and foremost, in metaphors" ... Archetype symbology ... [are] "Panofsky's points of reference for the symbolic use of perspective are ancient Greece, the Middle Ages, and the Italian Renaissance discovery of the vanishing point as the concrete symbol of the discovery of infinity itself"(p.5). (Curreri-Alibrandi, 1996, pp. 71–72)

What this means for communication in symbols through art and verbal communication becomes relevant to our argument in the subtle double-talk that is so much a part of the normlessness in an uncivil environment. Veiled in a cloak of double meaning, the "jesters" insult and degrade the intention of communication to avoid personal responsibility for uncivil conduct. For example, the artist's painting of a Madonna done in feces is more than a technique; it is a symbolic statement of contempt for the subject and symbol of the Catholic Church. It is the process of phenomenological hermeneutics that exposes the underlying meaning in the various forms of communication. Thus, a theology of beauty and past tradition of aesthetics is synonymous with the soul (Curreri-Alibrandi, 1996; De Man, 1971/1983; De Man, 1982; Navone, 1996; Zeltner, 1975).

The Strength of a Conclusion

Historical reviews of the philosophical leaders in the professions have been examined. Dewey was the principal educational philosopher for nearly fifty years and provided the structural beginning for the profession of home economics professionals, such as Hunt, and later refinement of those philosophies at the Lake Placid Conferences. In addition, the significance of aesthetics, within the larger historical context of knowledge in general, and the general educational theory of Dewey, has been examined. Aesthetics foundations in early home economics and later family and consumer sciences education were considered. Historical hermeneutic inquiry and transcendental phenomenological hermeneutics inquiry were implemented with the goal of understanding the communication of aesthetics as a method of symbolic social communication. The interpretive science was implemented for communication and social synthesis. The dialogue with others and the past is consistent with the historical transcendental phenomenological hermeneutics in the common concern of issues in daily life. The historical context of my own life and the current cultural situation and problematic social norms at the university level has been examined. A consensus may be achieved through rational criticism.

Discourse for Truth

Let us reconsider some fundamental statements regarding Dewey's educational philosophy as it was accepted and now challenged within the "new" modernity of a different kind of aesthetics phenomenology. To determine if this is an "old hat" philosophy resurrected under a cloak of seduction, as Farrar and Ferry might argue, we must then also decide if there is something wrong with that.

> A child, according to Dr. Dewey, is as evidential of the nature of reality as an electron or a star. For the purposes of philosophy the affairs of the nursery and the kindergarten seem to him as significant as those of the physical laboratory. This is in harmony with his general theory of existence, which holds that no level of experience— physical, biological, or social—should be given superior metaphysical status.
>
> The moral interest is also central in the philosophy of Dr. Dewey. Although resolute in the desire to understand and interpret the world solely on the basis of empirical findings, he is equally concerned to use these findings to *change* the world so that human goods may become more secure, more numerous, and more widely shared. (Schilpp, 1939, p. 419)

A philosophy that holds central the equal status of the human being founded on moral principles, with its aim the betterment of the condition of existence for mankind—this is Dewey's old hat traditionalism. As long as there are art lovers, there will be disputes as to their peculiarities (Mauron, 1935/1970). "Thus, when the leaves are falling from a tree, each may say to its neighbor: 'The physicists can think what they please, but I don't fall as you do.' Which, we know, easily becomes: 'I fall *better* than you.'" (pp. 109–110). Like Mauron, I am attempting to explain how I fall, in aesthetics. This is the nature of phenomenology.

When the broader perspective is considered in relation to a current global movement, his original theme becomes more significant in this current battle: "Education offers a vantage ground from which to penetrate to the human, as distinct from the technical, significance of philosophical discussions" (Mauron, 1935/1970, p. 421). Yet, his philosophy is about more than a method of teaching, via experience, as experimental inquiry. At a time when method also meant a preexisting understanding of a philosophical tradition of moral values, the same is certainly in question now. The importance of consequences of education follows from Dewey's presentation of his concept of the human mind and experience:

> The child acquires mind—a rational nature—as he masters the meanings of affairs in his environment. The meanings are not primarily his original creations. They have been developed by the long and painful experience of the race; they are funded in the habits, customs, traditions, tools, methods, techniques and institutions of his society. The child makes them his own through learning process. It is through learning by participation in ways of his community that he achieves mind—becomes a person. (Mauron, 1935/1970, p. 423)

If this is a valid assessment of learning for nearly fifty years, the current crisis of violence in the classroom, children killing children, is a reflection of the community in which the child has developed his mind, or "mindlessness." Without the logic of faith, children and adults dealt irrational "mean-spiritedness" have no foundations or recourse in an attempt to explain "man's power over man." Having been stripped of options as to recourse, they may choose the confusion of force against force. The reward for the virtue lies in their sense of righteousness. Otherwise, there is no logical explanation as to why they should not retaliate against their abusers.

In 1887, Dewey's *Psychology* was based on a conception of God as the "traditional biblical deity" and continued; though in somewhat modified form, throughout his career. In his 1934 book, *A Common Faith*, Dewey:

> expresses his reservations on both aggressive atheism and supernaturalism as being too exclusively preoccupied with man in isolation from nature ...Tuggle and Dewey also emphasize the importance of communication for enabling people of diverse cultures and backgrounds to work together ... Of all affairs, communication is the most wonderful ... And, of course, communication is not merely a matter of conveying statements through language. And may have a greater claim to universality. (Hahn, 1997, pp. vi–vii)

Are we to reject such logic simply because it contains implications for traditional standards being expounded by a "Eurocentric" heritage? When Dewey published "What Are Universal?" he challenged the linguistic illogic of a philosophy which did not consider humanity within its greater context and universality. For example, "Human beings comprehend Negroes ... while it would be a natural expression to say that the idea of humanity necessarily comprehends treating Negroes as human." With a universal logic, "Human beings would still have a meaning if no Negroes were known" (Tuggle, 1997, p. 18). The universality of humanity reveals the absurdity of classification of concepts of humanity based upon earlier notions of race. Thus, concepts tied to a theological philosophy are evolutionary in expression of humanity and commonality of humanness. To reject Dewey because he is from a traditional background would be to disregard a logic that is in the best interest of all humanity. Yet, he maintained his faith and his concern for "evil as a problem for humans" (p. 199):

> Philosophy is criticism; criticism of the influential beliefs that underlie cultures; a criticism, which traces the beliefs to their generating conditions ... Such an examination terminates, whether so intended or not, in a projection of them into a new perspective which leads to new surveys of possibilities. (Tuggle, 1997, p. 199)

Reciprocal Understanding Through Hermeneutics

If we are to use Dewey's philosophic rationale in the present context of a search for new perspectives, we must also consider the possibility that, by a lack of persistence as to a value base, we assist in its demise. We participate in our own reality, are impacted by it, and, likewise, impact that evolving reality. If the majority of citizens, once they become aware of the source of their current dilemma (and I am not so sure they are), decide to cast aside past traditions, this is the true nature of critical thinking and phenomenological hermeneutics. However, it is also true that the elite in education, the teachers of teachers of future generations, bear a greater responsibility for the serious critical reflection as to the impact of their decisions in curriculum development and course content. Yet, the voices of a few become silenced by the many.

Teachers are the gatekeepers of the future. Who are the gatekeepers of the gatekeepers? This reality presents collective dangers. For example, "Carl Jung once remarked that the group mind is the 'lowest' form of consciousness because individuals involved in a *negative* group action rarely, if ever, accept responsibility for their personal role and actions" (Myss, 1996, p. 109–110). Jung may be further quoted in relevance to art's role in society: "What is more, individualism can find avenues of expression—political, economic, and social— other than the arts. Similarly, when art's use is found in making manifest salient symbols and images, as in Jungian-influenced theories, one should be aware that the value resides primarily in the symbol or image: in its meaning, rather than in its vehicle" (Dissanayake, 1992, p. 91).

There can be no rational exclusion of "traditionalist" considerations and participation in the discourse for appropriate curriculum. As an elderly priest friend once told me (and I hesitate to say I have priest friends, as it could mean I will not be allowed to discuss these issues in a language of religiosity), "Don't listen for what you hear; listen for what you don't hear." The exclusion of one line of reasoning in the promotion of another is contrary not only to democratic philosophy, but critical theory, which underscore its foundation.

What is it that we do not hear in education? We can discuss every method of terminating life, every form of sensual pleasure, but we cannot discuss moral values. We can discuss families and how important it is for families to participate in education, but we have no choice as to where our families will be educated by the state, unless we are wealthy and can afford "values." Currently we find ourselves in a social debate in America over allowing vouchers for tuition for children in private schools. What is it those who are against vouchers for private schools really fear? That given a choice, the citizens would not choose public education, or that public schools cannot compete? If public education is so great, what difference does it make if "a few" parents choose private schools? If a large number of parents do choose private school vouchers given the opportunity, what does that say about our public school systems?

The long tradition of discussion of "experimental naturalism" outside the context of spiritual hierarchy in an attempt at organic evolution was central to Dewey's argument of a central process of learning. This process of learning occurs within rather than outside the total social reality.

> What are the educational consequences of this naturalistic
> interpretation of human personality [outside the context
> of spirituality]? This view of man's intellectual and moral
> nature certainly does not imply, as many assume, that the
> education of human beings is to be reduced to a process
> of animal training. (Schilpp, 1939, p. 423)

The continued debate seems also to indicate a continued interplay for power of position in curriculum development of traditions versus some evolving modified social order. What that social order will be has not yet been determined. If it is to be progressive rather than regressive, some lines must be drawn in the sand. To reject all civil discourse and behavior merely because such were developed by a white cultural dominance without some consideration of what limits should be set will result in a continued social decay. The centrality of aesthetics and beauty as a past tradition of theology founded on a belief in the potential for an evolved sensitivity becomes, then, another target for challenge of past tradition alone.

"Of what value are aesthetics and education in family and consumer sciences?" As Tuggle informs us in his text on the evolution of Dewey's philosophy, "To the surprise of his assembled 'horrified' students, 'who were more doctrinaire than the master,' Dewey 'joined with this gentleman (a visiting humanist from England) [*sic*] in proposing to establish some sort of humanist church in the United States ... [T]he historic men of wisdom felt that a religious ingredient was essential to their philosophy, though none of them were theologians, all found an intellectual ballast in traditional religious beliefs" (Tuggle, 1997, pp. 200–201).

> Beliefs about God, Nature, society and man are precisely the things that men most cling to and most ardently fight for ... [However] the "true" is indeed set up along with the good and the beautiful as a transcendent good, but the role of empirical good, of value, in the sweep of ordinary beliefs is passed by. The counterpart of this error, which isolates the subject matter of intellect from the scope of values and valuations, is a corresponding isolation of the subject matter of esthetic contemplation and immediate enjoyment from judgment ... Hence the primary function of philosophy at present is to make it clear that there is no such difference as this division assumes between science, morals, and esthetics appreciation. But it has the authority of intelligence, of criticism of these common and natural goods ... To note, however, contingency in connection with a concrete situation of life is that fear of the Lord, which is at least the beginning of wisdom. (Tuggle, 1997, pp. 201–202)

Critique of Tension and Conflict in Social Reality

Baldwin (1989) tells us, "Dewey employed the term 'God' throughout the course of his highly productive seventy-year publishing career" (p. 203). Further, the analysis of social context is primary when working through a critical inquiry. Interpretation of conditions "which have revealed distorted communication and lack of agreement," and through a philosophical reflection and critique of the historical sources of exploitative, repressive conditions, requires understanding of the history and conditions leading to the current debate (p. 203).

Beliefs held can no longer be justified in the current situation where a subgroup represses the interests of the whole group. The repressive domination and exploitation and present rationale for the current loss of norms and anomie has resulted in the violence we now find too common in the school classrooms (Brady, 2000). The normlessness and search for a restructuring social, cultural, and economic situation is evidence of the crisis in place. The repression of ideology requires action, which will result in change and rightness of norms and actions. Reaching intersubjectivity requires the right of each person to participate fully and participate in discussion as to the meaning and norms represented in aesthetics within a value orientation for educational curriculum. Baldwin tells us further, the weight of the stronger argument will dictate the outcome of this argument. Hopefully, enlightenment and consensus will lead to social action to overcome frustrating repressive conditions found in this evaluation.

A Concluding Call to Action

Baldwin establishes a clear analysis of the phenomenon of anomie with a loss of norms and consequent results. Her 1989 lecture at Iowa State University foreshadowed our current crisis in the American classroom (Baldwin, 1989):

> Disturbances and crises in the culture result from application of incorrect or inappropriate scientific inquiry to address questions of social norms. The current disturbances in the formation of new members of the society, the transmission and social reproduction of the culture and revision of the culture as the adolescent crisis are being experienced. The socialization of the individual along with the culture and the society experience certain detrimental effects if incorrect applications of empirical scientific methodology occur. Cultural tradition comprised of values, knowledge, attitudes and meanings, and standards of the times are ignored. If the domination of positivistic science inters the social traditions; the rationale of knowledge is at stake. The irrati.onal priorities result from the inappropriate scientific method of inquiry. Where there is a biased and dogmatic view of knowledge, meaning within the culture is lost (Baldwin, 1989; Jauss, 1982)

The society has a withdrawal of legitimization or shared standards or worthiness, as there is denial of public debate and loss of mass loyalty. The individual experiences a loss of orientation. There is a loss of any moral symbol for meaning in the culture. Value has been placed on the acquisition of material gain, without a counterbalance in consideration of human aspects of existence. The individual has no model of norm. This may be manifested, as has been discussed during this dissertation, in inappropriate conduct of communication or, as with the tragic killings in schools of late, total anomie or normlessness of a society in crisis. Science, in its attempt to become objective and value-free, becomes valueless.

The social solidarity at stake as a result of a lack of social integration through a cultural tradition of norms results in a loss of collective identity *Volkerpsycholie* (Wundt, 1921) and fragmentation of the culture. In addition, the isolation and specialization of knowledge, and our current debate regarding aesthetics, education, and "uncivil discourse" may be seen as a manifestation of this fragmentation of culture, to include the culture of education. Baldwin continues her analysis of the resultant fragmentation (1989):

> Without such social and professional interaction, the fragmentation of the society or the profession will continue. A lack of resolution to this critical problem will lead to continued disintegration of any social norms. Disenchantment in the social institutions will continue. There will be no reproduction of the society. The technical rationality will continue to cause disturbances in socialization and ego development of the child. (Baldwin, 1989)

Affective and motivational development will not continue, i.e., the spreading into institutions, such as that which was discussed by Dewey in child development and teaching (Dewey, 1922). There will be no development of political insight and social norms necessary for learning. The stability and continuity of society and formal operational thought in development of adolescents requires such norms. The transition of the culture to future generations requires analysis for issues as to what extent the current culture will be continued or terminated (Baldwin, 1989). The values and norms traditionally questioned by the adolescent require a transition with visible norms. The communicative environment (whether verbal, visual, or symbolic), could lead to a breakdown of the family structure, the Western culture, and psychopathology during the adolescent crisis. Through distorted communication, traditional communication and norms are being lost. The market can no longer sustain a normal distribution of wealth. As people lose faith in the market and in their God, there is no longer fair distribution of goods and education, and lack of appropriate employment opportunities further erodes the social structure (Baldwin, 1989):

> Disturbances in social structure, breakdown of cultural traditions, personal responsibility, and development of psychopathology have been the result of this imbalance in empirical methodology in scientific inquiry. The domination of empirical analytic inquiry has resulted in not only an imbalance, but also a distortion of method in the search for new knowledge. The current challenge for moral reasoning has ignored human and social ramifications of this scientific enterprise and loss of aptitude for social moral reasoning. The growth of technical knowledge has not resulted in similar growth of moral and human understanding (Baldwin, 1989).

In the beginning of the chapter on interpretation, I opened with statements of Bacon's concern for lack of moral focus in developing a method of scientific inquiry (Greenberg & Tobach, 1990). Through the early methods of scientific inquiry, knowledge could be obtained from nature. The illogical rationale for force was justified by the end, for, "laid up in the womb of nature are many secrets of excellent use. ... Hounded in her wanderings ... forced out of her natural state and squeezed and molded ... put in constraint ... bound into service ... (and made a) slave" (Greenberg & Tobach, 1990, p. 93). The abuse of nature and the domination of the female nature are obvious. Given this stated intent,

> It should come as no surprise that there is no proper place in the modern scientific paradigm for values that might restrict or constrain the abusive exploitation of nature for human ends ... The modern scientific worldview is frequently advertised as uniquely capable of providing a "true picture" of the world and its contents because it is

allegedly "value-free" with "moral and ethical neutrality," and "objectivity" (Greenberg & Tobach, 1990, p. 93).

The radical shift in thought of the earth, as separate from the context of a "purposeful whole" was a paradigm shift with scientific empirical inquiry (Greenberg & Tobach, 1990, p. 93). We are now re-establishing the historical context of inseparability of humanity and nature; we are also experiencing the conflict for supremacy with a deeper meaning. The "inhabited earth as a whole was frequently likened to the body of a living organism often personified as Gaia (or Ge), the original pagan mother goddess, whose etymological traces show up in such terms as geography, geometry, geology ... As long as the earth was considered to be alive and sensitive, it could be considered a breach of human ethical behavior to carry out destructive acts against it" (p. 92). The "assault on nature" was symbolically an attack upon the feminine mother earth.

Bacon is said to be the father of such methodology of thought in a search for new knowledge. Yet it is difficult to understand how such a critical component of scientific method could have resulted in the current crisis of an exploding technology, while at the same time, a disregard for the human component and goal of evolution. The loss of focus of a human context that has resulted in the fragmentation discussed above may be explained within the context of a hatred of the feminine. The same may be seen in the removal of the Madonna or Divine Sophia, the symbol of the female mother of God. That the empirical represents death and an assault on life and mother earth in its foundation would help explain the current struggle for supremacy in the current paradigm shift, which attempts to refocus issues on a "family of man" and a global "body" (Myss, 1996).

We are restructuring ourselves and our relationships to personal and spiritual authority. Inevitably, that restructuring will reshape every aspect of our world culture in accordance with the sacred truth *All Is One* (Myss, 1996):

> The fact that our global society is now saturated with crises that touch every nation, every organ, and every system in our global "body" has symbolic significance. Nuclear poisoning, the shortage of fresh water, environmental concerns, and the tinning of the ozone layer are just the first of many issues that are no longer national in scope

but global ... We have reached the end of the "divide and conquer" system of power, and that system is being replaced by an attempt to unite the powers of different nations in order to survive and move safely into the next millennium. Our interconnected "information age" is the symbol of a global consciousness. (Myss, 1996, p. 285)

The significance of this fragmentation is being manifested in family and consumer sciences and may be seen in the specialization, and now the potential elimination, of a core of its original philosophy, aesthetics and education. As the remaining activities of the profession further fragment and separate from one another in their empirical frenzy to be identified as the current gods of empirical science, the original purpose of both the specialists and the educators will be lost—the empowerment of individuals, families, and communities. Our mission will be modified to apply to a mere collective of activities without a cohesive core or fundament social moral political ideology.

One alternative presented for consideration in response to this crisis is school vouchers. The difficult debate on school vouchers was begun by Moe and Chubb in 1990 with their book, *Politics, Markets, and America's Schools.* That debate continues by educators and public policymakers in political scientists, religious and political leaders. To develop valid options, open communication must first be allowed to flow. For that to happen, there must be some restraint in regard to the current "uncivil discourse," which demonstrates the oppressive nature of anomie so well expounded upon by Baldwin (1989).

That this crisis is occurring in the most traditional branch of education is signal of a serious social anomaly in process. With all of the talk of concern for the American family, to allow the most traditional profession, whose training and mission is the empowerment of families, to be reduced to a memory, can only be intentional. Who will replace the family specialists? Crisis intervention through social workers has a totally different focus— crisis intervention, not preservation of those aspects of the family which are necessary before damage and suffering through loss of the family structure has occurred.

Philosophers such as Hultgren, Brown, and Baldwin cry the alarm for critical reflection through critical theory as to the current direction of a society in the process of continued fragmentation and loss of identity. The youth of our culture manifest this anomie and normlessness with such behavior and comments as discussed in this paper. They, however, are led by a generation older than they are in a perverse dominance of hedonistic self-centeredness, which despises all that is decent and caring of our fellows and our own dignity as humans. That art and aesthetics are the earliest manifestations of this society in decline is to be expected. Such is the nature and honesty of art. What that message is must be addressed by us all. Members of an elite academy of higher learning bear more responsibility in the guardianship of the society.

If we truly wish to empower individuals, families, and communities, we must also identify the process of our silencing in this crisis. What other profession states such a mission? What other profession is in the process of losing its voice by loss of funding and false representation of its history and function in the search for betterment of families through education?

I have labeled this profession the gentle child of academia. The silencing of the lamb may be in the process of the funding of the wolf. If our elected officials are truly concerned for the empowerment of families, for reexamination of cultural traditions through appropriate processes, why is the majority of funding being proportionally allocated to the advancement of a scientific technology without a balance of funding for social moral development of educational philosophy and curriculum development in such areas? Through the process of critical theory, a discourse for presenting sufficient reason for a call to action is completed. "Though the principle of sufficient reason sheds no light on reasons as such, it can nevertheless serve as our point of departure in characterizing the problem of reasons" (Heidegger, 1969, p. 12).

In the text titled *The Crisis in Human History: The Danger of the Retreat to Individualism,* Dewey (1946) wrote of a need for true "prophets" in our society. The isolation of the individual is the core of a loss of vital connection to fellows for identity of reciprocal need for survival. The potential for total social anomie and normlessness and the resultant danger to us all as a society have been clearly witnessed in the last few years. Children killing children has become not an infrequent and isolated occurrence, but a fear which all parents and teachers live with daily. As families lose control of their own identities and the most significant social "manipulators" become the institutions of learning, what will those examples be?

The gatekeepers of a society are controlled by the moneychangers who dictate what courses will be taught, by whom, and how. The power of the purse is the ultimate power of the society. The loss of a value core in education is hidden in the language of non-secularism. What the loss of educational values has resulted in is a value of normlessness.

The basic function of the family is for the connection of individuals for safety, protection, and identity beyond themselves against the social isolation of the individual within the world. It is not enough for a concept of a "family of man." The loss of intimate safety in the evolving development of a rationale for institutionalized daycare for small children in the bonding stages of development is another example of the move toward an "institutional society" outside the context of "tribal" or "family" identity. What is the ultimate goal of this normless priority, a society of slaves?

What is the role of family and consumer sciences in the twenty-first century? What is the need for aesthetics and education in family and consumer sciences in the twenty-first century? What is the role of Dewey's global movement in the twenty-first century? Who will be left to empower individuals, families, and communities in the twenty-first century?

When I began this journey of philosophical self-discovery, I did not realize the core values, which would be revealed and examined through concepts of aesthetics and education. Nor did I realize it would actually result in my making very strong statements about my own personal beliefs and concerns for the generation to follow. The role of the teacher educator has taken on greater significance in the course of the investigation. A concern for the inner core values of those who will teach our next generation not merely how to succeed, but how to sustain the many sorrowful realities that life automatically presents became an even more obvious issue as this study evolved.

The stronghold, "rock," or steadfast sense of self from which to stand in the midst of life's storms seems to be lacking in our educational system, whether in the lower grades or higher education. Where this sense of self is developed becomes the issue of values and morals in the development of key concepts in education. The transient nature of defining success in terms of status or money does not prepare the next generation for the bigger challenges of loss of health, family, or jobs, often by no fault of their own. Sometimes bad things happen to good people. Without a value core, these events cannot be met with a vision of options and alternatives. Not only do we *not* ask, *How well have you succeeded in life's process*, but also, *How well have you failed*? How do we teach individuals to respond to those things beyond their control?

Part of this lack of instruction may be found in our current empirical inquiry; we are still conquering our natural world, having dominion over all things. This makes the possibility of events beyond our control unlikely. They are, instead, some fault of our own, a bad choice, or lack of attention to detail. To assume all things are within our control also assumes we are the center of all things, like God. Thus, we take a higher power out of the context of the conversation. The value-free and objective logic holds fast to the notion that development of the right cognitive technique, the right formula, will result in control of everything—Man as God; No such thing as bad people, just bad choices; Evil is a concept that no longer exists. Then, beauty as a concept is without relevance to the soul.

> Lotze wrote: "Wherever in a certain favored phenomena there is an agreement (which need not generally occur) between what the phenomena ought to be to accord with the Idea, and what mechanistic necessity makes them, there we find beauty." The Idea (the world of values) must pervade reality (the world of form). This occurs when three conditions are met, corresponding to three standards within us. First, the object must please the senses—physiological condition. Next, the object must conform to the laws of our mental life—psychological condition. Finally, however, the object must also satisfy our ideas concerning the import and systematic unity of the world—the metaphysical condition ... So unity is a symbol of God's all encompassing essence, rest a symbol of his constancy and eternity; symmetry is a symbol of God's justice, purity a symbol of His will. Whoever can clearly see and reproduce this divine perfection is the great artist. (Dessoir, 1970, p. 151)

This is the fallacy of the imbalance of empirical thinking and its use in social context. Man has been held as God, with no recourse except to his own design. Now that the design has been found flawed, he seeks solutions in the void that does not allow for a higher alternative. He finds the lower source. A theology of beauty was the original meaning of aesthetics. Aesthetics in education became the link to the divine and the nature of the soul. When we find no recourse to the law, any policy or procedure to make a wrong right, what will be our choice? Will our recourse be to the Lord?

In the loss of a moral base in family and consumer science education and general education in the curriculum of higher education, my concern is that we are not preparing persons for the inevitable pain that happens in an imperfect world. As students seek protection or acceptance in a group of any kind, often their only alternatives are those which have no moral foundation, such as gangs, guns, and drugs (Brady, 2000). That public education has permitted and promoted this process by allowing our government officials to make these choices for us impliesthat we are not competent enough to make them ourselves. A clever manipulation and an attempt to create a diversion of elitist class warfare disguise the underlying problems in general education.

The overt manifestation of this created class war has been evident in the more open assaults and verbal abuses discussed in this dissertation. The seriousness of the underlying problem of anomie and normlessness are more evident in satanic murder cases such as those in Pearl, Mississippi, Tokyo, Japan, Maryland, Chicago, Florida, and many others in 1997. A generation after Dewey and his refusal to take God out of the context of educational discourse, I find hope in a past tradition with God as its center, in the absence of any other alternative.

Vampire cults, blood cults, pagan death rituals, with mutilation, and systematic and progressive violation of all laws, are out of control (Brady, 1997, p. 2). One of the latest examples of normlessness and anomie resulted in children out of control in Columbine. There are many more; their numbers and frequency continue to increase daily. Recently, when asked why he killed his parents and fellow students, sixteen year old high school student, Kip Kinkel responded, "I had no choice … I had to." Where do we go from here? That choice is ours. Either we move toward a "point of perfection" in another global enlightenment, or we progress toward the final stage of global disintegration and decay (Jauss, 1989. Again, let Hildegard von Bingen close this discussion with her ageless, prophetic, and, almost apocalyptic observation of truth:

Therefore, that man is blessed who is awakened to heavenly things through a miracle of God. And I heard the voice from heaven say: *The woman who says these things and who made them known by writing them down, sees and does not see, knows hot ashes and does not know them. And she brought forth the miracles of God not through herself, but through those things touched by God, just as a string that has been touched by the player of the lyre gives forth sound.* (Hozeski, 1994, p. 290)

APPENDIX: PORTRAYAL OF ARTS-BASED GENRE IN WORKS OF FINE ART

By

Dr. B. Marie Brady-Whitcanack

Acrylic Painting
"The Christ"
By: B. Marie Brady-Whitcanack, Ph.D.

Acrylic Painting
"Study of the Bellini Pieta"
By: B. Marie Brady-Whitcanack, Ph.D.

Acrylic Painting
"Peace Be With You"
By: B. Marie Brady-Whitcanack, Ph.D.

Acrylic Painting
"Pope Paul and Two Fatimas"
By: B. Marie Brady-Whitcanack, Ph.D.

REFERENCES

Abbs, P. (1994). *The educational imperative: A defense of Socratic and aesthetic learning*, 224. London: Falmer.

American Federation of Teachers. (1996, August). *Executive summary: Making standards matter* (Item no. 265). Washington DC.

Analytical Psychology Club of New York. (1962). *Carl Gustav Jung 1875–1961: A Memorial Meeting*, 29–30.

Ashfield, A. & De Bolla, P. (Eds.). (1996). *The sublime: A reader in British eighteenth-century aesthetic theory*. New York: Cambridge University Press.

Bacon, F. (1960). Preface to "Novu organum." In Anderson, F. M. (Ed.), *The new organon and related writings*. New York: Bobbs-Merrill.

Bacon, F. (1968). *The wisdom of the ancients*. Amsterdam: Da Capo.

Baldwin, E. (Speaker). (1989). *Searching for new knowledge: Is empirical science adequate to the task?* (Cassette Recording No. 003 222). Ames, IA: Iowa State University.

Baldwin, E. E. (1989). A critique of home economics curriculum in secondary schools. In F. Hultgren, F. H. & D. L. Coomer (Eds.), *Alternative modes of inquiry in home economics research: Yearbook, 9/1989* (pp. 236–250). Peoria, IL: Glencoe Publishing.

Baldwin, E., & Brown, M. (1995). *The concept of theory in home economics:*

A philosophical dialogue. East Lansing, MI: Kappa Omicron Nu, Inc.

Baldwin, E. (1997). Ethical Action for Policy Affecting Families: The Role of Critical Theory. *Family and consumer sciences teacher education: Thinking for ethical action in families and communities.* Peoria, IL: Glencoe/McGraw-Hill.

Beardsley, M. C. (1969). Reason in aesthetic judgments. In M. C. Beardsley (Ed.), *Introductory teachings in aesthetics* (pp. 245–253). New York: The Free Press.

Berg, B. (1998). *Qualitative research methods for the social sciences* (3rd ed.). Boston: Allyn and Bacon.

Berg, Y. (2006). *The red string book: The power of protection.* NY: Kabbalah Centre International.

Berger, G. (1972). *The cogito in Husserl's philosophy.* (K. McLaughlin & J. M. Edie, Trans.). Evanston, IL: Northwestern University Press.

Berleant, A. (1992). *The aesthetics of environment.* Philadelphia: Temple University.

Beyer, B. K. (1995). *Critical thinking.* (pp. 10–18, 28). Bloomington, IN: Phi Delta Kappa Educational Foundation.

Bourassa, S. (1991). *The aesthetics of landscape.* London: Belhaven Press.

Boyd, E. & Fales, A. (1983). Reflective learning: Key to learning from experience. *Journal of Humanistic Psychology, 23*(2), 99–117.

Boydston, J. A. (Ed.). (2000). *The collected works of John Dewey* (37 volumes). Found in website "John Dewey (Internet Encyclopedia of Philosophy)" maintained by Carbondale: Southern Illinois University Press, 1967–1991. Retrieved January 20, 2000 from http://www.utm.edu/research/rep/d/dewey.htm.

Brady, B. (1999, August). Aesthetics in education: The Scottish experience. Unpublished paper. Iowa State University, Ames.

Brady, B. (2000). America in Crisis: Mind control, ritual abuse, battered woman syndrome, and family violence. *The Journal of Family and Consumer Sciences, Vol. 92* (5). Alexandria, VA.

Brady, B. (1998). A search for beauty: Aesthetics in everyday life. (Unpublished manuscript). Iowa State University, Ames, Iowa.

Brady, B. (1997, December). Mind control/Ritual trauma/Battered woman syndrome and family violence (Also a case study currently under investigation satanic cult in Keokuk, Iowa). (Unpublished paper), Iowa State University, Ames.

Brady, B. (2001). Renaissance of aesthetic knowing and representation – Case study of Fort Madison, Iowa: A village of arts and restoration in a city of spires. (Submitted to *Proteus: A journal of ideas on community*). Shippensburg University, Shippensburg, PA. Submitted for publication February 22, 2001.

Brady, B. (2000). Uncivil discourse: A critical theory approach to reform in higher education. (Manuscript submitted for publication in *The International Journal of Educational Reform*). Lanham, MD: Scarecrow Press.

Brady-Whitcanack, B. M. (2000). Artist as Philosopher, Oil Painting, 24" x 28".

Brady-Whitcanack, B. M. (2005). Rachel. Acrylic Painting, 24" x 36".

Brady-Whitcanack, B. M. (2005) Rope Walkers, Poem.

A brief overview of progressive education (2000). University of Vermont. Retrieved from http://www.edu/~dewey/proged.html.

Bringmann, W., & Tweney, R. (Eds.). *Wundt studies: A centennial collection* (p. 19). Toronto: C. J. Hogrefe, Inc.

Brooke-Rose, C. (1992). Palimpsest history. In S. Collini (Ed.). *Interpretation and over interpretation: Umberto Eco, with Richard Rorty, Johnathan Culler, Christine Brooke-Rose* (pp. 125–138). New York: Cambridge University Press.

Brookfield, S. D. (1987). *Developing critical thinkers. Challenging adults to explore alternative ways of thinking and acting.* San Francisco: Jossey-Bass.

Brooks-Davies, D. (Ed.) (1996). *Alexander Pope: Everyman's poetry*. London: J. M. Dent.

Brown, C. (1981). Jung's hermeneutic of doctrine: Its theological significance. In H. Ganse Little, Jr. (Ed.). *American academy of religion dissertation series, 32* (pp. 1–4, 6, 7, 40–41). Ann Arbor, MI: Edwards Brothers, Inc.

Brown, M. (1993). *Philosophical studies in home economics: Basic ideas by which home economists understand themselves.* East Lansing: Michigan State University.

Brown, M. (1983). *Philosophical studies of home economics in the United States: Our practical-intellectual heritage*, 1–2, 264. East Lansing: Michigan State University.

Brown, M. (1989). What are the qualities of good research? In Hultgren and Coomer (Eds.). *Alternative modes of inquiry in home economics research: Yearbook 9/1989* (pp. 257–297). Peoria, IL: Glenco Publishing.

Buchanan, W., MacMillan, A., Macaulay, J., Trowles, P. & Rawson, G. (Eds.). (1989). *Mackintosh's masterwork: Charles Rennie Macintosh and the Glasgow school of art* (pp. 9 & 25). San Francisco: Chronicle Books.

Buescher, T. M. (1986). Appreciating children's aesthetic ways of knowing: An interview with Elliot Eisner, *Journal for the education of the gifted, 10(1)*, 7–15. In Arthur L. Costa & Rosemarie M. Liebmann (Eds.), *Envisioning process as content: Toward a Renaissance curriculum*, (p. 108). Thousand Oaks, CA: Corwin Press.

Bush, G. (1989). *Building a better America*. Washington, DC: President of the United States, Superintendent of Documents.

Cairns-Smith, A. G. (1999). *Secrets of the mind: A tale of discovery and mistaken identity*. New York: Springer-Verlag.

Campbell, C. (1991). Hildegard von Bingen: From the book of divine works. *German mystical writings* (p. 24). New York: Continuum.

Carr, D. (1999). *The paradox of subjectivity: The self in the transcendental tradition* (p. 13). New York: Oxford University Press.

Cassirer, E. (1946). Language and myth. In Gaetano Curreri-Alibrandi, *Beyond visual perspective.* (p. 71). New York: University Press of America.

Chitnis, A. (1986). *The Scottish enlightenment & early Victorian society.* (pp. 2–3, 26, 56, 101, 166). Beckenham, Kent: Croom Helm.

Chronicle writer. (2000, March 1). *A student's piece of performance art.* Retrieved March 3, 2000 from http:// chronicle.com/ daily/2000/03/2000030104n.htm.

Cohen, E. (1998, September). Making cooperative learning equitable. *Association for supervision and curriculum.*

Collini, S. (1992). *Interpretation and overinterpretation/Umberto Eco and Richard Rorty, Jonathan Culler, Christine Brooke-Rose* (pp. 3–4, 21). New York: Cambridge University Press.

Conforti, M. (1999). *Field, form, and fate: Patterns in mind, nature, & psyche.* New Orleans, LA: Spring Journal Books.

Conforti, M. (2008). *Threshold experiences: The archetype of beginnings.* Brattleboro, VT: Assisi Institute Press.

Conrad, D., & Shiman, D. (1974). Human rights, multiculturalism, peace and conflict resolution, environment, food and hunger, cross cultural understanding. *About the center for world education.* Center for World Education. University of Vermont. Retrieve January5, 2000 from http//www.uvm.edu/%/euvmcwe/mst.html.

Costa, A. & Liebermann, R. (Eds.). (1997). *Envisioning process as content: Toward a Renaissance curriculum.* Thousand Oaks, CA: Corwin Press.

Curreri-Albrandi, G. (1996). *Beyond visual perspective.* (pp. xxvi, 151–171). New York: University Press of America.

Daiches, D. (1964). A Scottish man of feeling, by H. W. Thompson (1931). *The paradox of Scottish culture: The eighteenth-century experience* (p. 74). London: Oxford University Press.

Daines, J. R. (1989). Verstehen: A more comprehensive conception of understanding through hermeneutics. In Francine H. Hultgren

& Donna L. Coomer (Eds.), *Alternative modes of inquiry in home economics research* (Yearbook 9/1989, pp. 69–79). Peoria, IL: Glencoe Publishing.

Davenport, N., Distler Schwartz, R., & Pursell Elliott, G. (1999). *Mobbing: Emotional abuse in the American workplace.* Ames, IA: Civil Society Publishing.

Delaney, R. (2010, September, 13). Sex: Christie Vilsak and others at FM gathering say it's time to talk the talk because many of our teens are already walking the walk. *The Fort Madison Daily Democrat,* pp. 1, 14.

De Man, P. (1983). *Blindness and insight: Essays in the rhetoric of contemporary criticism* (2nd ed.). Minneapolis: University of Minnesota Press.

De Man, P. (1982). Introduction. In Hans Robert Jauss, *Toward an aesthetic of reception: Theory and history of literature,* 2, vii–xxv. Minneapolis, MN: University of Minnesota Press.

Dendel, E. W. (Speaker). (1971). *Aesthetics and the quality of life.* (Sound recording). Ames: University of Iowa Lecture Series.

Dessoir, M. (1970). *Aesthetics and theory of art.* (S. A. Emery, trans.). (pp. 151, 1633–1664). Detroit: Wayne State University.

Devereaux, M. (1999, April). *The philosophical status of aesthetics.* American Society for Aesthetics, Marquette University, Milwaukee, WI. Retrieved April 8, 1999 from www.indiana.edu/~asanl/ideas/devereaux.html.

Dewey, J. (1904). The relation of theory to practice in education. *National society for the scientific study of education,* 3, I, 9–30. Bloomington, IL: Public School Publishing.

Dewey, J. (1922). *Human nature and conduct: An introduction to social psychology.* NY: Henry Holt and Company.

Dewey, J. (1925). *Experience and nature.* Chicago: Open Court Publishing.

Dewey, J. (1934, 1980). *Art as experience.* NY: Perigee Books.

Dewey, J. (1939). *Art as experience.* New York: Minton and Bach.

Dewey, J. & Glotzer, A. M. (1937/1968). *The case of Leon Trotsky; Report of hearings on the charges made against him in the Moscow trials.* By the preliminary Commission of Inquiry: John Dewey, chairman [and others] Introduction by George Novack. Preliminary Commission Coyoacan, Mexico, 1937. New York: Merit Publishers.

Dewey, J. (1946). The crisis in human history: The danger of the retreat to individualism. Latter works (Vol. 15. p. 223). In M. Tuggle, *The evolution of John Dewey's conception of philosophy and his notion of truth.* (p. 218). New York: University Press of America.

Dewey, J. (1979). *Reconstruction in philosophy* (15th printing). Boston: Beacon Press.

Dimbleby, J. (1994). *The Prince of Wales: A biography.* (p. 422). New York: W. Morrow.

Dissanayake, E. (1992). *Homo-Aestheticus: Where art comes from and why* (pp. xiv–xx, 91). New York: The Free Press.

Dolan (1999, August 13). Iowa State assumes a lead role in international consortium, *Inside Iowa State, 9*(3), 1. Ames: Iowa State University.

Drob, S. L. (2000). *Kabbalistic metaphors: Jewish mystical themes in ancient and modern thought.* Jerusalem: Jason Aronson Inc.

Drob, S. (2010). *Kabbalistic visions: C. G. Jung and Jewish mysticism.* New Orleans, LA: Spring Journal Books.

Dworkin, M. S. (1959). *Dewey on education.* (pp. 115–116). New York: Teachers College, Columbia University.

East, M. (1982). *Caroline Hunt: Philosopher for home economics.* University Park, PA: Pennsylvania State University.

Eaton, M. M. (1989). *Aesthetics and the good life.* Rutherford, NJ: Fairleigh Dickinson University Press.

Ecker, D. W. (1998, Spring). Navigating global cultures: A phenomenological aesthetics for well being in the twenty-first century. *Journal of Aesthetics Education, 32*(1), 5–10. Urbana: University of Illinois.

Eco, U. (1992). Interpretation and history. In S. Collini (Ed.). *Interpretation and over interpretation/Umberto Eco with Richard Rorty, Johnathan Culler, Christine Brooke-Rose.* (p. 30, 32). New York: Cambridge University Press.

Eiseley, L. (1973). *The man who saw through time.* New York: Charles Scribner's Sons.

Eisner, E. (1990, Spring). To the Association for Supervision and Curriculum Development. In B. Joyce, & M. Weil. (1996). *Models of teaching* (5th ed.) (p. 179). Boston: Allyn and Bacon.

Eckart, M. (1991). About disinterest. In K. J. Campbell (Ed.), *German mystical writings.* (p. 83). New York: Continuum.

Farrar, R. C. (1989, Spring). Phenomenology as a tool for aesthetic education in the multicultural college classroom. *Journal of Aesthetic Education, 32*(1), 43–45, 47.

Farrington, B. (1964). *The philosophy of Francis Bacon.* Chicago: University of Chicago Press.

Fay, B. (1987). *Critical social science: liberation and its limits.* Ithaca, NY: Cornell University Press.

Ferry, L. (1993). Between heart and reason: The decline of the avant-garde: Post modernity. In *Homo Aestheticus: The invention of taste in the democratic age.* (R. De Loaiza, Trans.) (pp. vii, 4, 5, 33–77, 192–246). Chicago: University of Chicago Press.

Findlay, J. N. (1981). *Kant and the transcendental object: A hermeneutic study.* (pp. 77–78, 80). Oxford: Clarendon Press.

Fiore, A., & Kimle, P. (1997). *Understanding aesthetics for the merchandising and design professional.* New York: Fairchild.

Fiore, A., & Paff, J. (1999). Facilitating the integration of textiles and clothing subject matter by students: Part One: Dimensions of a model and taxonomy; Part Two: Substantiating the applicability of proposed structures. Unpublished manuscript, Iowa State University, Ames.

Fourth "R". (1998, July). The fourth "R" the case for music in the school curriculum. Educational research http//www. Fourthr.com.

Freeland, C. (1999). *Cognitive science and the arts: An introduction to key topics under discussion.* Resources compiled by Dr. Cynthia Freeland, with assistance from the Cognitive Science Initiative, University of Houston. Retrieved April 8, 1999 from http//www.hfac.uh.edu/cogsci/index.html.

Gadamer, H. G. (1976). On the scope and function of hermeneutical reflection. In D. L. Linge (Ed.), *Philosophical hermeneutics* (p. 18). Berkeley: University of California Press.

Galloway, C. (1976). *The silent language in the classroom* (p. 9). Bloomington, IN: The Phi Delta Kappa Educational Foundation.

Gentzler, Y. (1999). What is critical theory and critical science? In J. Johnson & C. Fedje (Eds.), *Family and consumer sciences curriculum: Toward a critical science approach: Yearbook 19/1999*(pp. 23–31). Peoria, IL: Glencoe/McGraw-Hill.

Gibboney, R. A. (1994). *The stone trumpet: A story of practical school reform.* Albany: State University of New York.

Gilbert, K., & Kuhn, H. (1939, 1953, 1954, 1972). *A history of esthetics revised and enlarged* (p. ix, 8, 9). Westport, CT: Greenwood Press.

Gocsik, K. (1997). Elements of critical thinking. *Teaching critical thinking.* Trustees of Dartmouth College. Site maintained by J. Kalish. Retrieved January 12, 2000 from http//www.dartmouth.edu/~compose/faculty/pedagogies/thinking.html.

Graybosch, A., Scott, G., & Garrison, S. (1998). *The philosophy student writer's manual.* Upper Saddler River, NJ: Prentice-Hall.

Greenberg, G. & Tobach, E. (1990). *Theories of the evolution of knowing* (Vol. 4, p. 45, 5, 93). Hillsdale, NJ: Lawrence Erlbaum Associates.

Habermas, J. (1974). *Communication and the evolution of society.* (T. McCarthy, Trans.). Boston: Beacon Press.

Hacker, A. (2005, November 18). Preventing civil disturbances. *Inside*

Iowa State, a newspaper for faculty and staff. Retrieved October 10, 2010 from http://www.InsideIowaState.htm.

Hahn, L. E. (1997). Foreword by Lewis E. Hahn, Department of Philosophy, Southern Illinois University at Carbondale, IL. In M. Tuggle, *The evolution of John Dewey's conception of philosophy and his notion of truth.* (pp. v–vii). New York: University Press of America.

Halpern, D. F. (1984). *Thought and knowledge: An introduction to critical thinking.* Hillsdale, NJ: Erlbaum.

Hartman, G. (1989). The longest shadow. In D. Rosenberg (Ed.). *Testimony: contemporary writers make the holocaust personal* (p. 436). New York: Time Books.

Hawking, S. (1993). *Black holes and baby universes and other essays.* New York: Bantam Books.

Hawking, S. (1998). *A brief history of time.* New York: Bantam Books.

Heder, L. (1980). *Aesthetics in transportation: Guidelines for incorporating design, art, and architecture into facilities.* Washington, DC: U.S. Department of Transportation, Office of the Secretary, Office of Environment and Safety.

Heidegger, M. (1993). *Basic concepts.* (G. E. Aylesworth, Trans.). (pp. 43-44). Bloomington, IN: Indiana University Press.

Heidegger, M. (1992). *The concept of time.* (W. McNeill, Trans.). Oxford: Blackwell.

Heidegger, M. (1969). *The essence of reason* (T. Malick, Trans.) (p. 12). Evanston, IL: Northwestern University Press.

Heidegger, M. (1988). *Hegel's phenomenology of spirit.*(p. 5). (E. Emad & K. Maly, Trans.). Bloomington, IN: Indiana University Press.

Heidegger, M. (1972). *On time and being.* (J. Stambaugh, Trans.) (p. vii–viii). New York: Harper Torchbooks.

Heller, A., & Feher, F. (1986). *Reconstructing aesthetics: Writings of the Budapest School* (pp. 1–15). Oxford: Basil Blackwell.

Heller, S. (1998, December 4). Wearying of cultural studies, some scholars rediscover beauty; tentatively, they seek renewed attention to aesthetic criteria in criticism. *The Chronicle of Higher Education, 45*(15), 15–16.

Henry, W. (2000). *The peacemaker and the key of life.* Hendersonville, TN: William Henry. Retrieved January 28, 2001 from http://www. williamhenry. net/orderpage.htm.

Hicks, J. (1993). Technology and aesthetics education: A crucial synthesis. *Art Education, 46*(6), 42–47.

Hinterland (1990). The Artist. *Hinterland: Kissing the roof of heaven* [CD]. New York: Island Records.

Hofstadter, A., & Kuhns, R. (Eds.). (1976). *Philosophies of art & beauty: Selected readings in aesthetics from Plato to Heidegger* (p. 555). London: The University of Chicago Press.

Hofstadter, A. (1965). *Truth and art* (p. 87). New York: Columbia University Press.

Holgate, A. (1992). *Aesthetics of built form.* New York: Oxford University Press.

Horkheimer, M. (1941). Art and mass culture. *The social studies association, 9,* 290–304. New York: Social Studies Association.

Hospers, J. (1969). *Introductory readings in aesthetics.* New York: The Free Press.

Hozeski, B. W. (trans.). (1994). *Hildegard of Bingen: The book of the rewards of life (Liber vitae meritorum)* (pp. 52, 193, 256, 290). New York: Garland Publishing.

Hultgren, F., & Coomer, D. (Eds.) (1989). *Alternative modes of inquiry in home economics research: Yearbook 9/1989* (pp. 37–60). Peoria, IL: Glencoe Publishing.

Huntington, S. P. (1996/1997). *The clash of civilizations and the remaking of world order.* (p. 213). New York: Touchstone.

Hutcheson, F. (1973). *Francis Hutcheson: An inquiry concerning beauty, order, harmony, design.* The Hague: Martinus Nijhoff.

Jackson, P. W. (1998). *John Dewey and the lessons of art* (p. 163). New Haven: Yale University Press.

Jauss, H. (1982). *Aesthetic experience and literary hermeneutics.* Minneapolis, MN: University of Minnesota Press.

Jauss, H. (1982). *Toward an aesthetic of reception.* (Vol. 2). (Timothy Bahti, Trans.). Minneapolis, MN: University of Minnesota Press.

Jauss, H. (1989). *Question and answer: Forms of dialogic understanding.* Minneapolis, MN: University of Minnesota Press.

Jax, J. A. (1989). The need for interpretive science as a paradigm for home economics inquiry. In F. H. Hultgren & D. L. Coomer (Eds.), *Alternative modes of inquiry in home economics research: Yearbook 9/1989* (pp. 60–68). Peoria, IL: Glencoe Publishing.

Jervis, K., & Montag, C., (1991). *Progressive education for the 1990s: Transforming practice.* New York: Teachers College Press.

Jessop, T. (1969). The objectivity of aesthetic value. In J. Hospers (Ed.), Introductory *readings in aesthetics* (pp. 275–277). New York: The Free Press.

Johnson, M. H. (1998). Phenomenological method, aesthetics experience, and aesthetic education. *Journal of Aesthetics Education, 32*(1), 32–41. Urbana: University of Illinois.

Jones, P. (Ed.). (1988). *Philosophy and science in the Scottish Enlightenment.* (pp. 217–219, 202, 203). Edinburgh: John Donald Publishers.

Jung, C. (1992). *The Gnostic Jung.* Princeton, NJ: Princeton University Press.

Jung, C. (1995). *Jung on alchemy.* Princeton, NJ: Princeton University Press Jung, C. (1964). *Man and his symbols* [by] *Carl G. Jung* [and others]. Garden City, NY: Doubleday.

Jung, C. (1969), *Modern man in search of a soul.* (W. S. Dell and Cary F. Baynes, Trans.). New York: Harcourt, Brace & World.

Jung, C. (1970). *Mysterium coniunctionis: An inquiry into the separation and synthesis of psychic opposites in alchemy.* (R. F. C. Hull, Trans.). Princeton, NJ: Princeton University Press.

Jung, C. (1966). *The spirit of man, art, and literature.* Princeton, NJ: Princeton University Press.

Kabat-Zinn, J. (1994). *Wherever you go, there you are.* NY: Hyperion.

Kaelin, E. F. (1970). *Art and existence: A phenomenological aesthetics* (p.65, 191, 194). Cranbury, NJ: Associated University Presses.

Kainz, H. P. (1983). *Hegel's phenomenology, Part II, The evolution of ethical and religious consciousness to the absolute standpoint* (p. 170). Athens, OH: Ohio University Press.

Kandinsky, W. (1948). *Concerning the spiritual in art: The documents of modern art* (p. 75). New York: George Wittenborn.

Kappa Omicron Nu Honor Society. (1995). *The concept of theory in home economics.* East Lansing, MI: Kappa Omicron Nu.

Kaufmann, Y. (2009). *The way of the image: The orientational approach to the psyche.* NY: Zahav Books, Inc.

Kenyon, J. H. (1998). Waking up to lead: An investigation into the relationship between the development of aesthetic cognition and the development of leaders. (Doctoral dissertation), Peabody College of Vanderbilt University, Nashville, TN.

Kivy, P. (Ed.). (1973). *Francis Hutcheson: An inquiry concerning beauty, order, harmony, design.* (pp. 6–7, 44, 46). The Hague: Martinus Nijhoff.

Kockler, D. (2004, April 18). Will riots end VEISHEA? Retrieved from http://www.WillRiotsEndVEISHA-DesMoinesNewsStory-KCCIDesMoines.htm.

Kohak, E. (1978). *Idea & experience: Edmund Husserl's project of phenomenology in ideas* (p. 12). Chicago: University of Chicago Press.

Kolodny, A. (1998). *Failing the future: A dean looks at higher education in the twenty-first century.* London: Duke University Press.

Kreitman, N. (2006, Feb. 23). The Varieties of Aesthetic Disinterestedness. *The Journal of Contemporary Aesthetics*. Retrieved April 23, 2010 from http://contempaesthetics.org/newvolume/pages/artoicle.php?articleID=390.

Krippendorff, K. (1980). *Content analysis: An introduction to its methodology* (Vol. 5). London: Sage.

Kung, H., & Jens, W. (1995). The encyclical *evangelium vitae* and the problem of help in dying. *A dignified dying: A plea for personal responsibility*. (J. Bowden trans.). (p. 114). London: SCM Press.

Kurtis, B. (2000, February 22). Dangerous obsessions. *Investigative reports*. South Burlington, VT: A & E Television Network.

Lahey, B. B., (2007). *Psychology: An introduction*, 10th ed. Chicago: McGraw Hill.

Lamont, W. D. (1934). *Introduction to Green's moral philosophy*. Westport, CT: Hyperion Press.

Le Baron Hilton, H. (1972). *Families of the future*. Ames: Iowa State University Press.

Lorraine, R. (1999, April). *Review of Mann's, Aesthetics*. Retrieved April 13, 1999 from http://www.aesthetics-online.org/ideas/lorraine.html. American society for Aesthetics, Marquette University, Milwaukee, WI.

Lotze, H. (1885). *Outlines of aesthetics: Dictated portions of the lectures of Hermann Lotze*. (G. T. Ladd, Trans.). Boston: Ginn & Company.

Lovitts, B. E. (2001). *Leaving the ivory tower: The causes and consequences of departure from doctoral study*. Lanham, MD: Rowman & Littlefield Publishers, Inc.

Mallery, J. C., Hurwitz, R., & Duffy, G. (1987). Hermeneutics: From textual explication to computer understanding? Selections of short abstracts on various topics of hermeneutics. *The encyclopedia of artificial intelligence*. S. Shapiro, Ed. New York: John Wiley & Sons.

Markowsky, J. (ed.) (1994). *Sequenctia: Hildegard von Bingen: 1098–1179 canticles of ecstasy* [CD]. New York: BMG Music.

Marzano, R. (1992). *A different kind of classroom*. Alexandria, VA: Association for Supervision and Curriculum Development.

Mauron, C. (1935/1970). *Aesthetics and psychology* (R. Fry & K. John, Trans.). (p. 69). Port Washington, NY: Kennikat Press.

McCann, K. (2000, November2). Artivcle: SIU Halloween riot ends with tear gas. Retrieved November 25, 2010 from http://www.highbeam.com/doc/lP2-4561001.html.

McCormack, T. (1982). Rethinking women's culture: From de Beauvior to Clause 28 (p. 3). *The CRIAW: Women's culture: Selected papers from the Halifax Conference.*

McKenna, W. R. ((1982). *Husserl's Introductions to phenomenology: Interpretation and critique.* The Hague: Matinus Nijhoff.

Mezirow, J. (1977). Perspective transformation. *Studies in adult education, 9*(2), 153–164.

Michaels, L. (1989). To feel these things. In D. Rosenberg (Ed.). *Testimony: contemporary writers make the holocaust personal* (p. 12). New York: Times Books.

Mish, F. C. (Ed.). (1994). *Merriam Webster's collegiate dictionary* (10th ed.). Springfield, MA: Merriam Webster, Inc.

Morgaine, C. (1997). Reflection and ethical action: A critical theory of self-formation. In Janet F. Laster and Ruth G. Thomas (Eds.), *Thinking for ethical action in families and communities: Yearbook 17/1997* (pp. 78–90). Peoria, IL: Glenco/McGraw-Hill.

Morris, G. S. (1885). *Hegel's aesthetics: A critical exposition.* Chicago: S. C. Griggs.

Muelder Easton, M. (1997, Fall). Aesthetics The mother of ethics? *The journal of aesthetics and art criticism 55:4*, 355–364.

Murdoch, I. (1970). *The sovereignty of good.* London: Routledge & Kegan Paul.

Myss, C. (1996). The energy consequences of belief patterns. *Anatomy of the spirit: The seven stages of power and healing* (pp. 109–110, 285). New York: Three Rivers Press.

Navone, J. (1996). *Toward a theology of beauty* (p. v). Collegeville, MN: Liturgical Press.

Nettleship, R. L. (Ed.). (1906/1969). *Works of Thomas Hill Green.* (Vol. II. p. 239). New York: Longman, Green (1906); Kraus Reprint (1969).

Nervi, P. L. (1965). *Aesthetics and technology in building.* Cambridge, MA: Harvard University Press.

Ogose, T. (1989). *Hume and Smith in the method of philosophy.* Unpublished manuscript, Institute of Economic Research, Kobe University of Commerce, Tarumi, Kobe, Japan.

Ogden, C. K., Richards, I. A., & Wood, J. (1929). *The foundations of aesthetics* (pp. 18, 49, 50). New York: International Publishers.

Olson, I. (1997). The arts and educational reform: More critical thinking in the classrooms of the future. *Journal of Aesthetics Education, 31*(3), 194–199. Urbana: University of Illinois.

O'Reilly, R. (1999, October). The public philosophy and charter schools: Alberta's charter schools. *International journal of educational reform, 8*(4), 342–351. Lanham, MD: Scarecrow Press.

Paul, R. (Speaker). (1989). *Critical thinking in elementary school.* ASCD. February 6–8, 1987.

Paul, R. (1990). *Critical thinking.* Rohnert Park, CA: Center for Critical Thinking and Moral Critique.

Paul, R. (1995). *Socratic questioning and role-playing.* (pp. 709). Santa Rosa: CA. Foundation for Critical Thinking.

Paul, R. & Nosich, G. M. (1991). *A proposal for the national assessment of higher-order thinking at the community college, college, and university levels.* Commissioned by the United States Department of Education, Office of Educational Research and Improvement, National Center for Educational Statistics.

Paul, R. (2000). Call for proposals: 20th international conference on critical thinking and educational reform. *Foundation for Critical Thinking–A study of college instruction of critical thinking.* A report prepared for the legislature of the state of California, Sonoma State University web page. Retrieved April 26, 2000 from http://criticalthinking.org/ eentsisc/proposal/html.

Paul, R. (2005). *Creative and critical thinking.* Dillon Beach, CA: Foundation for Critical Thinking.

Pender, P. (1999, July 25). Home of the Holy Grail? *Sunday Herald,* pp. 1, 4. Glasgow, Scotland.

Persell Elliott, G. (2001, February). Driven beyond endurance: Workshop of workforce abuse. Presented by Gail Persell Elliott, Ames, Iowa.

Piantanida, M. & Garman, N. (1999). *The qualitative dissertation: A guide for students and faculty.* Thousand Oaks, CA: Corwin Press, Inc.

Pieper, J. (1963). *Leisure: The basis of culture* (A. Dru, Trans.) (p. I). New York: Random House.

Posner, G. & Rudnitsky, A. N. (1997). A survey of Western art, Appendix B. *Course Design: A guide to curriculum development for teachers* (5th ed.) (pp. 229–248). New York: Longman.

Proutist Universal. (1998). *Economics for human development: Davos conference challenged by 20 million.* Retrieved January 5, 2000 from http://www.prout.org/.

Radnitzky, G. (1973). *Contemporary schools of metaphysics.* Chicago: Henry Regnery.

Raskin, M. G., & Bernstein, H. (1987). *New ways of knowing: The sciences, society, and reconstructive knowledge.* Totowa, NJ: Rowman & Littlefield.

Raymond, G. L. (1906). *The essentials of aesthetics in music, poetry, painting, sculpture, and architecture* (pp. 30–36, 286). New York: G. P. Putnam's Sons.

Redfern, H. B. (1986). *Questions in aesthetic education* (pp. 1–4, 22, 23, 97). London: Allen & Unwin.

Reitmeyer, C. (1999, April 1). *Family and consumer sciences curriculum committee meeting, April 1, 1999.* Meeting minute notes presented for evaluation and discussion with notations of questionable need for aesthetics and education to curriculum committee members.

Roberts, L. (1987). *The theological aesthetics of Hans Urs von Balthasar* (pp. 2, 36, 238). Washington DC: Catholic University of America Press.

Robertson, P. (1996). *Charles Rennie Mackintosh: Art is the flower* (p. 6.) London: Pavilion Limited.

Romano, C. (2000, October 20). A philosopher's examined life: It's worth forgiving. *The Chronicle of Higher Education,* p. B11.

Rosslyn, Earl of (1997). *Rosslyn Chapel.* Roslin, Scotland: Rosslyn Chapel Trust.

Roth, R. J. (1962). *John Dewey and self-realization.* Englewood Cliffs, NJ: Prentice-Hall.

Ryan, A. (1995). *John Dewey and the high tide of American liberalism* (pp. 22, 89–107, 257, 328). New York: W. W. Norton.

Santayana, G. (1896, 1955). *The sense of beauty: Being the outline of aesthetic theory.* (pp. 162–163). New York: Dover Publications.

Seidel, G. (2000). *Toward a hermeneutics of spirit* (p. 9, 13, 17). Cranbury, NJ: Associated University Press.

Schilpp, P. A. (1939). *The philosophy of John Dewey.* (Vol. 1, pp. 419, 423). Chicago: Northwestern University.

Schubert Kalsi, M. L. (1978). *Alexius Meinong: On objects of higher order and Husserl's phenomenology.* The Hague: Martinus Nijhoff.

Sherman Epprigh, E., & Storm Fergus, E. (1971). *A century of home economics at Iowa State University: A proud past, a lively present, a future promise* (pp. 12, 105, 275). Ames: Iowa State University Home Economics Alumni Association.

Sharp, D. (2009). *Glossary of Jungian terms.* Toronto: Inner City Books Studies in Jungian Psychology.

Shamdasani, S. (Ed.). *The red book: C. G. Jung.* Verona, Italy: Philemon Foundation.

Shlain, L. (1991). *Art and physics.* (pp. 30–31). New York: Quill William Morrow.

Siler, T. (1990). *Breaking the mind barrier: The artscience of neurocosmology* (pp. 15, 17, 35, 189, 217, 334, 335). New York: Simon and Schuster.

Singer, J. (1994). *Boundaries of the soul: The practice of Jung's psychology.* New York: Doubleday.

Sim, S. (1992). *Beyond aesthetics: Confrontations with poststructuralism and postmodernism.* Toronto: University of Toronto Press.

Smith, T. P. (1988). *The aesthetics of parking: An illustrated guide.* Chicago: American Planning Association.

Sokal, A. (1996, Spring/Summer). Transgressing the boundaries: Toward a transformative hermeneutics of quantum gravity. *Social text, 46/47, 14* (1 & 2). Durham, NC: Duke University Press.

Sorokin, P. (1928/1956). Studies of the fluctuations, rhythms, and cycles of social processes. *Contemporary Sociological Theories,* 728–741.

Spira, J. L. (2000). *Integrating progressive education into technology-based distance learning.* Retrieved January 5, 2000 from http://horizon.unc.edu/projects/monograph/CD/Professinal_Schools/Spira.asp.

Stage, S., & Vincenti, V. (Eds.). (1997) *Rethinking home economics: Women and the history of a profession.* Ithaca: Cornell University Press.

Strickland, A. & Coulson, L. (1997). Learning creative process: A basic life skill. In A. Costa & R. Liebmann (Eds.), *Envisioning process as content: Toward a Renaissance curriculum* (pp. 163–184). Thousand Oaks, CA: Corwin Press.

Temple, W. (1951). *Nature, man and God: Being the Gifford lectures delivered in the University of Glasgow in the academic years 1932–1933 and 1933–1934* (p. 62, 254). London: MacMillan and Company.

Thompson, A. (2005, November 17). Survey Says: SIUC resembles Animal

House". *Daily Egyptian*. Retrieved November 25, 2010 from http:// newshoundde.siu.edu/onlinestories/storyReader$4936.

Topp, R. (1999). Critical thinking: A challenge for professionals and students. (pp. 156–166). In J. Johnson & C. Fedje (Eds.), *Family and consumer sciences curriculum: Toward a critical science approach: Yearbook 19/1999.*

Tuggle, M. (1997). *The evolution of John Dewey's conception of philosophy and his notion of truth* (pp. 21, 37, 199). New York: University Press of America

Turner, F. (1991). *Beauty: The value of values* (pp 1–5, 116). Charlottesville: University Press of Virginia.

Usener (1896). Gotternamen Versuch Einer Lehre von der Religiousen. In Gaetano Curreri-Alibrandi *Beyond visual perspective* (p. 71). New York: University Press of America.

Van Manen, M. (1990). *Researching lived experience: Human science for an action sensitive pedagogy.* London: State University of New York Press.

Van Manen, M. (1991). *The tact of teaching: The meaning of pedagogical thoughtfulness* (p. 41, 143, 205, 213, 217, back cover). New York: State University of New York Press.

Vermont Intercultural Dialogue. (2000). *The Vermont intercultural dialogues & encounters initiative: Building global links for youth empowerment.* Retrieved January 5, 2000 from http://www.uvm.edu/~dewey/youth.html.

Wall, T. F., (2003). *Thinking critically about moral problems.* Belmont, CA: Wadsworth/Thomson Learning.

Wallace-Murphy, T. & Hopkins, M. (1999). *Rosslyn: Guardian of the secrets of the Holy Grail.* Shaftesbury, Dorset, UK: Element Books Ltd.

Water Resources Planning and Management Conference. (1997). *Aesthetics in the constructed environment: Proceedings of the 24th Annual Water Resources Planning and Management Conference, Houston, Texas, April 6-9, 1997,* sponsored by the Water Resources Planning and Management Division of the American Society of Civil Engineers.

Co-sponsored by the ASCE Urban Planning and Development Division.

Weaver, R. (1948/1984). *Ideas have consequences* (pp. 15, 26, 27, 125, 127–129, 170–171). Chicago: University of Chicago Press.

Weber, R. P. (1990). *Basic content analysis* (2nd ed.). London: Sage.

Wechsler, J. (1978). *On aesthetics in science* (pp. 1–2, 143). Cambridge, MA: MIT Press.

Weinberger, J. (1985). *Science, faith, and politics: Francis Bacon and the utopian roots of the modern age: A commentary of Bacon's advancement of learning.* Ithaca, NY: Cornell University Press.

Westbrook, R. B. (1991). *John Dewey and American democracy.* Ithaca, New York: Cornell University Press.

White, G. (2002, December 5). Athletes videotaped in buff due $506 million. *The Burlington hawk eye.* Burlington, Iowa. P. 4A.

Whitmont, E. C. (1978). *The symbolic quest: Basic concepts of analytical psychology.* Princeton, NJ: Princeton University Press.

Wilks, S. (1995). *Critical & creative thinking: Strategies for classroom inquiry.* Portsmouth, NH: Heinemann.

Witt, C. (1997). *Barbarians on the Greek periphery? Origins of Celtic art.* University of Virginia, dissertation proposals on the web. Retrieved from http://www.faraday.clas.virginia.edu/~umw8f/Cze/HomePage. html.

Wolff, J. (1993). *Aesthetics and the sociology of art* (2nd ed.). Ann Arbor, MI: University of Michigan Press.

Wolfsonm, E. L. (1995). *Along the path: Studies in kabbalistic myth, symbolism and hermeneutics.* Albany, NY: State University of New York Press.

Wright, W. A. (Ed.). (1873). *Bacon: Advancement of learning* (5th ed.) (p. 89). Oxford: Clarendon Press.

Whybrow, K. (1997). Intersubjectivity: Establishing an understanding. In Janet F. Laster and Ruth G. Thomas (Eds.), *Thinking for ethical action in families and communities: Yearbook 17/1997* (pp. 65–77). Peoria, IL: Glenco/McGraw-Hill.

Wundt, W. (1921, April). *Elements of folk psychology: Outline of a psychological history of the development of mankind.* (E. L. Schaub, Trans.). New York: The MacMillan Company.

Zeltner, P. M. (1975). *John Dewey's aesthetic philosophy* (Vol. 12). Amsterdam: B. R. Gruner B. V.

ACKNOWLEDGMENTS

I wish to thank my personal friends, religious leaders, and guides who have provided the stamina and determination to state the unstated and meet the enemy head on. Thank you, Dr. Edward McKenney, Father Gerald Hoenig, Mr. Lex Whitcanack, and Dr. Michael Conforti. In the words of Brown: "This 'chaotic' state of affairs would seem to counsel us to adopt one of two courses: either resignation to an opportunity now lost or the fashioning of a new line of approach" (Brown, 1981).

www.ingramcontent.com/pod-product-compliance
Lightning Source LLC
Chambersburg PA
CBHW030305290526
45785CB00001B/218